To Paul,
Thanks for
and questions at the presentations.

The Book in the
Dresser Drawer

Lord's richest blessings!
Brian Lee Miller

Brian Lee Miller

Amazon Reviews: Brian Lee Miller
Facebook Like: Author Brian Lee Miller

ISBN-13: 978-1518823022
ISBN-10: 1518823025

Front Cover & Inside Pictures – Author's Collection

In Memory of Davey Lee

Contents

Disclaimer

My narrative relays my nonfictional escapades while growing up as a child and the journeys that have continued in my adult life. The actual physical setting is in Michigan, Minnesota, Arizona, and Wisconsin. The time frame includes the 1960s to the present.

The characters in my personal account involve immediate and distant family members, close friends, classmates from high school and college, coworkers from various employments, and casual acquaintances from all walks of my life. In some cases I have changed the names of individuals.

The activities described in the book are fifty years' worth of my recollections and are retold from my sincere point of view. I have tried to be as accurate as possible and to avoid any embellishment concerning the details. I have tried to check for accuracy through research, photos, the Internet, and conversations with individuals involved with the events.

Acknowledgements

I extend a thank you to my friends and family members for their support and for implanting in me the belief in this writing adventure. I notably thank my daughter, Jenny, for listening to my retelling of the events as they developed over the years. As my enthusiast she aided me with inserting the memories in my mind.

I appreciate the students who were the audiences of my portrayals. In our classroom discussions I longed to bridge together my chronicles and their learning processes. I now realize the stories were beneficial for me as a teaching aid and the presentations were my rehearsals for future editing of the descriptions.

Holding a unique role in my motivation to compose the volume were the freshmen and sophomore girls at Winnebago Lutheran Academy (WLA) during the 2013-14 school year. The fifteen short stories I voiced in our Friday's physical education class were managed as the basic outline of the book. The girls' encouragement furnished me with the inspiration to commence at my computer and form the manuscript.

I am grateful to all the students I have encountered in the school districts of Lomira, Mayville, Oakfield, and WLA. The two years of substitute teaching and witnessing the students' smiles, laughter, and questions entrenched in me an assurance that the features were meaningful for all readers.

I graciously thank my wife, Kris, for her faithful teaching for over thirty years, and I specifically thank her for consenting to my daily book time. Without her concessions I could not have organized my reflections and pecked away long hours at the computer. Thank you, Kris, for your love, patience, and support.

Finally, I hold dear to my heart my loving parents. They were the two people in my life cheering for me in my high school years, marriage, college pursuits, and employments. They encouraged me in all my endeavors even if it was daydreaming of writing about my life's adventures. My parents shared with me their faith in Jesus and their unconditional love.

To God be the glory!

Introduction
THE BLUE SPIRAL NOTEBOOK

In third and fourth grade I was notorious for spending a fair amount of my school day in the corner of the classroom or in the hallway observing a time-out due to my misbehavior. I often received discipline in the form of either writing sentences or receiving a paddling from my teacher. I was occasionally guided to the principal's office for a round of sterner discipline.

In fifth grade I had my first male teacher. The improper incidents declined in the schoolroom as I improved my behavior, increased my study sessions, and progressed in my academic successes. My fifth-grade teacher kindled a flame in me to read the books *Where the Red Fern Grows, Old Yeller,* and *My Side of the Mountain.*

Through my teacher's influence I wanted to express my sentiments using the writing process. My written words were intended to be a collection of my nine years' worth of events. I anticipated the text to contain stories about my parents, siblings, and friends.

The storyline would be the neat times I treasured with my grandparents while on fishing trips, playing cards, attending a Friday fish fry, or viewing the TV show "Gomer Pyle".

I was dedicated to capturing my stories in written detail and my preferred method of authoring was with a black pen and a blue-covered spiral notebook. I clumsily wrote in print and cursive as I employed both sides of the college rule paper. The grammar and spelling were demanding as the concepts lingered in my mind while I ached to construct a mountain of features for others to read and enjoy.

In my work I was extremely zealous and was exhausted from etching six pages. Wanting a break and storing the manuscript in our shared bedroom, I had to slyly conceal it from Mike.

My brother, Mike, was unwavering at scaring me as I lurked down our long dark driveway to rescue the daily newspaper. My sibling was proficient at locking me outside of our rural house or locking me in the cellar when I was retrieving vegetables.

Mike found considerable humor in kicking my top bunk bed from underneath causing me to flop over or to tumble off the side. Mike was ecstatic about teasing his brother about my reading books, my Beatles haircut, and my recesses spent skipping rope with the girls.

To preserve the spiral notebook from exposure, I placed the book in the bottom right drawer of my wooden dresser. I positioned the pages under my clothes and I assumed I would return to the writing task in a little bit, maybe in a few days or a week.

The recess period from my writing was twenty-two years, yet I had stimulating undertakings during those years which could have been a portion of my memoir. Instead of putting the events on a sheet of paper in the blue notebook, I filed them in my memory bank. I planned to pluck them out and utilize them within a future platform.

The long concealed notebook was brought out from the drawer's hiding place after twenty-two years and three months before the beginning of my second career as a teacher.

I had concluded my college student teaching tenure at the age of thirty-one years old. As I relayed a teaching classroom moment to my dad, he uttered I should record the incident's highlights in a journal. His theory was that the sequel would make pleasant reading within a complied document of my future teaching deeds.

I seized my dad's suggestion and I scrawled down the specifics of the teaching outcome in the notebook. I contemplated transcribing the book that summer and I feebly made an effort to author it.

However, I could not develop the storyline, as my authorship would wait another twenty-two years before I could muster my ideas and switch on the creating process with my thoughts.

In my life my dad would reveal his satisfaction in my actions by an ordinary nod, smile, or a laugh. Dad did express his love through his considerate words to me, and I garnered later in life another common means used by Dad. To show his admiration Dad would often share instances with others of my life's ups and downs.

My dad was raised on a farm, graduated from high school, and served in the US Army in the Korean War. Dad's occupations included working full-time as a custodian, working part-time as a carpenter, and dabbling in investments. Davey Lee was a prosperous entrepreneur, a fabulous dad, an outstanding grandfather, a devoted Christian man, and a tremendous husband for forty-nine years.

I inherited from Dad his indulgence to articulate stories. Davey Lee enjoyed narrating stories and he was an exceptional storyteller. The story I recounted to my dad was produced at St. Paul's Lutheran School in New Ulm, Minnesota.

As a college requirement for my teaching degree I student taught at St. Paul's for nine weeks. I was assigned to a fifth-grade classroom under the supervision of Mr. Blauert. Mr. Fritz Blauert had been in the teaching profession for over thirty years, and he had mentored countless student teachers.

With me being an older college student, Mr. Blauert quickly allowed me to progress into the teaching aspects. I had plenty of latitude with my teaching duties and I cherished the time with the students. I was enraptured with leading the students in their lessons.

After our first reading lesson most of the students didn't bother to read the story. They polished off their vocabulary and context worksheets by guessing, copying answers, or barely skimming the pages. The students were persistent at bluffing their way through our discussion, yet I rummaged for a way to motivate them and instill in them a passion for embarking on adventures in books.

My attack was activated when the students had a study period in between the math and reading lessons. I exited the classroom and when I returned I instructed the children to clear their desk tops.

I swaggered into the room barefoot, and jumped up on the teacher's desk. Wiggling my toes in view of the fifth graders, I was dressed in filthy blue jeans with frayed cuffs, grass stains, and holes in the knees. I snatched their attention with my meaningless suspenders and a flannel shirt with torn sleeves and missing buttons.

My disguise continued with my unshaven face produced from dots formed by a washable black marker. A gunny sack was tied shut with a piece of twine and slung over my shoulder while I was trying to keep a white railroad cap on my head. I had reappeared in the chirpy room as the fictional character Johnny Appleseed.

My gunnysack was stocked with chocolate treats intended to be a reinforcement to the children if they correctly answered the review questions. There was no doubt my inquiries were complex enough that there was no faking by the noncompliant students.

Within a microscopic time frame, the students who hadn't read the story had a dilemma. After our discussion the mutinous students went back and read the entire story as they were entranced by the book's tale and the highlighted points we had discussed.

After the Johnny Appleseed spoof I was never filled with tension wondering if the students would read their assigned stories. When we had a selection with fictional or non-fictional characters the students asked if Abraham Lincoln, Attila the Hun, Tom Sawyer, or Paul Bunyan were visiting our classroom the next day.

My blue spiral notebook had a new rendering. The Johnny Appleseed visit was an entertaining anecdote to transpose, yet I did not anticipate the intriguing chronicle that emerged in the fifth-grade room two weeks after Johnny's visit. The presentation had the two most provocative questions I have ever witnessed in a conversation.

Chapter 1
THE TWO QUESTIONS

Of the twenty-one students in my student teaching classroom Seth caught my undivided attention through his peculiar perception of worldly notions. Seth was a thinker outside of the box and he was well beyond his years when defining vocabulary words and using the skillful terminologies in his everyday speech.

Rarely, did I face discipline concerns with Seth. My concern with Seth was to keep him on track with us during our lessons. If I said white, Seth would think and say black. If I said up, he would think and say down. If we were in a lesson envisioning a drinking glass, Seth might visualize a pair of eyeglasses.

Seth's academic achievements were above average, but he sparred with math problems as it was a challenge to unlock his mind to the math concepts. Seth would tussle to solve a one-step problem and it was the luck of the draw whether to add, subtract, divide, or multiply. The math facts were dull and impractical calculations to him.

Seth's frustration led to his viewing math lessons and math homework as bothersome. The fifth grader would rush through his work, writing down any answer to dispatch with his math. He then could move on to what he perceived as more important topics.

Seth was a keen student in the field of world history. He delighted in studying significant people and events even though this was an age before the Internet and the endless fingertip data. Seth with his messy hair and loose fitting eyeglasses, routinely traveled the extra steps to research encyclopedias or history books.

Because of his unusual way of observing issues, Seth quarantined himself from the other students during the school day. Missing out on social happenings didn't bother Seth, and he was at harmony with the status quo of existing alone.

One day we had a guest in the classroom arranged by Mr. Blauert. The local man's address was centered on World War II. Twenty of the twenty-one fifth-grade students were immediately bored with the man.

But Seth was engrossed by the man's hello, and Seth was on the edge of his chair from the start of the speaker's introduction.

During the speech the students were slouching in their chairs or resting their lethargic heads in their hands. Within minutes it was evident the elderly narrator had turned the tide with the students. The presenter had pushed the unspecified switch opening the students' minds to being alert and responsive.

The man announced that as a young soldier he was in a shattered European city near the conclusion of WWII. The ex-soldier spoke about a grim moment in his life as a warrior. He communicated in his speech to the students that the particular occasion in the war was a turning point in his service in the army and in his life.

Our guest speaker vocalized to the pupils his military squad members were scattered throughout the battle zone after the recent bloody skirmishes. Many of his brothers-in-arms did not make it through the clash as he watched them die from enemy fire. Some of his dispersed buddies ended up isolated, alone, and lost. Other soldiers in his disassembled company had become prisoners of war (POWs).

The infantry soldier stated he was actively defending himself and attempting to live through the unfolding chaos. The man conveyed that his enemies were hammering down on him while he was persistently in a state of retreat.

The draftee was concealing himself in abandoned, dilapidated, and shelled-out buildings. He was utilizing space behind doors, under stairs, and among the concrete rubble. The runaway soldier was striving to hide anywhere to stay ahead of the enemy soldiers and the thundering tanks rumbling through the ruins.

The retreating soldier withdrew to within a short distance of the open sea with its docks and harbor surrounding him. As he had herded himself into a compromising position, he was starting to let himself contemplate surrendering and facing the cruel consequences as a POW.

The speaker relayed to the students and their student teacher the specifics of a possible path for him to take to escape. The warrior stumbled upon a captain of a merchant ship in the harbor. The confused soldier had bargained for an opportunity of boarding the cargo ship and sailing away from both the war and his enemies. The combatant debated about the extreme cost as he had to swap his one prized possession for the ship's passage. He was bewildered about his decision within the pivotal seconds.

The elderly gentlemen told the attentive students he attempted to pray to God for guidance in regard to the crucial moment, and frustratingly, he could not mutter a simple prayer due to his trembling fear caused by the mayhem exploding around him. The fledgling individual recognized comfort in his considerations through the singing of hymns—the hymns of praise, thanks, and worship he had memorized, enjoyed, and sung as a youngster in his Lutheran grade school.

The fighter's persistent enemies were continuing to close in on him. He knew he would not be treated kindly as a POW after hearing the horror stories within the war's pipeline of information. He did not fancy himself in the position as a detainee by his ruthless enemies.

Finally, the worn down soldier unfastened his military-issued pistol confirming the decision to make the trade in exchange for his passage out of the country. The semi-automatic pistol would be worthless against the steel armored tanks, but on the other hand the pistol was an irreplaceable object as a defensive weapon in individual assaults. I wondered if there was a hidden motive with the soldier wanting to keep the pistol. Could the handgun be exploited as a last resort to end the soldier's life through suicide?

The fugitive agreed to the exchange, and he embarked on the merchant ship and was hidden in the bowels of the departing vessel. The lonely escapee was evading the demolished city and was retiring from the shredded country. He was navigating away from the vicious war while sidetracking his malicious enemies.

The frightened teenager was alone in the boat's damp bowels. However, under the heavy canvas tarp he enjoyed a reprieve from the war. The soldier was voyaging farther from land. He was relaxing for the first time in months, and was feeling a genuine sense of liberation. He had no clue where he was heading, but any place was probably better than what was behind him.

All twenty-one fifth graders in their desks were wide awake and entrenched in every word from the speaker. The students were glued to their seats with their eyes fixed on his eyes.

This was as worthy as it could develop in a classroom. For the students and me this was retelling of a significant time in world history. The account was not an ambiguous story in a lackluster textbook, and not an exaggerated fake Hollywood production. The man and his presentation were real, uncensored, and electrifying.

This was a soldier acknowledging the intimate points of an unsurpassed global war. He was distributing the facts of himself as a combatant of World War II in Europe on the run. The soldier was a campaigner of the war with no other belongings besides his well-worn out uniform.

But then the ex-soldier told the details of how he had become a fugitive exposed by his enemies. Dejectedly, the merchant ship was detained two miles out to sea. Within seconds the soldier was lead up to the top deck of the merchant ship. He was searched and held as a captive by his enemies. The foreign soldiers were now in total control of him. Despite the soldier's best effort he had become a POW.

The dignified man took a short break in speaking to the children, and he asked if there were any questions from the students. As a silent monitor I was situated in the back of the classroom, and I examined Seth calmly raising his hand in the air.

My first reaction was to hustle over to Seth's desk in the middle of the rows and whisper to Seth to put down his hand. But Seth didn't raise his hand like a macho high school male student. Most teenage boys have just enough energy to raise their index finger two inches from their original resting position on their desk.

Also, Seth didn't exploit the tactic a normal fifth grader uses to gain attention. Fifth-grade students have refined the technique of waving their hand side to side resembling a person lost on a raft. They appear to be frantically attempting to gain the attention of the rescue aircraft directly above in the sky or low in the distant horizon.

Seth wasn't going to blow his opportunity by raising his hand like a second grader either. The students in second grade add to the rescue wave the grunts, groans, and pleading howls resonant of a dog panting after a vigorous run. "Oh! Here! Please! Me! Ahhh!!!"

Instead, Seth raised his hand straight above his head. There was no gesturing and no pleading. Seth sat upright and motionless in his desk generating eye contact with the speaker.

I believed Seth was not going to embarrass himself, the speaker, his student teacher, or his peers with an ill-advised question. I was quite certain Seth would not ask a question to reap attention, to be the funny guy, or say words that would be insulting.

When I substitute teach, I introduce myself to the students by sharing with them information about myself. In a bid to become acquainted with the students, I will permit them to summon questions about my life, family, friends, and hobbies. They may ask anything.

From the second graders I am often asked, "What's your favorite color?"

In the fifth-grade classroom, I receive the slightly more motivated question, "Do you have any pets?"

From the independent high school teenage students, I retrieve nothing unless I develop a trusting relationship. Normally, I am the one who converts to the pleading routine. The inquiries do eventually come from the teenagers as, "Are you married? Do have any children?"

I was moving to the conclusion Seth's probe would be inquisitive. I was confident Seth wasn't going to ask the man, "Are you wearing underwear?"

The speaker spotted Seth's raised arm and while rendering visual contact with Seth the man asked, "Yes, young man?"

4

Seth stood up out of his chair and pushed the metal chair under his desk while standing straight with his arms behind his back. Hours later I came to recognize Seth's actions and position was from a respectful student, who was standing at full attention while addressing the distinguished soldier.

Seth's dialogue had two points. The first part of his query was Seth mentioning a question he communicated after he decoded the particular situation. The second part of his prodding was his way of receiving confirmation of his evaluation. In his delivery Seth was not sarcastic or challenging with his words and actions.

Seth breathed in and solicited in a polite audible voice, "You were a Nazi…weren't you?"

Seth pulled his chair out and sat down in it. Seth scooted himself up snug to his desk while never losing eye contact with the ex-soldier.

My heart sank as the room became mute. The other students were stumped and they had the jaw dropping expression of "what just happened" on their faces. Seth was perhaps the only student in the room who figured out the true identity of our guest speaker.

Our guest lecturer with his thick German accent replied to Seth and everyone in the classroom, "Yes, I was a Nazi soldier."

Seth was captivated with the man as soon as the man had greeted the students with his vibrant and cheerful "Guten Tag." Seth had recognized the tanks bearing down on the young German soldier as Russian tanks. Seth characterized our orator as a teenage soldier who underwent the face-to-face fighting against the Russian troops.

Seth had gleaned from his studies that the Russian soldiers near the war's end showed no mercy towards their enemies. The captured Germans, whether officers or soldiers, were treated with repulsive rage by the Russians.

Seth used the clue regarding the treasured belonging, the Luger pistol, to stamp his final assertion of the man's identity as a German soldier in WWII. The elderly man with his short, stout frame was long ago a combatant exiting his fatherland attempting to save his life.

Seth analyzed this information while the elderly man narrated his imprisonment and revealed his being incarcerated, because of a United States Navy unit patrolling the sea outside the destroyed European city.

This was not material expressed in our institutions from an American soldier's perspective. The presentation was authentic German history, reiterated in the presence of the eleven year olds in New Ulm, Minnesota.

I was speculating if the students comprehended the definition and connotation of the word Nazi. Seth understood the term, and he had put the pieces of the puzzle together while contemplating the name. Seth retained the facts, as this was his dream come true opportunity with a pronounced figure who was involved with a gigantic historical event.

The man talked of his time as a POW. The ex-prisoner explained the United States government was not concerned with the deported German soldiers manufacturing plans of escape from their confinement. In the government's thinking, the German POWs would be treated well and they would be content in their imprisonment. The soldiers would be retained in a camp in the heartland of America surrounded by German immigrants.

The veteran soldier expanded on the intimate release from the prison compound after the war as he shared the essentials of his marriage, children, occupation, and present life to the students.

When the next break came in the man's presentation Seth again had his hand straight up. This time my decision to allow Seth another question was irrefutable. I was urging Seth with an inward thought, "Go for it."

In front of the class, the orator once again acknowledged Seth.

Again, Seth conferred his respect to the soldier by pushing in his chair and standing at full attention. Seth was exploiting the available primary source and without any qualms Seth imposed upon the narrator his examination. The fifth grader used the form of a statement while tacking on his question to validate his own conclusion.

Seth stated, "You killed people...didn't you?"

Seth returned to his seat, and the man waited until Seth was settled into his seat and desk. The man peered into Seth's eyes. The ex-Nazi rival confessed to everyone in the innocent setting, "Yes."

There was a moment of silence in the room, but the soldier did not wait long to continue with his dialogue of the accounts.

The elderly man recalled that as a teenager in Germany he was attempting to be an obedient citizen serving in the German army out of love and loyalty to his country. He explained in many circumstances as a soldier he was following direct orders, and that at other times he was striving to stay alive.

Our narrator explained that the facets of the war besieged him with complications concerning moral issues. By the end of the war he was mindlessly dodging tanks, bombs, and machine gun fire.

The contrite sinner admitted his undeniable acts within the war and that his feelings were in turmoil for years. In time, he confessed to God his guilt, sorrow, and remorse. The ex-soldier found peace and forgiveness through God's Word, prayer, and his Savior, Jesus Christ.

I had a lump in my throat and a wave of compassion in my soul. I had witnessed a stirring question and answer in spite of the off-limits subject matter.

Introduced into our discussion was the topic of taking another's person life. The phrases of murder, homicide, or execution were not mentioned, but the connotation of those thoughts were floating around in the room. In most social circles it is considered to be offensive to publicly discuss with soldiers the topic of the deaths or killings that occur within wars.

The man continued his address by speaking about his time in the POW camp, which I understood as he was explaining the location. The previous fall I had participated on the college football team at Dr. Martin Luther College in New Ulm. As a husband and a dad, I was playing football in my senior year at the non-athletic age of nearly thirty-one. I displayed no imposing physique at five feet-eleven inches tall and two hundred pounds. I had no athletic ability to be at that level of competition.

Our football team had spent our first week of training camp residing at the Flandrau Group Camp outside of New Ulm. The week was used as a team bonding exercise to achieve our physical conditioning. In the diverse environment, we were also inaugurating our team's goals.

The players and coaches were divided into teams for competition in good-hearted games as we exploited the park's pool for additional workout drills. In the group camp's building in the evening, we performed entertaining skits and slept in the hard bunk beds.

We concluded our NAIA college football season over two months later. Our team had an unsettling season record and a bizarre one of a kind sideline play in a close game. The 1991 Lancer football team of DMLC had an once-in-a-lifetime venue for our season's last game, but a gloomy end with a scornful listing in an issue of the magazine *Sports Illustrated*.

As our speaker was relating the basics of his prison barracks, my brain made the connection to our football camp. The elderly man was detained in a POW camp in the 1940s at the Flandrau Group Camp. Nearly fifty years later, I lodged in the ex-POW camp and living quarters. I was stunned by the inexplicable association.

Our speaker was transported miles from his home and family with his detention in New Ulm altering his life. I traveled miles from my home with the hope of training to be a Lutheran elementary teacher. My time enrolled in college in New Ulm would transform my life forever.

Seth's questions steered our narrator to display his confession, repentance, and faith. Our special narrator spent time as a German soldier in WWII and as a POW in the United States. He had become an American citizen with family and friends, while living his life as a forgiven child of God believing in his Savior, Jesus Christ.

My inspiration to teach children was supported by the classroom presentation, and my love of stories in general was reaffirmed. The day's activity underscored my desired interactions with people, even though I have my characteristics of being reserved in certain social environments.

In the years since the presentation in Mr. Blauert's classroom, I have been enticed to make public the story to friends, relatives, students, parents, and colleagues. I have yearned for the people receiving the interpretation to be nurtured spiritually and compassionately.

The issues in this world of bullying, racism, stereotyping, and disagreements will constantly surround us and be within our boundaries. Crucial life decisions will always confront us on this earth.

May the Lord grant us the will to serve Him, and may we treat our fellow humans with love, understanding, and forgiveness.

Chapter 2
THE NEIGHBORHOOD

The characteristics individuals display as adults are visible at an early age in their childhood. Our youthful memories never fade away as we carry them with us throughout our lives. Our traits direct us in establishing our hobbies, in our choices of occupations, and in selecting our companions.

We may discover, complement, or abandon selected behaviors in our life, but our childhood connections extend a sizeable influence in creating who we become as spouses, workers, and members of society. We may think we are just another brick in the wall, though each person is distinct within their childhood experiences.

On a cloudy day in January 1973 my cousin Paul and I would encounter an adventure in our outdoor playground that would define my exclusive characteristics. I didn't grasp it then, because of my pronounced immature lack of vision. After many years, I have ascended to appreciate the epiphany of the moments involving one coveted hill. The day would help my subconscious comprehend why I had certain achievements, regrets, and dreams in my life.

Paul and I proudly label ourselves home-grown Michigan boys, born and raised in the Great Lake State. We lived in the Lower Peninsula and were raised in the Genesee Valley Area. Even though manufacturing factories, commercial businesses, and large residential cities were within twenty miles of our homes to the south and north, our immediate territory was unquestionably rural.

Since our birth, we lived in Montrose Township in Genesee County. Paul and I lived approximately one mile apart as the crow flies, or as a kid stumbles through plowed fields, tangles in overgrown fence rows, and wanders confused in deciduous forests. In the physical world of young children on bikes or in the family vehicle we were one and one-half miles apart. The distance didn't seem daunting to us.

We had a marvelous neighborhood to build forts, hunt, fish, and roam. All the same Paul and I were proficient in discovering mischievous activities. Paul's family lived on an acre of our grandparents' farmland. Paul's family members were my Uncle Ward and Aunt Joanne, his seven sisters, and his younger brother, Don. The Dowells were my childhood version of *The Waltons*.

Diagonally from the Dowells' house, lived the Belill family. The Belills' house was surrounded by forty acres of farm land. The homestead contained a metal pole building, a chicken coop, a wood plot, and a farm pond. The Belill family consisted of the parents, Emerson and Donna, and their six children. One of the six children, Tim, was the same age as Paul and me. Tim, Paul, and I would remain close friends during our childhood and even today.

On the north end of Belill's farm Emerson's brother, Jim, and his family had a farmhouse. Jim and his wife, Pauline, had three girls.

There were other families within the one-mile square, but our connected group was my family, the two Belill families, and the Dowells. Most of our parents were raised in that proximity, so our four families blended together and celebrated together summer vacations, birthdays, high school graduations, weddings, funerals, and holidays.

All of the families' children were required to perform the household errands of preparing meals, washing dishes, and cleaning floors. Our daily chores included making beds, completing the laundry, and taking out the garbage. There was nothing unusual in our duties as we mowed our lawns, cleaned the garages, and weeded the gardens.

The girls in our neighborhood were acquainted with traditional female perspectives, yet they joined in our sports activities and delighted in hunting and fishing. On occasion they would outshine the boys casting a shadow of shame on us at our assemblies.

When my siblings Mike and Yvonne, and I would journey to our grandparents' we would hook up with the Belills and the Dowells. Our grandparents' house was between the two Belills' dwellings and a few hundred yards north of our cousins, the Dowells.

As a four-year-old, I remember riding a rusty red framed tricycle from my grandparents to the Belills or the Dowells to hang out with my cousin Paul and my friend Tim.

At the Belill's farm we would pick teams for football games, tag contests, snowball fights, hockey matches, baseball contests, or basketball competitions. Choosing teams was the most grueling aspect, and once the physical action began we seldom had arguments.

A tackle football game could be intense with flea flickers and blitzes while halting the competitive games when members of a family had to take a time out for mealtime with their entire family.

We continued basketball playoffs by porch lights, football thrashings in pitch-black, and baseball in the moonlight of a summer evening. We were so forward-thinking, we had 3-on-3 basketball tournaments well before the start of the popular competitions now held at festivals and fairs.

As children it was commonplace for us to have sleepovers, play hide-and-go-seek in the midnight hours, shoot billiards in our basement, and watch televised athletic events at each other's houses.

Three of our four families had pool tables in their basements. Our dads had bought them, traded for them, or received them as gifts. Shooting billiards in an age lacking video games was a perfect distraction when wretched weather entered the picture. We were well trained in our billiard shooting, with only the lack of a suitable pool stick tip shutting down our contests.

As an eight-year-old boy I can easily trace my footsteps back to the Apollo 11's spacecraft landing on the Earth's moon. On July 20, 1969 Neil Armstrong spoke the legendary words, "This is one small step for [a] man, one giant leap for mankind."

On the historic day I was at the Dowells' ranch-style home. Paul and I earmarked moments keeping tabs on the Apollo 11 mission as we spent most of the hours playing games, running around, and riding bikes.

In the afternoon, Paul made a miserable trade with his sister Angie. Paul's infamous trade was his highly respectable red bicycle in exchange for a plastic ring Angie had uprooted from the bottom of a cereal box. Paul has authorized the embarrassing "I can't believe I made such a dumb trade" as his encouragement while establishing himself as a prosperous business owner.

After our day's routines, we had baths and changed into our pajamas. With Paul's family, I watched man's first steps on the Earth's moon. In the living room eating popcorn, we were mystified as the event unfolded on the twenty-five inch wooden console television set.

My cousins' house was located in the southwest corner of our grandparents' field with one tall tree on the entire allotment. The lack of mature trees made it a tough situation for our gang of young boys. We needed trees to escape aggressive dogs, and to build camps on the main trunk and its branches. We desired older trees to climb for spying on our enemies and avoiding the feisty girls.

When I was eleven years old, Paul's parents sold their first house and moved one mile south on the same road. I assumed the move meant the forfeiture of compiling time with my favorite cousin, Paul. The second house, for the eleven member Dowell family, was situated roughly one hundred yards off Marshall Road.

The Dowells' new house was difficult to view from the road due to the abundance of trees in the front yard. Most of the trees were conifers planted in rows parallel to the street. Among the evergreen trees was an assortment of poplar trees adding diversity to the setting.

The dirt driveway was straight and the final approach to the garage was a concrete pad about forty-five feet by forty-five feet and referred to by everyone as the turnaround area. There was a basketball hoop at the end of the turnaround pad and any wild, errant basketball shot during our passionate games would tumble endlessly down the hillside.

The Dowells' two-story abode was grander in square footage than their first house as the house did seem appropriate in the neighborhood. Nearly, all the homes in the vicinity had hefty dimensions and were situated far off the road while being enclosed by a plethora of trees.

The rear expanse of the acreage had an arresting hill dotted with a range of deciduous trees. There were maples, walnuts, ash, and oaks evident in the woods. The trees were mature and had appeared after the logging commerce of the early twentieth century.

The hill was the real deal, and it was the setting of many ruckuses by our relatives and neighbors. The paramount activity was sledding down the hill in the winter. The glorious sledding season went from November to March depending on snowfall and temperatures.

On the far north side of the acreage was the junk pile. The heap of scrap consisted of lawn mowers, firewood, and scrap lumber and metal. Stacked alongside the official junk pile was a dog house, a wire-fenced pen, and a hodge-podge of objects long ago abandoned.

The main attraction at the locale was the trail blazed out from hauling of firewood up from the valley. When the snow came we had a sledding run measured by the neighborhood as a high-risk course. To gaze down to the bottom would make children tremble in their boots, doubt their sanity, and stutter through their last testimony.

The conservative participant could begin halfway down the hill, thus avoiding the death-defying velocity. Or the wary aviator could get underway at the top of the hill and bail out halfway through the course to avoid the ghastly accumulation of momentum.

Reluctant sledders could use one of the first models of sleighs, the wooden slat frame with metal blades. In the 1970s, the sled was still manipulated with the aging dinosaur considered old-fashion and was reflected by us as a device used by wimps. The blades dug into the snow with the sudden stops leading to painful finales.

Steering was futile as the sled was legendary for making its own path. When the sled veered off track and bulldozed through fresh snow, the moisture sprayed in the rider's face was blinding. Enduring the deviation, navigators tumbling sideways were common occurrences.

Another option providing far-reaching foolishness was replicated through a plastic saucer. The saucer existed in a variety of colors and were three feet in diameter with two weak handles on the side.

I envision a kid with a garbage can lid, and the gadget won over their gang of daredevils as the neatest fad. Then someone with the brains, funds, and luck, marketed the gismo for millions of dollars.

The saucer would begin down the hill unflustered, then suddenly advance to a whirling bedlam with guiding the saucer being impossible. Another annoyance was when the saucer would rotate 180 degrees and would stay in that position while soaring down the decline. The aspiring show-off sledder would rocket along unable to discriminate the snow run, stationary trees, or returning sledders.

The light saucer was easy to carry up the hill and the inexpensive contrivance had no contenders in the speed category. I was a saucer person through and through, with the innocent piece of plastic being my chosen nightmare for spiraling down the hill.

Another means for embarking down the hill was the toboggan and the Dowells regrettably had one of the implements. With the long wooden sleigh with a curved front the world was opened for massive groups to practice kamikaze sledding. Steering the toboggan did not exist, and the timid velocity made speed a non-concern.

The palpable test for the riders was to remain on the toboggan to the end of the run. Most rides with the toboggan concluded with human bodies piled up, interspersed, and snarled together. The whole topsy-turvy mess resembled a juvenile delinquent train wreck.

With inventive minds, we exasperated avenues for descending down the hill as we flopped our rear ends on a chunk of cardboard or a plastic bag when in a bind. We also experimented with discarded tire tubes from various makes of cars, trucks, and tractors. The steering perils still existed with the air-filled tubes, and an added irritation was the rigid stem stabbing your body parts.

To swell the hazards, we had no hesitancy with excursions at night with blindness bringing a novel suspense to the affair. At the onset of winter, sledding runs were manageable and pleasant due to the fluffy snow. As the snow became packed, the vulgar ruts and mounds were cultivated. Landings from airborne flights were unpredictable and a flyer truly hoped to avoid smashing into the dreaded trees.

I experienced as a child several bangs with my noggin causing concussion-like symptoms. I was diagnosed with a concussion by my parents or a physician three times before I was sixteen years old.

My first incident with a concussion resulted from falling off a dock at Lake Gogebic in the Upper Peninsula of Michigan. On our family vacation, I fell headfirst into a boulder under the water's surface. As a seven year-old, I occupied time at the hospital being monitored. That night and the next day, I struggled with bouts of vomiting while sleeping long hours at our rental cabin.

My second head trauma case was playing ice hockey on Belills' pond. As a seventh grade monster, I was bodychecking an opponent and I entirely missed the person. Performing a perfect nosedive while striking my head on the ice, I again surrendered the night hours disoriented, struggling to sleep, and with fits of vomiting.

My third occurrence of a head banger was in a pre-Thanksgiving holiday basketball game. As a puny point guard on the varsity team, I had weaved into the lane scuffling with the giants and received a shrill elbow to my skull. The game, ride home, and the following two days were never placed into my memory bank.

As children we wobblingly stood after a collision and would be inept at reciting our names or location. Yet, we would stagger back into action proclaiming, "I just got my bell rung, I'm alright."

We just did not perform proper treatment unless our bodies forced us. Concussions from sledding or mountaineering the hill were possible, and onlookers not in the crashes were snappy with their Olympic-style scores.

Our only guidelines on the hill or in the neighborhood involved being aware of strangers, avoiding the Flint River, and returning home at the proper time. There were exceptions as we explored *near* the river and we devised our own timetable. Relying on landline phones we often snuck back home in the cover of darkness.

We were granted plenty of freedom and we were responsible for our schedules. Child kidnapping was rare, terrorist threats were non-existent, and getting lost was inconceivable. However, being struck by a car, drowning in water, and falling from a tree were possibilities. The Millers, Dowells, and Belills had an alluring neighborhood with lots of prospects. Besides, nothing could happen to us, we were invincible.

Chapter 3
THE VAST PLAYGROUND

The Dowell's official backyard was the area where the shrubs were trimmed, the green grass was mowed, and the vegetable garden was within a short walking distance from the house.

Behind the civilized all-American dominion was the vast non-fenced in backyard. This extended wilderness started with the sledding hill and contained a valley, creek, and pond. Within the array of forested land were water puddles, fallen logs, and adjoining properties.

On a specific day in January, Paul, Don, and I grabbed two trajectories down Dowells' hill. We proceeded to wander in the valley as a liberal portion of the land was the Dowell's property. When we entered the unsuppressed acres, I started my normal questioning. My main hypothesis involved the mysteries of the opposing hill.

My curious mind was haunted to investigate the hill across the interfering creek. The creek flowed along the back side of Dowells' land as their property's borderline. At no time had we ever crossed the creek, because we often debated if we could legitimately tread within the region. We were still in the process of pinpointing the owners as we had been deliberating for months the feasibility of crossing the free-flowing creek. My constant emphasis was on that unchartered hill.

We did have concerns with moseying around as intruders. We determined through our investigations the acreage we should cautiously stalk, and the territory we could freely enter. If there was a "No Trespassing" sign, we didn't assume the section was off-limits. The warning was meant for strangers and not intended for the good ole boys like my cousin Paul, my friend Tim, or myself.

Then again, we entered some designated land in the neighborhood as if it were our own estate. On those properties we would receive permission for entrance from our inherited friendship through our families. From time to time in life it's not what you know that counts, but it's who you know that matters.

As we wandered on a fraction of the acreage in the valley, we would be vigilant and on the lookout for the owner. We may have branded who owned the parcel, yet we did not have permission to be there. To dodge detection and avoid a confrontation, we became proficient at sneaking behind trees, hiding in bushes, and blending in with the surroundings.

Judiciously, our gang determined the homesteads we would never penetrate. If the owner's reaction was calling the authorities for our encroachment, we stayed well away from the area. When we reasoned the landowner might discharge a warning shot with his shotgun or send out his growling dogs, we only dawdled on the other side of his boundary.

Most of time we ignored the unwritten strategies of boundaries. Our biggest factors of entering the land or not, were based selfishly on the wildlife prospects or the possibility of generating undisclosed forts.

Throughout the valley, Brent Creek flowed from the south to the north. The stretch on the back side of the Dowells' land was straight. On the other adjoining properties, the creek meandered its way through the countryside creating steep and gradual inclines on both sides of the valley. The base of Dowells' hill was one hundred yards away from the creek. Dissimilar, the opposing hill was ten yards from the watery creek.

The difficulty spanning across the creek was the depth of the water and the strong current. Swimming to the other side of the creek was unmanageable due to the frigid temperatures. Even by wading across the creek on a warm day, the odds of trouble were understandable when incorporating the debris comprising the creek. There were hidden rocks, sticks, and loose gravel in the water. Adding in the fragile soft banks meant traversing the water was unfeasible without a miracle.

Perhaps, the decisive element in the vast playground was the pond. The pond did not exist on that January day as Paul, Don, and I roamed the valley. The water hole was fashioned as a byproduct of a sewage line created in the 1970s. A twenty-mile concrete underground line was installed from the populated city of Flint to our rural neighborhood in Montrose Township.

The concrete tiles were approximately four feet in diameter, and prior to their installation, we rode our bikes in the cylinders stored along the valley. The results of us being brave munchkins were skinned knees and bruised knuckles. My funky bike with its banana seat and monkey-bars survived unharmed, and the bike functioned well with an ideal design for the strange endeavor.

The destination of the water treatment and sewage plant was controversial from the start. As a boy being raised in the county, the construction and operation of the water facility was prominent in my life. The treatment plant was front-page news, a dinner table hot topic, and the main focus among the rumor mill. Gossip of the treatment plant was overheard at the grocery store, post office, schools, hardware store, and coffee shop.

The residences surrounding the proposed water treatment plant were vehemently opposed to the development due to high traffic volume, deteriorating roads, and environmental concerns.

After the construction of the water treatment plant, the main road passing through the facilities had to be repeatedly resurfaced due to the heavy circulation of semi-trucks.

There was another controversial decision when it was resolved to build a bypass around the treatment plant through the middle of a private woodlot. The bypass was named Keewadin Road, in connection with the past influence of Native Indians in the vicinity. The debated alternative route would increase by two miles the trip to the town of Montrose for school, shopping, and work.

Due to the absence of residential homes along the road, the bypass regularly chaperoned as a charming lovers' lane in the wee hours of the night. The straightness of the road also ushered in an unaltered drag strip.

As a teenager, I undertook drag races on the asphalt with my black Camaro bolting up and down the scandalous road. I offer no comment on my personal involvement with the secluded parking proposition.

Whether driving on the main road or the alternate route, it was impossible to escape the musty odor from the treatment facilities. Our fresh rural outdoor environment frequently resembled the smell of the wet, moldy socks lying in the corner of the guys' locker room.

When the workers installed the sewage line, there were controversies with the labor force practices along the route. In my relatives' woodland area, there were discussions of the departure of established walnut trees. The result of the backroom settlement was the appearance of a pond on the Dowells' site.

Downstream from Dowell's property, Brent Creek drains into the Flint River. The Flint River leads to the Saginaw River with the concluding destination of the drainage system being the Saginaw Bay, which is an enormous segment of Lake Huron. The connection to one of the Great Lakes meant a diversity of fish throughout the year in the creek and the pond.

We had unparalleled times fishing northern pike in the summer, and migrating salmon in the fall. Paul and I once freaked out as a monstrous pike rolled across the surface with its toothy jaw opened. After the sighting we were cautious in the water barefooted, yet we continued to cast for hours to entice the nasty fiend to attack our red and white daredevil lures on our fishing lines.

Excluding the potential presence of Jaws a summertime dip in the pond wasn't out of the question. Being growing competitive children, we found skipping stones in the manmade pond helped develop and test our throwing skills.

Besides the pond, we had many other wonders and occupants of the natural setting to inspect. As curious young varmints, we would canvas for frogs, snakes and any other hidden critters. As teenagers we hunted rabbits, squirrels, and deer. Being outdoor fanatics, we had bonfires, camp-outs, rodeo competitions, and a dog barking contest.

The bonfires were matchless because they were held in connection with our nighttime sucker spearing. A bonfire during an outing was our home base where we warmed ourselves, roasted hot dogs, and relaxed between tramps through the creek. The sucker spearing was a revered annual event and was anticipated at the first sign of spring. The obscure adventure with lanterns, wood-handled spears, and waders would be undertaken when the spring thaw arrived in March.

The suckers were a species of fish migrating from the Great Lakes into the creek to spawn. We would spear the suckers by lurking through the creek's shallow sections carrying our lantern as a non-alarming guide. During our slow steps upstream we would clutch our four-prong spear and cast it at the swimming fish.

In spite of suckers being classified as a rough fish, our crew's proposed to clean the fish and slow-cook them in a homemade wood smoker. But we could not convert our preconceived notions of the undesired table fare. The speared suckers developed into garden fertilizer, or they were slung on the creek's banks as a treat for the raccoons, skunks, and opossums.

In our wonderful playground the unplanned dog barking contest commenced one wintry day. As we were wandering in the valley, Paul and I recognized two beagles expressing passionate howls in the distance. Without any predetermined proposal we started imitating the dogs. We whooped like we were hot on the trail of a cottontail rabbit, and after a minute I won the challenge due to Paul's relinquishment of the loud wailing.

I continued with my yowls with the baying action becoming clever between the beagles and me. In plain view Paul and I beheld on the opposing hill a pair of beagles surfacing with their tails wagging. They were sniffing and examining the hill as they uncovered two bewildered boys standing in the valley. Paul and I were perplexed at the phenomena which had come about, though we were flattered we had coaxed the dogs into our humble domain.

We arrived back in reality with our minds spiraling with nervousness as we identified behind the beagles a rabbit hunter with his intimidating shotgun. Instead of his determined mutts chasing a rabbit back to him, two absentminded lads had bribed his hounds over to the hill's edge for a mindless game.

Shrewdly, we hid behind trees and slipped away avoiding any eye contact. By no means did we stick around to stockpile verbal accusations from the hunter. The bump into the dissatisfied hunter wasn't my first or last embarrassing moment as a child, but it was the last dog barking contest I entered.

On a tract of land south of Dowells in the valley, Paul and I had another awkward incident. At a secluded pasture Paul and I crawled under the hot wire fence. We advanced toward the lone tenant in the enclosure, a retired white horse named Fred. The stallion was unyielding in his afternoon grazing as he continued with the green alfalfa. He did check his radar once by raising his head and spying us sneaking along in the grass.

Through our uncomplicated tactics we were able to arrange me in position to climb aboard Fred's sagging back. However, there would be no ride for me on Fred into the sunset. I lasted under six seconds on his crude, skeletal back. One raise of Fred's head and a short gallop positioned me on the ground sidetracking his wandering hooves. I picked up my pride and body, and I solicited to Paul whether he wanted a round on the rodeo circuit. In between Paul's laughs I snatched a solid no answer.

The immense playground or valley was the setting for an extra educational opportunity for the cousins and our mutual friend, Billy. Billy resided about a quarter of a mile from Paul's house and he was the same age as Paul and me.

One spring day, we three yahoos brainstormed the idea of constructing a raft. The recent rain and melting snow had increased the creek's water level and had created the ideal condition for whitewater rafting down the waterway.

We had plenty of ambition in designing the raft as we gathered the ingredients and equipment needed for our creation. My dad had worked as an independent carpenter, so lumber and tools could be borrowed from my house. Paul also had a generous supply of provisions available at his house because of their ever-growing junk pile. Additionally, Billy had the prevailing reputation of somehow placing his hands on anything we ever wanted or needed.

The three bandits hoarded numerous items, and after constructing the vessel, the next business was to enlist a volunteer as our fearless trailblazer. Billy, the person with the most energy and drawing the shortest straw, was commissioned our admiral. Paul and I declared we were not willing guinea pigs, while we gladly accepted the role of lowly shipmates.

Serving as shore hands, Paul and I had the maritime duty of holding on to the rope secured to the raft. On the maiden voyage our admiral and main navigator issued one command, "Hang on to the rope guys. Don't let go of it."

The shipmates muttered an agreement while Billy climbed onto the magnificent contraption. Upon launching our Queen Mary of Brent Creek, Billy and the gorgeous yacht swiftly drifted out into the middle of the creek. The young lad, Billy, was a self-portrait of Peter walking on the Sea of Galilee.

Our commander was bursting with pride in his valiant adventure as a suave seafarer. Billy's natural facial set-up was usually a smirk and he often added the display of a mischievous façade. His expression was comparable to a cat's inflated mouth declaring, "I ate the canary and there's nothing you can do about it."

Within seconds the craft began sinking, with Billy instantly losing his firm child-like faith. First, the water began to conceal his tennis shoes as the raft was lowering itself in the water. Next, the water level rose above the cuffs of his blue jeans. Billy downright lost his enraptured glow and demanded of his cadets, "Help me!"

Paul and I have been able to communicate with each other with scarcely a glance and we execute as we sense the need. In this case, we yanked on the rope with all our might. Between the current carrying the marine craft downstream and us tugging on the raft against the current, the vessel took a serious deep plunge into the water.

Billy screamed louder and reiterated his authoritative shouts of, "Help me! I'm drowning! Pull me in!"

After two more heaves on the rope the wood blob continued to descend. Paul and I were unruffled as we simply flung the nylon rope toward the raft.

With the rope falling short of its destination, streams of tears and a frown appeared on Billy's face.

I was pretty sure I wasn't diving into the evil current, so I began praying for Billy's strength to swim to shore. I was envisioning standing with the grieving parents at Billy's funeral. In light of my actions, I was positive I would be grounded until I was twenty-nine years old.

Apparently, the observation of the sinking craft was an optical illusion. Upon further review we detected the apparatus was holding its own. The glorious vessel had a chance to survive and be docked.

Paul and I rushed to the grassy bend and we stretched out our arms and hands towards the homemade raft. The two deckhands, now promoted to rescuers, grasped the distressed ferry and annexed the apparatus to the solid portion of the creek bank.

The mighty seadogs involved with the voyage went wild and crazy. Upon Billy stepping on shore there were high fives given out by all members. Nevertheless, Billy became serious, non-talkative, and pouty.

As part of Billy's debriefing, he offered his earnest comments, "You guys promised not to let go of the rope. I almost drowned. Why did you throw the rope at the raft?"

Paul and I could not reply to our admiral with a sophisticated answer, except to murmur we thought it was the right thing to do at that time.

The evaluation of the chartered cruise was ruminated differently by the naval crew, and I can reflect that Paul and I were never thanked by Billy for saving his life. Billy never again mentioned the voyage, though Paul and I frequently recited the story to our friends and family.

Paul and I attempted to render the narrative's account as theatrically as we could, although we would often near the story's conclusion and end up chuckling and laughing about Billy's reversed reactions. I reminisce on the unstable event now with thankfulness, but back then I foolishly imagined ourselves as invincible.

Famous for perilous acts one summer day Billy turned while urinating and sprayed the pasture's hot wire fence. Billy received an instant jolt and plunged to the ground. Through the direct revelation Billy was uninjured, and after the exhibition I needed no further lessons about dangerous electrical fences.

In our childhood Paul and I highly regarded our escapades with Billy. I think Billy was the one guy banned as much as me from the Dowells' residence.

As an adult Billy was married and had no children. One day while driving home from work a vehicle on an intersecting street ran a stop sign and slammed into the side of Billy's vehicle. Billy died at the young age of forty-two years old.

   ***

On that specific January day in the valley, Paul and I had no grand plan. At the bottom of my cousin's hill, Paul and I at twelve years old had only one responsibility to watch over Paul's younger brother Don. We were free to roam the vast playground with Don tagging along with us.

The wonderful things to explore in the spring, summer, and fall did not exist in the winter so my attention was obsessed with dominating the opposing hill. Standing upstream of the launching site of the renegade raft, I vowed to be a valiant explorer in the valley. Paul and I were going to investigate the daunting hill. But in order to cross the deadly creek, we would need a miracle.

Chapter 4
THE OPPOSSING HILL

Paul and I spotted a trace of ice forming along the edges of the creek. In this stretch of the creek the current was too rapid to allow the forming of an ice bridge. Winter weather would not permit the manufacturing of a bridge. Plus, building a manmade structure would provide visual evidence of our infringing on the forbidden soil.

I was flabbergasted at the transformation in the creek since the last time we were there. Toward the creek's south end, a bulky tree had become lodged between the two opposing creek's banks. About two feet in diameter, the fallen tree was forced into a snug position as a natural bridge over the water. The ruckus continued in my mind as I observed the tree was hefty enough to support a person's weight. We now could scamper across the creek with minimal effort, and without finding ourselves wet.

With no "No Trespassing" signs in sight on the opposing hill, and miraculously a bridge in front of us, I was itching to use the abundance of daylight hours to investigate the steep unknown incline. With all the hurdles eliminated I proceeded into my impromptu dance of jumping up and down. Paul wasn't amused and he was mute while seeming to be unconnected to the plan.

After my questioning, Paul admitted he had hesitations about his younger brother. Don was four years younger than us and Paul knew Don didn't have the balance required for crossing the log or the strength for climbing the abrupt hill.

Unlike the east side of the valley where the Dowells' hill had a gradual grade and lots of trees, the opposing hill was much brasher and had fewer trees. Within the west gradient, the ground surface had loose sandy dirt and even from a distance we recognized the climb would be a challenge for Paul and me. Factoring in the steep incline and the concern about the poor leverage caused by the loose dirt, the circumstances meant something unattainable by Don.

The dilemma was dampening my mood and the issue was schooling me about perseverance. Paul and I worked through several possible solutions as we didn't fancy taking Don with us and we couldn't send him back to the house. Back at the Dowell's abode we could not trust Don to preserve our classified undertaking.

Our theory developed to have Don remain on the Dowells' side of the creek with him being permitted to play in a defined area. Don could frolic around the nearby trees or sit on a dry log while we scaled the hill. Paul's brother was not to meander around in the valley, but Don was permitted to throw sticks, stones, and snowballs. Under no circumstances was he to wander near the creek's bank. Above all he was not to crawl out on the tree bridge and take a stab at crossing the icy log hanging above the treacherous creek.

Paul used all the intimidation his young mind could rally and he launched it on Don. I added my unsympathetic thoughts with the nastiest glare I could formulate. Paul expressed to Don two more times he was not even to touch the log bridge.

As soon as I sensed the Don situation was dealt with sufficiently, the matter was out of my mind. My focus reverted to my year-long allure involving the opposing rise.

The crossing of the bridge was a minor distraction and a pleasant bonus as I didn't injure myself, fall in the creek, or perform something dweeby that I would sometimes do in those situations. After crossing the creek Paul reminded Don of the instructions for the fourth time.

Paul and I were two healthy, curious, and brave boys entering a world of exploring. The scramble up the hill was a complicated crawl, and as expected there was limited leverage. The unstable dirt miserably failed as we often lost our footing and slid backwards. Halfway up the quest I was taken aback with the task as my breathing became erratic and my calf muscles tighten.

After all my fabrications during the past months, I was ascending to the summit of the mysterious mount. I would calculate my future engagements with my eyes gazing across the seized stage. My feet would tread bit by bit over every inch of soil as I would examine all the trees and creatures of the hilltop. Paul and I would contemplate the prospects to build a fort or hide while I would seek out all the riddles concealed from me until now.

The climb was not a racing contest to the summit, but I did ascend to the crest of the hill before Paul. I was pleased by accomplishing the scuttle with no cuts, scrapes, or bruises. This was my moment of euphoria as the conquering hero and I wanted to stake a flag into the ground marking my victory. I was motivated to thunder out a whoop, yet all I did was stare at the site before me.

Within seconds Paul was standing alongside me, and I delivered a sideways glance in his direction. I then deployed my full undivided attention back to my captured realm when I oddly became suspicious of a flash of movement.

I twisted sideways noticing Paul had revolved 180 degrees and he was facing the defeated hill. Without any words or explanation, Paul began to dash down the hillside toward the wintry creek.

My mind was thrown into neutral gear with my body frozen in the stationary gear of park. My eyes attempted to keep up with the action as I squinted down the hill viewing Paul in a runaway stampede. My cousin was hurtling downward with gigantic strides while I was preparing for the sight of a horrible tumble.

In awe of my cousin's balance and amazed at his speed, I examined the spectacle associating Paul's sprint with his feet being on fire. In my mental haze I was interrupted by a sound I couldn't decipher at first. The screeching sound wasn't an animal nor was it automated. I heard it again and I decrypted the message as a boy's scream. Through my auditory senses I heard, "Help! Paul! Help!"

The phrases altered in volume while I confirmed the yelling was from Don. His voice was shrill at times then muffled and almost lost.

My leaping bounds down the routed hill were not of the caliber of Paul's mindless sprint. By the time I had galloped back to the tree crossing, I viewed Paul deep in the frigid creek. He was below the tree bridge battling his way back to the shore. Behind Paul being tugged by his arm was the eight-year-old disobedient Don.

If Paul's feet were on fire sprinting down the hill those same feet were now doused in freezing water. The fire had moved to Paul's speech as a heated discourse developed between the big brother and the little brother. As is the case among most brothers, the older brother was dominating the conversation. Don was whimpering and crying, while from my view it didn't appear Don was assisting much in the rescue operation.

After I took the conservative and dryer route across the jammed tree bridge both of my cousins were on the bank of the creek shivering. During the entire ordeal this was the first time I was considering the fearful possibility of death visiting our kingdom. My terror of losing one or both of my cousins far outweighed any thoughts of exploring the other side of the hill.

The chattering of their teeth and the violent tremors were frightening to my world. In the moment of immediate jeopardy, we had the logic to start removing their wet outer layer of clothes. I contributed my outer coat to Don and my flannel shirt was donated to Paul. I kept my long-sleeve thermal T-shirt as I was not close to the vulnerability of endangerment comparable to Paul and Don.

My concentration was fuzzy and my first inclination was to start a fire. By creating a fire we could dry the clothes and warm the icy brothers by the fire's heat. For us it wasn't unusual to have matches or a cigarette lighter to start campfires, to burn piles of leaves, or to dispose of our household trash in a burning barrel.

However, in this case it would be chancy to initiate a fire as Paul's siblings or parents might spot the fire and become suspicious. In actuality, starting a fire would be improbable due to the winter snow on the kindling and logs.

As three young boys we didn't recognize *hypothermia* by the actual term. All the same, we clearly understood if we were wet and it was freezing cold, we could die. The concept of freezing to death alarmed us to make quick decisive decisions.

Our small entourage did not have any choice except to retreat to the house and risk our arctic jaunt being unveiled. Heading towards the house, the long trek up the hill was more demanding than the descent to the valley earlier in the day. Trudging our way back to the two story house, the long shadows from the sun and our adolescent attitudes had been altered.

Our threesome was unassuming while being downcast in our steps and in our speech pattern. We ascended up the grade as we were cautious of being spotted remaining to the north end where the sledding path was outlined. We strove upward possessing the framework of the trees between us and the windows of the dwelling.

Paul and I were operating as a duo dictatorship. We would enter the basement by going through the Bilco doors at the home's north end. The metal doors hung on a thirty degree angle with three steps to the cement flooring of the basement. The hinged red doors were the type seen in movies that a person is accessing during a tornado warning.

Our underhanded path was a no-brainer as the entrance allowed us to avoid passing through the main door and kitchen, thus refraining us from being detected, or leaving evidence of our shenanigans.

Upon entering the basement Paul and I gathered the drenched clothes and we cycled them through the laundry machines. We had no trouble in operating the washer and dryer while we occupied our waiting time by shooting games of billiards and walloping the punching bag in the basement.

The transition from the edge of devastation back to being vulnerable children in a world of innocent deeds was subtle. After about ninety minutes all evidence of Paul and Don plummeting into the frigid water was dismissed. Paul and Don were dry and warm with all of the dry clothes back on their rightful owners. Among the three voyagers we did not have one sniffle, sneeze, or cough.

Everything was fine except for one tiny detail. To conceal our wayward stunt, we were not to blab to anyone concerning the incident. An allegiance was formed and our main goal was to keep the information of the mishap from leaking to our parents. Punishment from our parents could be grounding, banishment from the other person's house, or a belt to our backside. Paul and I made the oath with us delivering our demands to the weak link, Don.

Life did continue for Paul, Don, and me. We attended school, completed our homework, and participated on our sports' teams. We accomplished our daily chores at home, ate meals, and slept in warm beds. On Sundays we went to church and spent time with our families. We even found time to slide down the hill, hunt in our infinite playground, and compete in our pick-up games on Saturdays.

Weeks after the death-defying incident Paul was eating a snack and Don entered the room. Boldly, Don asked Paul for some of the treat and Paul responded with his short answer of no.

Don threatened to tattle to their parents about the unscheduled and illegal polar plunge in the creek. I'm not for sure if Paul didn't take the threat serious or he wasn't going to be intimidated, but Paul calmly and without hesitation called Don's bluff during their poker game.

Don walked out of the room and went straight to their parents. Don went on to divulge all the simplified details of our top-secret quest to his mom and dad. Don did not leave out a single specific in his narration.

Consequently, Paul was quizzed and rebuked by his parents. My aunt and uncle were indeed uneasy about us crossing the dangerous creek. Yet, they did not mention our covering up of the charade by the using the basement's appliances. I think they attained a fraction of assurance in our rescue mission and with us taking responsibility for our actions by using the laundry machines.

Definitely, Don was presented with the bulk of their parents' wrath. Don disobeying the direct orders of his older brother was their prime area of opposition. Neither Don's nor Paul's disciplinary punishment became public knowledge. However, I can verify Don did not contest Paul's authority the rest of our childhood.

Being the youngest or the alleged golden child of my family, I received no punishment from my parents for the exhibition. I did receive news from Paul the next day on the phone that I was banned from Paul's house for a month. In my optimistic outlook I figured I wouldn't be expelled from their house and land by the time the upcoming sucker spearing season began.

Memories of that cold January day has made me realize I have an appetite for searching out unidentified elements. My adventure with my cousins, the precarious creek, and the cagy hill became life-threatening, but overall the ordeal was satisfying for my inquisitive mind.

Nearly all of my undertakings in my life have cultivated insights and enjoyment within me. In limited feats I have been presented with confusion and hurt. While most of my exploits have been planned, certain ones have spontaneously developed.

I do cherish all of my adventures and hold them in special spots in my memory. My life consists of steps planned by a loving and protective God.

There are magnificent adventures waiting in classrooms, during a vacation, or on a daily run in a neighborhood. My curiosity to discover what's over the next hill is unrelenting.

Chapter 5
THE JOURNEYS

For my high school senior class trip at Michigan Lutheran Seminary, we traveled to locations in the states of Wisconsin, Minnesota, and Illinois. Thankfully, we were transported by a chartered coach bus as we toured schools, churches, and institutions associated with the Wisconsin Evangelical Lutheran Synod (WELS).

My kindergarten through twelfth grade instruction began as I attended Montrose Public Schools. At the age of four years old, I began kindergarten as my mother preferred I was with the older five-year-old children that I connected with in our neighborhood. The early start to kindergarten was solely activated for the development and expansion of my social skills.

I concluded my freshmen year at Montrose High School, and for my tenth grade year of high school I enrolled at Michigan Lutheran Seminary (MLS). Located in Saginaw, Michigan, MLS is a preparatory school preparing graduates for studies in the ministry in the WELS.

During my three high school years at MLS, I resided in the campus' dormitory. The night before the senior trip three seniors and I snuck out of our dormitory on a wayward mission. In the middle of night we toilet-papered the residences of a professor and the school's president. The incident was the lone time I have participated in the midnight art of toilet-papering.

In my teaching vocation I have been on the other end of receiving donated toilet paper. To wake up in the morning and scan a lawn full of toilet paper in the trees is predictable at certain times. The task of cleaning up the art display is annoying whether it is homecoming week or prom night. The retrieval of the paper is never completed until weeks later.

With a lawn mower mulching the toilet paper in the yard, nothing is accomplished except creating more white fragments clinging to the green lawn. The transformation to the winter season finds the paper camouflaged on the snow-covered driveway and sidewalk, yet the aggravation reaches a new level as the strands of paper become clogged in the snow blower's auger.

Maybe the toilet paper act was a modest caper before our senior trip, but it was agreeable to this insubordinate teenager. We sure did have muted laughs as we chucked the rolls up in the trees.

The next morning we refocused on the upcoming expedition, and I was anticipating the road trip with my fellow students. I was enthusiastic because I had been fortunate to have a taste of traveling outside the state of Michigan before, and I had reveled in the experience.

As a nine-year-old boy on a week-long vacation, our family visited my father's childhood family farm in South Dakota. In addition we traveled to Nebraska to visit distant family members. My parents, my older siblings, and I were crammed into a suffocating station wagon for the family vacation.

We occupied our nights in an Apache pop-up camper we towed behind the station wagon. I prized our camping-out in the county and state parks, and we did creepily stow away one raining night in a parking lot of an abandoned gas station in an unidentified locality.

On the summer vacation I met a number of my great-aunts and great-uncles, and their immediate families. The excursion was a getaway with fresh inspections of new and unfamiliar sites. To occupy our time, we engaged ourselves in the travel game of identifying state license plates on vehicles. During longer stretches on the road we competed against each other in the alphabet letter contest using words on the roadside billboards. And of course in the station wagon we took naps, whined, and repeatedly asked if we were there yet.

Besides the roadside diversions, camping out, and the car games, we uncovered pleasure in the modest whims as rural kids. We found it superior to spend long hours swimming in an indoor pool in Omaha, Nebraska. We could have inhabited the pool for days as swimming tadpoles if we were permitted.

From the trip I processed my most award-winning memory of manhandling a twelve-ounce glass of draft beer in a hole in the wall saloon. While in the dark bar in downtown Gary, South Dakota, I was a pipsqueak boy transforming into a scandalous buckaroo.

Our senior class voyage would be similar to the family vacation because both outings covered several Midwest states of the United States. Both trips were recreational excursions with minor objectives thrown in to validate the jaunts.

Our family journeyed to Nebraska to retrieve a muzzle loader gun my father had inherited. The school's senior trip was a recruitment visit to the two WELS ministry colleges and the WELS theology seminary.

On the first morning of the senior tour I was on luggage duty. I was one of the first people to be on the sidewalk next to the bus. I wore a smile on my face and dragged my family's gray vinyl suitcase along in in my hand. I procured my first picture using my disposable Kodak 110 camera. Another classmate snapped a picture of two senior buddies and myself lounging in the piled-up baggage. All three of us were behaving like macho teenage boys whereas we were convinced the world was in our adolescent grasp.

On the school's chartered bus we proceeded through Michigan, Indiana, and Illinois, with certain intervals becoming brutal due to the extended hours on the highways. In Wisconsin and Minnesota we visited the two WELS colleges and the WELS seminary. Furthermore, we dropped in on WELS high schools, grade schools, and churches.

Mixed in our agenda we investigated the WELS publishing house, an assisted living institution, and the past AAL or current Thrivent Insurance organization and building. Being a curious teenager I seized the stopovers as appealing.

When our bus commenced west across the Mississippi River on our way to a recruitment tour at Dr. Martin Luther College in New Ulm, Minnesota, I was positive we had strayed to the other side of the world. On that day in Minnesota I finally understood the belief of ancient civilizations about their journeys. Many ancient voyagers believed that if they traveled too far on land or by sea, they would fall off the earth's flat surface.

Our routine on the school trip was to motor by bus during the day and file off the motor vehicle for a hurried sidetrack tour. After the short excursion off the bus we would continue on to a church or school, consume a meal, and occupy the night slumbering on a gym floor or in classrooms.

The whole commotion of inspecting the buildings and meeting the different faces was stimulating. I intended to absorb and take pictures of everything. I aimed to scrutinize what was over every hill. But after heading east back over the Mississippi River, I was positive I would not be attending college on the other side of the world.

For my contemporaries and me the last two days of the school trip overshadowed the beginning days of the spree. Our itinerary had the final two days and nights in downtown Chicago, Illinois. We would be lodging in the world-renowned Palmer House Hotel in the loop area.

In Chicago, we toured as a school group the Museum of Science and Industry, and the Sears Tower. The Sears Tower was the tallest building in the world at the time, and we jockeyed the elevators to the roof to assess the city's skyline. We were aghast at the skyscrapers and the uninterrupted Lake Michigan. Previously, I had ridden in plenty of elevators, but this was the first time I was in an elevator covering ten floors in one cluster in a matter of seconds.

In the Windy City, we were allotted our free time and I did not have a lack of proposed pursuits. On one tenure, a friend and I indifferently funneled onto a metro subway. We did not have a destination in mind, and in hindsight that could have been a precarious situation for two immature boys.

Once on the subway, we whizzed through Chicago and headed north to the suburbs. By chance we departed from the subway within the campus of Northwestern University.

After being at small colleges in Wisconsin and Minnesota, Northwestern University was remarkable. Northwestern's campus contains stately structures positioned within the shores of Lake Michigan. The setting of the university's grounds was further enhanced with the scattering of mature trees. If the buildings were able to relay the stories of their past they would have some intriguing tales.

Northwestern was the third Big Ten campus I would wander through as an adolescent. As a Michigan native, Michigan State University and the University of Michigan were my first visits of Big Ten universities. I had also explored the campuses of Eastern Michigan University, Western Michigan University, and Central Michigan University.

Another initiative to occupy my free time in downtown Chicago was when two buddies and I visited the Chicago Playboy Club. As teenage boys from a blue-collar working culture, seeking out such an enterprise was thrill-seeking. Without a shred of discussion from the doorman we were not allowed to enter the lounge due to the age requirements.

As a consequence we tried our best to sneak a peek inside as the lounge doors swung open and shut. Without giving the impression of promoting the activity, we did observe patrons entering and leaving. With wonderment we recognized waitresses transferring between their occupations and their leisure interval. We were savvy as witnesses of the off-duty bunnies in their casual clothes and winter coats.

As our consolation prize we were competent enough to buy souvenirs at the gift shop. There is no eye-popping story to tell about the Playboy Lounge, except that as a primitive adolescent it would be a head-nodding credit to boast about with the boys for years.

For the evening's amusement my girlfriend and I, plus another couple, went to an Italian restaurant on Michigan Avenue. We were dressed for the evening with the cultured gentlemen sporting dress pants, shirts, and ties. The glittering ladies were revealed in their beautiful dresses with highlighted portraits and pampered hair. All dressed up we dined on my seventeenth birthday as if we were affiliates of the elite upper crust.

On the second evening our plans were unassuming. Six friends and I devoted our evening to hanging out at the hotel pool. For dinner we grabbed a pizza from a local pizzeria. While chilling out around the pool we became aware of a rumor being tossed around the hotel's hallways. The detail of the allegation stated there were three famed people at a charity event unfolding at a dining room in the hotel.

The historical background of the Chicago's Palmer House Hilton built in the 1800's is well scripted on the hotel's website. The narrative tells of the Chicago business magnate, Potter Palmer, who built the hotel in downtown section. Thirteen days after opening the hotel the building was destroyed in the Great Chicago Fire.

Potter Palmer refinanced and rebuilt the hotel presenting the structure to his wife as a wedding present. Throughout the years, Bertha Palmer, decorated the luxurious hotel with art paintings, chandeliers, and furniture. In the early 1900s, the Palmer House was a buzzing social spotlight while hosting U.S. presidents, Charles Dickens, and Oscar Wilde.

In 1933, the Golden Empire Dining Room of Palmer House was converted into an entertainment epicenter. Legendary entertainers visiting the Palmer House include Frank Sinatra, Judy Garland, Ella Fitzgerald, Harry Belafonte, Louis Armstrong, and Liberace. In recent years the historic Chicago hotel, the Palmer House Hilton has undergone a multi-million renovation.

The organizers of our high school trip booked reservations for a stopover at the Palmer House Hotel by electing to populate the thirteenth floor. On the annual trip our school through the years had learned potential quests habitually avoided lodging on the thirteenth floor. Because of the occupants' superstitious beliefs we were able to acquire affordable rates.

The evening's hoopla turned out to be a dinner honoring the "Outstanding Chicagoans of Today." We heard that two of the three celebrities were Ann Landers and Howard Cosell. Ann Landers was recognized for her syndicated advice column. Howard Cosell was distinguished for his commentary of boxing matches and Monday Night Football. The third star of the celebrities was the one that really caught my attention because of his athletic accomplishments.

While poolside, a master plan was developed by two flamboyant students to inspect the banquet being held in the Golden Empire Dining Room. As self-acclaimed charity crashers, my friend Steve and I proceeded up to our separate rooms. I hustled through a shower and I ensued through my actions to showcase my best appearance as a successful businessman.

My head of hair was nearly shoulder length impeccably parted down the middle and feathered back on both sides. In that era young men packed their own handheld blow dryers for styling purposes, and I had one along as I operated it in my hotel room that evening.

To spruce myself up, I squeezed into my best duds. My senior picture attire consisting of a three piece suit was hanging in my hotel's closet. The Caroline blue getup consisted of matching suit coat, pants, and vest.

First, I threw on my blue dress shirt and tucked the polyester shirt into my dress pants. My pants smoothly clung to my legs until they passed the knee territory. The pants were loose at the calf region and reached the ground in the form of large, fluttering, bell-bottoms.

In the mirror's reflection, I twisted a white tie into a knot with the tie's tail falling short of my waist. Slipped through the pants' loops was a black belt, and my vest was snugly fastened around my midsection.

My suit jacket assimilated comfortably over my shoulders and through my arms. The ensemble came to a polished close with the zipping up of my two inch, high-platform shoes. The outfit was no retro getup as this was cool stuff for the fashionable 1970s.

Stepping off one of the elevators in the lobby, I overheard Howard Cosell's booming discourse. I lifted a peek into the decorative hall with its stylish tables decked out with dishes, silverware, and glasses. Even as a crude schoolboy, I took notice of the flower arrangements, napkins, and candles. Overwhelmed, I stared at the large assembly of people sporting tuxedos and elegant evening gowns.

Steve and I had the strategy to saunter in the ballroom and engage first-hand everything with our eyes. Taking four footsteps through the banquet hall doors, we were immediately targeted by one of the sharp waiters. When we spotted him sizing us up and gliding our way, we knew we had been targeted as frauds. Jumpy in regards to our deception, we shifted gears and veered away from him in the opposite direction.

As a middle-aged man he was beginning to show gray streaks in his thinning hair. Apart from his appearance and age, he was quick, persistent, and closing in on the offenders. When the devoted employee cut us off and stopped us between the round tables he inquired in a firm voice, "Good evening gentlemen. Your appearances are quite grand for tonight's affair. May I please observe your tickets?"

I was evading eye contact and my face was heating up mutating to a shade of red. I was making every effort to stall and before I could invent a believable excuse the attendant continued his discourse.

"If you gentlemen need tickets, they may be purchased at the designated area near the door," he stated the proposal as he pointed with his open palm. Near the entry I noticed the area for quests' coats and ticket purchases. The waiter then tacked on the intimidating factor, "The price for admittance is $1,000 per person."

My ridiculous thinker was mulling it over for a second, but the extravagant cost engraved on my forehead that we were way out of our league. Our masquerade was unmasked and we now would be paying the price, or in this case the penalty. I was agonizing over washing dishes or receiving a loitering fine. I did not want to be escorted out of the room by a security guard or arrested by a police officer.

The domineering server nodded to the door while he summarized our retreat through the doors we had pranced through. The watchdog capped off his speech by warning us of attempting another devious re-entry. Another unauthorized visit would not be tolerated and there would be undesirable consequences enforced.

We nodded our agreement as we slurred a thank you and we began to skedaddle across the dining room. As only teenage boys can pull off, we acted placidly that our gig was revealed. Steve and I withdrew from the room swiping a piece of humble pie on our way.

Entering the lobby dejected I was not abandoning our crusade. The lobby served as a transitional zone and the elevators carried passengers between the floors. As we stood in the foyer our new approach was conceived. We would dillydally in the area, and we would star gaze at the legendary guests when they exited the event.

When we had first heard about the occasion in the hotel there was a fidgety buzz among the people. Now one hour later, the newsflash was fading. There was a fair amount of traffic in the chamber by the hotel's staff, yet by most interpretations the region was deserted.

One African-American woman, who was in her mid-twenties, was sitting on a bench. As we loitered in the area I initiated a conversation with the woman. Another student, Lemano, joined in the dialogue as the lady alleged she was waiting for the third superstar that was in the ballroom.

The very celebrity was at that moment addressing the audience of the charity event, explaining the details of him winning a gold medal in 1960. Even though the celebrity was known as a boastful talker, he seemed quite humble and reserved at the microphone.

I had doubts of a relationship between her and the third member of the prominent celebrities. Candidly, she went so far as to state she was not an ex-wife, the current wife, or mistress of the most celebrated personality at the dinner. She said, "I am his girlfriend."

Setting aside her romantic saga, we did have a pleasant discussion. Another hour sluggishly passed and in reflection I should have been engineering tactics for my next possible action. Up to that moment my lackluster blueprint was to catch a glance of the third megastar and move as close to him as possible.

The banquet was terminated and the guests entered the vestibule. Listed at six feet-three inches his height may not be intimidating, but he was encompassed by the swarms of admirers. The cheerful and energetic people were seeking photos, autographs, and handshakes. They wanted a moment with the celebrity and the three-time heavyweight boxing champion of the world, Muhammad Ali. He clearly stood out among the gathering. Muhammad Ali, who was garbed in a black tuxedo, was the focus of everyone's attention.

The spotlight was on "The Greatest".

Chapter 6
THE GREATEST

I am flabbergasted that a second-grader can finish Ali's trademark phrase, "I will float like a butterfly, sting like a _." In the same way, I think it is amazing that most adults from any part of the world can recognize a picture of Muhammad Ali.

At the charity event in the Palmer House Hotel it may have been his prestige, charisma, or accomplishments as he was the main attraction. Everyone was drawn to him and they were gripped by his presence. Muhammad Ali had the magnetism to pull people into his presence. Even with that particular decade not having the social media and bombardment of news sources of today's world, the general public back then could still identify Ali.

Muhammad Ali was born Cassius Clay and at eighteen years old he won a gold medal in the 1960 Summer Olympics held in Rome. In 1964, Clay won his initial World Heavyweight Boxing Championship by defeating Sonny Liston. Cassius Clay joined the Nation of Islam and changed his name to Muhammad Ali. In 1967, Ali refused to be drafted or serve in Vietnam. As a result of his actions, he was arrested and stripped of his boxing title.

Ali was a controversial and outspoken celebrity, who labeled himself "The Greatest". Having the status as a talker he was known to converse before, during, and after his professional fights. In his boxing career he had matches in the United States, Europe, and Africa, and he had distinguished bouts in Madison Square Garden. Later in his career, he utilized a boxing strategy coined as rope-a-dope. Muhammad Ali is the only heavyweight boxer who lost and regained the world championship title three times in his illustrious career.

When Ali exited the Golden Empire Ballroom he moved with a confident composure. When he stopped and signed his name on a piece of paper, I was whacked sideways in my thoughtless brain. In stupidity I had not arranged the necessary paper and pen to retrieve an autograph. I had wasted over an hour doubting a stranger's tale of her connection to Ali. I had blown the once-in-a-lifetime opportunity to acquire a signature from a world-famous celebrity.

I was contemplating my failure when I heard an announcement by Ali's personal staff, "Ali will not be signing any more items."

The crowd in the foyer was informed the champ had to be on his way in lieu of other commitments. He had signed two autographs and had lingered in the lobby for one photo opportunity. For a moment I had comfort realizing even if I was prepared for obtaining Ali's signature, it was a good chance the implementation would have been pointless as he was not signing items. Misery does love company.

Up to this point I was part of the masses attempting to progress near Muhammad Ali, and I had slithered my way within one person between Ali and me. I did have my disposable camera with me, but I could not take a photo due to being pressed in by the mob of fans. I figured I had assimilated sufficient bragging rights being in same the room with Ali and being within an arm length from him.

As Ali entered an elevator with his bodyguard, the inkling of shadowing him dawned on us. My friend, Steve, and I conjured up the idea to take a substitute elevator and hook up with the champ on another floor.

Choosing an elevator was no setback as there were several in the lobby. We pushed the button on four panels on the outside of the four elevators, and we besieged the first unsealing sliding doors. Steve and I nearly trampled over each other as we scurried into the opening compartment.

Then came the first genuine test of the infiltration. Inside the elevator we were being inundated with multiple selections of possible floors. My instinct was telling me there wasn't enough turmoil in the other areas of the hotel to reason Muhammad Ali was staying overnight in a hotel room. So I mentally eliminated the floors with only overnight rooms.

Dissecting the other options on the panel, the choice became obvious between two possibilities. The main floor (M) contained the check-in desk, hotel services, and meeting rooms. The basement (B) was the location of restaurants, shops, and stores.

Important to our predicting process was the fact that both the main floor and the basement level had public exits to the outside world. Without conferring with Steve, my verdict became B.

The Palmer House Hotel elevator Steve and I occupied was as moody as Dr. Jekyll and Mr. Hyde. At first we fired off like a rocket, and there was not adequate time to cultivate an assault in my mind. Without notice the descending elevator transformed into an apathetic snail pace as I was perceiving Muhammad Ali exiting his elevator and fading from my existence.

After the familiar stomach-flop halt the elevator doors sluggishly began to breach apart. As soon as I detected enough space to squeeze through the doors, I was wiggling out of my fickle imprisonment. Vaulting into the corridor I skimmed left, right, close, and far. Sadly, I sanctioned no Muhammad Ali in the immediate area near the elevators.

I accepted my failure and I stepped back into the elevator. I ached for one chance to amend my mistake, but time was against us. As I prepared to make my second choice on the panel, I engaged one last gander into the corridor. Across the way an elevator situated in the correct orientation of Ali's elevator was beginning to open. Leaning out of the elevator, I rubbernecked at the opposite doors and I said a short hopeful prayer for Ali to appear from an elevator.

As if in a dramatic movie scene, the bodyguard and Muhammad Ali emerged from the easygoing elevator. In a heartbeat I went from uncertainty and pessimism to confidence and optimism.

My sought after celebrity strolled down the large corridor with a body language of self-assurance. The atmosphere of the area was hectic and the patrons were immersed in their interests. However, in the bright passageway the public's reaction was engaging as they identified the renowned boxer.

There were shopping customers who gasped and held their mouths open as if to catch houseflies. A handful of innocent bystanders twisted their necks to follow the icon with their skeptical eyes. Women, both young and old, pointed at him and hardened as cold statuettes in a lonely museum.

No one monitored the star with vigorous footsteps, except two high-spirited teenage boys. Steve and I trailed behind the prominent personality for a few seconds, and then we boldly and smugly promenaded beside the champ and his bodyguard.

About the time I gathered the nerve to pose an interchange with Ali, he made a surprised right turn. The ex-titleholder swung open a hinged glass door leading into a restaurant, and inside the entry chamber he turned right again while pushing a solid wood door. Ali entered the adjoining space and in a flash the star had maneuvered himself completely from my presence and sight.

My maddening credence was hoping Muhammad would not be detained for an extended stretch in the restaurant. I knew he had dinner back in the ballroom and I could not envision Ali in the restaurant for another speaking engagement.

I began aimlessly drifting around in the walkway trying to pass the nervous moments. I was disgruntled with myself for being reluctant and not approaching Ali earlier. Ali's bodyguard had not entered the establishment and had remained outside the door in the corridor.

Without thinking I advanced to the personal assistant and summoned, "How long do you think the champ will be in the restaurant?"

The gigantic bodyguard continued to scan the hallway as he recognized my ramblings. The stoic man relayed in a low audible level, "I can't say for sure, but Ali should be back out in a few minutes."

With sprouting poise I asked, "Can I try to get an autograph?"

My pristine buddy answered me without even a glance at my longing face, "You can try."

With a renewed spirit, I began stirring in the role of an offensive autograph and photo-seeking fanatic. In my first pirating canvas of the area, I swiped a writing utensil in the form of a pen from the restaurant, and I scraped up an old envelope from a nearby trash container.

When Muhammad Ali returned from the restaurant's bathroom I was waiting in the passageway. The bodyguard, Muhammad Ali, Steve, and I were the only people in the immediate area. I stepped closer to Ali and I maturely inquired, "Muhammad, would you be willing to sign this?"

I held toward him the borrowed pen and recycled envelope. From his lack of facial variations and words, I had no indication about his intentions or future interchange with me. Doubting if he had heard my request, I was unsure if he even knew I was there in front of him. But I was optimistic he would surrender his non-signing agenda broadcasted outside the ballroom.

Decisively, Muhammad Ali reached out for the writing implements. Once the items were in his grasp, he began scribbling his name diagonally on the recycled remnant of paper. All the while as he wrote, Muhammad Ali panned the corridor and he seemed unconcerned with my existence.

As he handed back the pen and the priceless artifact, Ali looked at me and provided me a head nod. I didn't say a word as I received the treasured signature. I securely placed the autograph, plus my recently acquired pen, in my suit jacket's front pocket.

Ali began to stride down the hall and I was more relaxed in ambling alongside my two contemporary associates. The next phase of the master plan was simple to employ. Steve seized my camera and he rushed out twenty feet ahead of Ali and me.

In my high platform shoes I paraded alongside the superstar and I thanked him for the autograph. Feeling brave I voiced my congratulations to him on his past victorious fights and his remarkable boxing career. I relayed a grownup "good luck" on his upcoming boxing contest, and I continued soaking up the moment and my adoring gait with Muhammad Ali.

After a few steps I had nothing else ready to express, so I extended my arm and offered my hand as a thank you token. For the handshake I presented 90 percent of the effort toward the gesture. To my amazement Muhammad Ali reached over and seized my hand. Muhammad Ali contributed the other 10 percent as we shook hands in the corridor. I acted as if we were two close friends meeting after we had attended a classy cultured event.

While I occupied Ali's hand, I posed with a smile as I trickled my attention to Steve. My friend clicked the camera's button, and Steve's anticipation and action were carried off in perfect timing. Ali and I were both eyeing the camera, and I was grinning ear-to-ear. The photograph would be magnificent with the handsome Ali in his black tuxedo and me in my blue three piece stylish attire.

The boxer Muhammad Ali was in top shape and his stature was dignified. Ali's physique was solid and I knew standing next to him, I would have no longing to confront the hostile athlete in a boxing ring. I honestly sensed his poise, showmanship, and acceptance of his acquired role as a celebrity.

Ali's obliging handshake was firm and his hand engulfed my paltry extremity. Ali did not squeeze, radically shake, or pull my hand. The handshake was professional, and the size of his hands were gigantic.

"Thank you and good luck on your next fight," I replied.

Ali and I disconnected our grip and I began to float along the hallway suspended in the air. As I took deep breaths, I assumed the world had stopped spinning, or I was rotating as fast as the earth's spinning.

Steve returned by me and we gradually condensed our steps while quietly fading behind the exiting Muhammad Ali and his assistant. Ali continued the path to the exit while Steve and I re-examined the astonished reaction of the guests.

The often controversial Muhammad Ali walked through the opened glass doors at the passageway's end and he stood outside the hotel on the sidewalk. The outside atmosphere was awakening me out of my magical high. The clamor of society indulged in its moaning and groaning was obtuse to my ears. An awareness about Ali returning to the outside world presented me with a sudden cold detachment.

Muhammad Ali's life of world fame with a high-profile lifestyle was not in my realm of thinking. Ali's involvement in politics, media coverage, and interviews were incomprehensible. The amount of training sessions, televised bouts, and exotic travels were beyond my adolescent perception.

Granted, I could infer he faced challenges, difficulties, and setbacks as an occupant of this sinful world. Likewise, the street was reality for my classmates and me with our trepidations over future education, vocations, and marriages. Our lives would soon be assaulted with concerns over the economy, politics, and wars. We were just beginning to dive into the uncertainties of our health, safety, and existence.

The automated doors had slid shut and I could view outside the hotel a white stretch limousine parked alongside the curb. A dapper chap exited the driver side of the vehicle and rapidly proceeded around to the sidewalk. The chauffeur handled the back door of the automobile and Muhammad Ali began to bend down and position himself into the vehicle. Ali hesitated and retreated back one large step. He stood stationary for a brief second as a person glided into the backseat of the automobile.

Ali and his tux were within inches of the mysterious passenger while descending into the vehicle. The astute chauffeur closed the door and he scurried around to the driver's side of the vehicle. Within seconds the driver was behind the wheel and steadily accelerated the limousine into the hectic street. Muhammad Ali was gone from my life.

The encounter of shagging down Ali had taken about three hours. I had been blessed to breeze down the corridor with the most legendary athlete and celebrity in the world. I was honored to shake his hand as I relished our one-on-one arrangement. There were no interruptions from anyone and the unplanned rendezvous was surreal.

The person who snuck in the limousine with Ali was the young lady from outside the ballroom. She had specified being Ali's girlfriend and she did not plead with us to be believed. The situation in the lobby was a golden opportunity squandered by me regarding her confidential relationship with Muhammad Ali. I missed out on obtaining personal particulars I could have recycled as exciting future narratives.

After gallivanting around with the autograph and my camera for about an hour, I had a small predicament when I did retire to my hotel room. For safekeeping overnight I had to decide where to retain the autograph I had toiled so hard and long to obtain.

I deliberated about placing the signature under my hotel pillow, but I did not want to wrinkle the autograph. While weighing the thought of placing the inscription in my suitcase, I discarded that thought because I wanted to view the signature first thing in the morning. I even considered folding the envelope and placing it in my wallet, yet I didn't want to put a permanent crease in it.

I decided to place the signature on my nightstand alongside the bed. I wouldn't wrinkle it, and I could observe it first thing at dawn.

In the morning I was exhausted from the previous night's pursuit and I woke up late. The first thing I did was survey the nightstand for my autograph and I was alarmed to notice the piece of paper missing. I skimmed the room for my relic while inspecting the area around the nightstand. My examination did not disclose the paper under my pillow, in my suitcase, or in my wallet.

Again I eyeballed the area of the nightstand. This time I lifted the table, lamp, and alarm clock. I thoroughly combed behind the table, as the autograph apparently had vaporized overnight.

Taking a rushed shower, I dressed in my t-shirt and jeans then finished packing my suitcase. I was hoping I had moved the envelope during the night as I crisscrossed the floor. With a roving eye I began a search again under the bed and behind the TV. For the third time I diligently examined my bed, suitcase, and wallet.

I was confused as there was no way I was thinking about any dimwitted superstitions. I was not going to inaugurate any connections with the missing autograph and the number thirteen.

When my roommate returned from breakfast, Karl informed me our chartered coach bus would be departing for Michigan in a matter of minutes. As a last resort I asked Karl if he knew the whereabouts of the paper. Nonchalantly, Karl replied he had cleaned the room and he had thrown unwanted garbage in the trash.

Bounding towards the blue receptacle and dumping the contents of the container on the room's floor, I rummaged and filtered through every worthless piece of paper including the fascial tissues. In the middle of the rubbish I observed my crumbled piece of paper. My salvaged autograph and envelope had returned to my custody.

After our bus trip back to Michigan, I strived to have the photos on my camera developed as soon as possible. After three days I claimed the color photos at a pharmacy store. My plan was to take the photo of Ali and me to be enlarged to an eight by ten copy. In my preparations I had purchased a wood picture frame, and I planned to mount inside the glass the surviving envelope with the signature.

On the tour there was a glitch with the forwarding button on the camera. The grooved dial had little snags or hang ups while being rotated. The camera had been stored for months in our family's junk drawer. Naively, I wasn't worried about the camera's function, but I was apprehensive about the photo capturing my handshake with Ali. I was longing for the photo to be centered and focused.

I chuckled at the first three by five print which was my friends and me in the heap of luggage acting masculine on the trip's first day. When I checked the next print I was sickened by the blank glossy paper. The same result was on all of the remaining photos. I owned twenty-three imageless photos. I even scanned the film's negatives and found no evidence of my shaking hands with Muhammad Ali.

The facts plainly related I had no proof of my handshake with Ali as we strutted down the corridor at the Palmer House Hotel in Chicago. There wasn't even a selfie of Ali and me.

For years I could read the unbelief in certain people's reactions as they took note of my glamorization of the day after my seventeenth birthday. The cross-examination reaction has disappeared from my audience as I am now a believable, gray haired grandfather. And even in my old age, I still receive pleasure in reminiscing about the incident.

Since the chance encounter I have noticed the creased lines on the twice-discarded envelope have made the autograph even more exceptional in my manifestation. In the Chicago Tribune's archives, I discovered a photograph from the evening of the chance meeting. Ali is throwing a punch at Howard Cosell. Ali and Cosell are in their tuxedos while Ann Landers is good-humoredly breaking them apart.

As I unfold the adventure with second graders or teenagers, they enjoy solving the identity of the third star. The students' eagerly vote for M or B with their eyes widening with anticipation in the elevator scene. My audiences are astonished with the aspects of Ali's colossal hands and the listeners come up with guesses of who slipped into the limousine. Finally. I join with my students as they groan out loud over a non-existing photo of "The Greatest" and me.

Thank you, Lord, for the unexpected surprises and pleasing adventures in our lives!

Chapter 7
THE OCD MISFIT

In the animated movie *Rudolph, the Red-Nosed Reindeer*, which first aired on television in 1964, Rudolph is made fun of because of his bright red nose. We witness as Rudolph is not allowed to join in any more reindeer games. Rudolph sulks and runs away from home, and by way of an iceberg, arrives on the Island of Misfit Toys.

There were the absurd, impractical times in my childhood when I made the decision to run away from home by packing a suitcase and heading to the back woods. I would enjoy my snacks and my accommodations until dinner time or darkness.

At times in my life I have declared myself a misfit. I have perceived I don't comfortably fit within my environment. My persistent inner voice pressures me to think of myself as an oddball or a misfit.

When I was starting a summer factory job while attending college I was in my orientation procedure with a young lady conducting the vision examination. During the process she rose up out of her chair and rushed out of the room. I was stumped and all I could do was wait for her to return.

After two minutes she marched back into the room. She wore a stumped look on her face and she asked me in a prying voice, "Do you realize you are color blind?"

"Yes," I replied. I was wondering why she didn't ask me before her bursting reaction out of the room. I would have conveyed to her that I have battled classifying certain colors for decades.

Colors are tricky for me to distinguish and rightly name. For years I have had insecurities about identifying the correct color of everything in my life. My world of sight is not black, white, and gray as I perceive many colors. Though the forms may appear as a merger of various hues.

I regularly find myself erroneously categorizing a color. Through my elementary school days I questioned if I had missed the day in kindergarten when we were taught the names of the assorted crayons.

There are three basic variants of color blindness, and Red/green color blindness is the most common deficiency affecting eight percent of Caucasian males. The young lady at the cheese factory categorized me as having the effects of red/green blindness. Teasingly, I prefer the politically correct phrase, color deficient.

In my early childhood I suffered through two personal conducts that were humiliating. My thumb-sucking and bedwetting were traumatic incidents, but the thumb-sucking was erased when Mike began teasing me at an early age about the thoughtless practice.

My mother and I tried two approaches to the more difficult bedwetting. One strategy maintained I was forbidden to drink any liquids after 6 PM. The other tactic was my mother would wake me in the middle of night to use the bathroom. I would have a random accident until I was seven years old, and the acts left an abrasion on my self-esteem for several years afterwards.

In second grade I was diagnosed with speech sound disorders. At six years old I was informed I would receive assistance through speech therapy with Mrs. Rye. I would unite with Mrs. Rye three times a week for twenty minutes during the morning.

At first it was cool to veer off to Mrs. Rye's room as I would be released from the normal subjects. I idolized the personal attention and praise from Mrs. Rye. She was kindhearted and my favorite adult at the time would present to me treats for being a dedicated student.

My enthusiasm for the dismissal declined after two conferences. The degrading stares, pointing fingers, and mocking murmurs accumulating from my classmates were noticeable. I also surmised that I had to make up the lessons I had averted. A second graders' work is not exhaustive, but it did seem like a burden to my strong-willed mind.

After four speech sessions it was determined to adjust the speech classes to coincide with my morning recess. The alteration was a mammoth mistake as recess was in my top three activities at school. The other two items fluctuated between reading and science to gym and lunch depending on my mood for the day.

The other children were heading off to the playground or gym, as I sulked off to speech. Even treats from Mrs. Rye couldn't remedy being deprived of my tag games and swinging contests.

Being active with making sounds of the letters r and w wasn't obliging in second grade, yet I was granted a reprieve when my speech program was switched to the school day's conclusion.

With the new time frame I vowed to identify the acceptable sounds, practice the techniques, and verbalize the noises. I was motivated when I appropriately enunciated my "th" or "str." My successes came by listening to my speech therapist, following her instructions, and repeating over and over the correct articulation.

The reality was the instruction was brought to a halt after one year. I'm not sure if the stoppage was due to budget cuts or my testing out of the instruction.

To this day I struggle with specific linguist sounds and speaking various words in our English language. My pronunciation of certain words can be comical, mortifying, and a merciless struggle. Every day I try to practice with pronouncing a wide range of words.

Idea and ideal will be elusive to me as I agonize adding the letter l to both of the words. To avoid an embarrassing error I will revamp sentences. "I have an idea for supper," becomes "I have a thought for supper."

At times I scuffle with the words of wrestle, risky, Alzheimer, explicable, and tour. In contrast, I can dazzle myself while rolling off my tongue the exciting words of aluminum, Massachusetts, continental, evangelical, and supercalifragilisticexpialidocious.

When my high school years came rumbling along, I added to my misfit sensitivity my clashes with acne. My outbreak of acne symptoms was not severe. Nonetheless, there are remaining obvious facial marks. I have adjusted about being self-conscious when an individual will implore about the depressions. There is nothing in my explanation which is heroic while I can't decree the marks are from a knife scar or me overcoming a disastrous disease. I reply to stares by declaring the truth. The scars are teenage skin irritations that did not heal properly.

I have inquired of dermatologists regarding laser surgery to improve the situation. I have been presented the impression it is an expensive procedure and I have been advised against it.

Over the years, I have reasoned I feel like a misfit at times because of my color deficiency, speech impairments, and acne scars even though I had a wonderful childhood and years in school. I had devoted and loving parents. I was encompassed by marvelous relatives, friends, classmates, teachers, and pastors. My grade school, middle school, and high school years were beneficial, educational, and a firm foundation for my life. Through it all I was a big dreamer.

Growing up as a youngster and as a young adult, I imagined being a cowboy, a professional singer, a songwriter, a pianist, a magician, a pastor, a soldier, or a truck driver.

I had visions of playing or coaching football, basketball, or baseball at the high school, college, or professional level.

There were the daydreams of racing stock cars, or being employed as a hunting or fishing guide in a remote area like Montana or Alaska.

Crossing my mind was the prospect of being a world-renowned chef, a teacher in a foreign country, a caring nurse, a valiant pilot, a patient social worker, a world traveler, and even an author.

The possibilities were magnificent to dream about in my youthful mind, but I perceived myself as abnormal and uncertain about life.

I had attended Montrose public schools for grades K through nine. In a mixture of ways it was an agreeable setting for me. I valued Montrose schools, yet through the years I had a nudge from my conscious for more challenges on my plate.

My dad, my Aunt Marilyn, and my sister, Yvonne, attended Michigan Lutheran Seminary (MLS) in Saginaw. They had resided in the dormitory or housing provided by the school. The family members were enrolled at MLS for three years of high school, yet they did not attend their senior year at MLS. For their senior year, my family members attended and graduated from Montrose High School.

I decided to transfer to MLS starting with my sophomore year. The dynamics leading to my decision were initiated since I was familiar with MLS from my family's connection. Also, our WELS church in Montrose was an affiliated member of MLS.

In sixth grade I expressed an interest in a Christian based education. My parents and I explored a neighboring Lutheran elementary school, but transportation and scheduling didn't allow the realization of the educational goal.

As a freshmen in high school I had considered preparing for the pastoral ministry. After consulting with my parents and our pastor, I visited MLS in my freshman year. Completing the school tour I filled out the application form that day.

Nearly all of the students at MLS entered school with established friendships from their elementary schools and churches, and the freshmen students had bonded with their social groups or peers their first year at MLS. When I enrolled in my sophomore year I did not know one student. As a shy rural boy, I was vacated of friends the first few weeks of school.

Without a Lutheran elementary school background the memorization of Bible passages was taxing for me. My high school religion courses were alluring, albeit I didn't have the expertise of the Bible stories. The time frame I blocked out for my religion homework had to be extensive and rigorous.

I was homesick my first year at MLS, but it was exhilarating to meet my professors and classmates while also discover the city of Saginaw. After an initial academic shock I did gain modest academic successes. I adapted to the routine by generating a wholehearted effort towards my homework, sharpening my study skills, and wisely monitoring my time.

For my first year at MLS, I was in the pastor track of studies and one of the requirements was four years of Latin. Professor Spaude worked with me during my lunch hour on my first-year Latin course in the library. After a year, I faced the truth that the foreign language study was unsurmountable for me. In my junior year of high school I switched from the pastor track to the teacher program.

At MLS in tenth grade I was a step behind the majority of students academically and socially. Because of being homesick, a new environment, and lacking a similar background as my new friends, I once again had the reoccurring theme of feeling like a misfit.

I will admit I was not always a model student in high school as I had my share of setbacks, agonizing moments, and ill-advised decisions. Uncharacteristically for MLS' classrooms, I was ousted from a physical education class for being a whiner and complainer as I became angry about the lack of fouls whistled in our basketball game.

During my high school years I was blessed to be on the varsity football, basketball, and baseball teams. All the same, I elected four basketball games into my senior season to quit the varsity team due to disagreements with the coach. As a result I received scorn from various students who took exception to my decision.

In my senior year I could have been dismissed from MLS as I made a hideous decision in connection with an off-campus Christmas party. MLS had recently adopted a zero tolerance to alcohol consumption by students. After taking responsibility through my confession and apology I did receive campus detention for two months. I was placed on probation for the remaining months of my senior year.

During the three years at Saginaw my friends and I spent weekend evenings visiting the nearby ice cream palace, attending athletic events, or packing in a movie night on our gym floor with pajamas, pillows, and sleeping bags. On some weekend evenings off campus I delighted in watching television and devouring popcorn with Professor Birkholz's family at their residence.

One Saturday morning at MLS a friend and I decided to walk the three miles from the school's campus to Fashion Square Mall. We had missed the school van to the mall and I was content with the hike. Along the trek I figured out there were potential transporters zooming by us on the hectic four-lane road.

Our school's policy strictly prohibited hitchhiking by the young students living far from their homes in the populous city. Trudging along between the chaotic road and the sidewalk I turned and faced the oncoming traffic. I commenced to place my fist out sideways with an extended thumb begging for a ride with any willing stranger. I strode backwards watching prospective drivers declining the offer of our delightful company in their vehicle.

After several minutes a mid-size sedan car pulled into a parking lot and indicated by a wave out of the front window he was offering us a ride. I was pleased in my accomplishment of obtaining a means of transportation besides walking. I elbowed my friend and said, "I told you I could do it!"

Jogging to the car and opening the passenger's door, I was greeted by Professor Birkholz. Professor Jerome Birkholz was a tall, intimidating man and I had no aspiration to lose his favor.

Without blinking an eye, Professor Birkholz provided our passage to the mall. On the ride to outskirts of the city there was no preaching or lecturing as he did remind us of our school's rules. Furthermore, he suggested alternatives to hitchhiking. My professor was stern, yet evangelical. I appreciated Professor Birkholz and the great Christian role model he was for the students.

Spotting most of my errors during high school, I did aim to be a respectful, hardworking student. At MLS I was blessed with valuable life lessons and academic accomplishments. Most importantly, my high school days strengthen and nurtured my faith in my Savior, Jesus.

I embraced the social aspect at MLS and my life in the big city. In the course of the seasons I would roam through the city inspecting the suburbs, downtown area, and other schools. On longer outings I explored the industrial sectors and city parks.

In the fall I wasn't shy about earning money by raking leaves in the neighborhoods of the city. I would travel as a loner, door to door pitching my available service. I would occupy the winter weekends at Hoyt Park being whacked during ice hockey games and then offering my service for snow shoveling afterwards while walking back to school. In the springtime I wandered in rougher regions of the city hoping to stumble on a basketball game.

Prior to high school I was at ease and content playing basketball, hunting, singing, and building camps by myself. Equally, I would entertain myself by playing solitaire, shooting billiards, or running away from home.

In high school I uncovered I had an unnerving time speaking in front of large gatherings or to individuals. I am still reserved around persons I'm meeting for the first time, but once I plow through the preliminary introductions and the ice-breaking conversation I do receive enough poise to fuse into the standard dialogue. I now enjoy speaking to larger audiences, smaller groups, and individuals.

When I was young child I rejoiced in being organized. As an energetic preteen youngster I instituted pride in my personal areas of play, sleep, or work. While a high school dorm rat I preferred my spaces structured and tidy. My childhood was probably the beginning of my mild undiagnosed case of obsessive-compulsive-disorder (OCD).

I am notorious at being a sanitary freak in the kitchen using lots of paper towels in cleaning the sink and countertop. Another quirk is scrubbing the meal's pots and pans before I seat myself to begin consuming the prepared grub. Along the same line, once I get polishing up an area I sometimes can't retreat or rest until I expand into perfecting other far-reaching capacities.

Moving to my dealings in the outside arena I do methodically mow my lawn striving for the manicured green carpet appearance. Never mowing back to back in the same weekly pattern or direction, I validate a rotation of four different weekly patterns in my lawn care.

Maybe it's a weekend testosterone build up that causes me to pamper my truck. I am compelled to scrub the exterior, polish up the tires, vacuum the inside carpet, and sparkle up the windows.

In my bedroom I have liberated most of my dressers thus eliminating the folding of clothes and cramming them into drawers. On white plastic hangers my wardrobe is suspended in the closet according to the garments' styles, while spanning across the closet from darkest apparel to the lightest items.

In the wardrobe system I am denied the correct spectral presentation. My color deficiency is the cause of only black or white socks on the closet shelves, and I have been playfully informed by people observing my bedroom closet that I'm a sick person with my logistic arrangement.

Washing my laundry in a timely matter may be my primary oddity as a household chore. I am legendary for not checking the pockets of my pants, shirts, and jackets. I have routinely laundered my wallet over the years in our washing machine. There are a thousand other objects I have tumbled through the appliance.

Nothing is safe from being tossed into the laundry contraptions. My personal top five non-living items thrashed through my washing machine are shotgun shells, referee whistle, tube of super glue, two Christmas light bulbs, and a spark plug from my lawn mower. I tend to stifle electronic devices being inserted into the washer and dryer as I have never washed the TV remote control or my phone.

Setting aside my OCD, I do have a terrible pattern of misplacing my wallet and keys. Rarely, do I lose my phone, but when I do misplace the device, I do it well. A few years back I released my smartphone from my hunting pants as I plodded through knee deep snow.

On Christmas day I examined every inch of my quarter mile path for five hours. Through the administration of a metal detector, I stumbled on the dead phone within seconds of ending the search.

Whenever my son-in-law, Josh, is in need of a sales pitch, I am manipulated as his example. As a Sprint manager, Josh will listen as a customer requests an economical phone and a simple plan. Josh negotiates the transaction by sharing my past theme concerning a phone. Josh seals the deal my testifying his father-in-law has been re-born, and I exhaust my phone for tons of everyday activities.

I wear my OCD misfit badge with honor. After years of self-examination to pinpoint my characteristics, I am esteemed at being diverse with my odd traits. Every day I examine my purpose in life, while I stumble around not always distinguishing my proper pathway. My concentration digresses and I deliberate where I should be or where I'm heading. I do get lost in my life, but I will keep dreaming big.

God has blessed my life and I am grateful for everything.

Chapter 8
THE OCCUPATIONS

My life during my high school years was a typical American existence and it wasn't a constant blur of misfit emotions. Though due to my indecisiveness after my high school graduation, I began working full time at Furstenberg Building Center (FBC) in Montrose. The work environment was agreeable with my fellow employees and employers playing an implicit role in my life. Before working at FBC, I had several employment relationships that were merely performed as the needs arose or to provide an income.

At eight years old, I began assisting my dad out with his carpentry jobs. At first my tasks entailed cleaning up at the building sites and gathering up the scraps of lumber, shingles, and drywall. Similarly, collecting the discarded nails, cardboard boxes, and plastic coverings were my responsibilities. I cleaned and organized tools, and throughout the process I was a dependable errand boy.

Years later as I developed my trifling carpentry abilities I labored alongside my dad and my brother Mike in our dad's business. We were an industrious team installing new roofs, building garages, and remodeling residential and commercial structures. Dad equally built patio decks, acquired demolition jobs, and performed masonry projects.

Our prevalent accomplishment each year during the summer months was the sale of a residential dwelling constructed by us from the basement to the finished product.

My first paying enterprise outside of working for my dad was at the age of thirteen years old. I was riding the school bus home and Billy mentioned he was fired from his part-time job the previous day. Billy's employment was providing provisions for two horses.

The Phillips' house was located diagonally from my cousin's Paul's house so I jumped off the school bus at my cousin's home to inquire of the job. I nervously muddled up the Phillips' lengthy driveway and knocked on the elaborate wood door. I was not acquainted with the Phillips nor had I consulted with my parents about the job opening.

Tom Phillips interviewed me while giving me a tour of the barn, horse stalls, and pasture. He explained the position's requirements and finished his presentation by offering me the job.

I accepted the job opportunity on the spot. My obligations would now entail working at the barn every day of the year even on Sundays and holidays. The daily chores would take an hour and the non-negotiable pay was one dollar-per-day.

When I conveyed to my dad the new undertaking Dad was not aroused by my enterprise. My father informed me the means of my transportation would be my responsibility to determine and implement. In my pursuit of my first independent job, I had no problem with sourcing out my ten-speed bike as my means of transportation.

The route was five miles round trip and the total interlude needed for travel and work was two hours. My dad's concern was not my daily exercise on the rural roads; his uneasiness was my losing focus of my homework, school sports' teams, and chores at home.

The errands of tending to the horses and the barn were serviceable for a young boy. Cleaning the stalls, filling the water buckets and feed troughs, and spreading out fresh straw were matter-of-fact duties. The aspect of tending to the horses was not my preferred assignment as the pampered horses were selfish, rude, and stubborn.

Over a year's span I rode my bicycle to the barn with severe trials on many of my passages. The tests in the fall season were the spells of heavy rain or gusty winds. In the winter months, the white-out conditions and below freezing temperatures were miserable.

On a few trips, I wiped out in the ditch, walked my bike through snowdrifts, and was soaking wet from start to finish. I managed my self-directed journeys except for a hand full of days when my mom provided safe, warm migration in her yellow Grand Torino.

The following summer I sweated at the Phillips' residence baling hay, painting the barn, and performing various repairs. I worked on an hourly basis for an increased wage of $2 per hour.

Besides tending to the horses, another task I performed was tending to a flock of Rouen ducks. The ducks are comparable to wild mallards with the tame Rouens being brighter in color and larger in size. I was swayed by the ducks and bought two ducklings to raise.

As a novice duck farmer, I produced in our family's backyard an enclosure fashioned from two by four lumber and chicken wire. In the pen I placed a Kmart acquired child's wading pool. A homemade duck house or coop was fabricated from lumber in my dad's scrap pile. The stylish coop had insulated walls and a shingled roof.

The genders of the baby ducklings were unidentifiable due to their equal appearances. When the ducks became adults with colorful feathers, I recognized I had received a male and a female, and my ducks were bestowed the names Bonnie and Clyde.

My morning tasks included watering and feeding the ducks while collecting the eggs in the coop provided by Bonnie. My mother used the eggs in her baking, but I had to expand my occupational field because of the over-abundance of our duck eggs.

As a short order cook I scrambled, hard-boiled, and fried the eggs on a regular basis. The duck eggs were not just for breakfast as I learned other recipes and prepared various dishes. Even with my best efforts the supply of eggs became out of control, so I attempted to sell or donate duck eggs to our relatives and neighbors.

Clyde was handsome sporting a shining green head, a smooth white neck collar, and black curly tail feathers. His breast was gray, and his brown feathered wings had blue and white bands.

Often the ducks were released from their pen to roam our property scavenging for bugs and grass as part of their feeding routine. The alpha male, Clyde was legendary to peck at people's heels and pursue intruders with his deep quacks. An insult to me was being put on his list of trespassers, regardless of my daily testimonial that I was his main provider for food and water.

The pair of ducks was contained in the roofless, three-foot-high pen without clipping their wings. My strategy was to retain them as plump ducks unable to lift themselves in flight off the ground. As a duck entrepreneur I combed the bordering farm fields for the non-harvested ears of corn. My dad even purchased for me an antique, hand-cranked corn shucker to detach the kernels from the cobs.

The ducks went wacky over the shelled corn that I stored from the garage's rafters in gunny sacks. The duck's demand for food was overwhelming. In the late fall months my grain supply inventory ran low and the drop in my inventory necessitated me to find another source of reasonable priced and obtainable feed.

Through the local grapevine I garnered the hidden knowledge to get hold of free discarded food at the IGA grocery store in Montrose. The contention for the expired products was waged among the township's hobby farmers raising pigs and chickens.

I joined in the rivalry on Tuesdays and Fridays by scrolling through the back storage room. The fifty gallon blue barrels were filled with day-old merchandise of bread, rolls, and buns. Flanking the barrels were green bins containing assorted vegetables.

I had two well-satisfied ducks during the winter months. Sporadically, the supply line either became thin or my busy schedule didn't always allow me to collect the fare. The situation became disorderly as my ducks became slim and agile. In the spring they began to escape the pen by flying over the short walls.

In the sanctuary of our yard, Bonnie and Clyde roamed as outlaws. The two renegades became a frenzied gang when one day I chanced upon Bonnie with her ducklings milling around the overly-populated pen. On assorted spring days Bonnie had formed a nest behind their pen among the tall weeds and had laid several eggs.

In the summer, the nine fugitives made raids in our garden and napped on our front porch or on the rear concrete patio. The snoozes were not disagreeable until the ducks' deposited waste products drew my mom's displeasure. The ensuing weeks I was exhausted in trying to sustain an adequate food supply. The band of insurgent ducks was making life a challenge at our contemporary dwelling.

Throughout the following weeks the immature ducks were close to being undomesticated. The unruly ducks were tenacious and they had total authority over our cats and dogs. Our normal pets hid in the garage, house, and in the trees from the obnoxious waterfowl. The rebellious flock dropped squishy trails everywhere, with not even the bribery of food enticing them to retreat back into their pen.

As a deadline for drastic measures approached due to their proposed airborne flights, the flock of juvenile ducks developed botulism. I emotionally struggled as the disease caused the ducks to lose control of their feet, wings, and neck. Over a span of five days I undertook minor campaigns with no improvement. The adolescent ducks one-by-one died, leaving me with only Bonnie and Clyde.

My adult ducks according to outward appearances weren't affected by the loss of their family, but they behaved differently. My reign over the ducks was tested as the romantic duet had embraced their freedom. The pair had uncovered the small stream at the back vicinity of our property as they waddled and splashed in their profound paradise. While in their trance, they had no clue of the impeding dangers.

Bonnie and Clyde spent most of their days at the seducing stream out of sight and away from the safety of our jurisdiction. Their returns to the open pen and coop at night were less frequent, and I was speculating I would soon lose my ducks to the wild.

One morning while managing my ducks, I perceived an unwary quietness. I spotted only Bonnie in the pen with no Clyde in sight. For a week I held spirited combs in the brushy waterway, neighboring fields, and fence rows. There was no trace of my drake duck, as I suspected Clyde had become a feast for a neighborhood red fox.

Over the next days, Bonnie was lethargic and she avoided eating her food whether it was placed in her pen or in the yard. Bonnie would only eat the corn if I sat with her and hand-fed her.

Two weeks later Bonnie was lying dead in her coop. In my examination I unearthed no suspicious signs of violent activities and my validation is she had died due to a lonely heart.

My duck-raising farm excursion came to a sad end, yet I have fond memories of Bonnie and Clyde. They taught me accountability in an occupation while providing me with a pleasing hobby and teaching me the many responsibilities pertaining to animal care.

In my sophomore year of high school, I did not work at the Phillips' residence due to me being twenty miles away at Michigan Lutheran Seminary. During the school year I performed the jobs of raking leaves and snow shoveling mentioned earlier.

The next summer at fifteen years of age I shifted to a higher paying job and an employment providing me with sufficient working hours. I labored at a strawberry and Christmas tree farm in rural Montrose. Once more I depended on my ten-speed bike for transportation as the round trip was now seven miles.

The weather was suitable for bicycling in summer, but my yellow ten speed bike was showing signs of wear. I had to walk home as the department store bike showed up once at the end of a rainy work day with a flat tire. Also, after one exhausting Friday, I was focusing on the weekend when halfway home the bike's chain broke.

At Rumble's Tree Farm, my main requirement was swinging a machete knife to trim and shape the spruce, fir, and pine trees planted for future Christmas trees. In the fields I self-educated myself in regards to being alert as snakes slithered and hissed in the conifers.

The summer job of trimming trees was satisfying due to the cash flow into my bank account while also working with my cousins and friends. The lunch periods in the strawberry fields with my male and female counterparts were bonus social pastimes. As teenagers we chatted about movies, cars, dating, and the opposite gender.

The summer before my senior year of high school I made strides up the professional ladder. I was hired as full time summer employment at a retail lumber business and hardware store in Montrose's city limits. My dad was a regular customer at Furstenberg Brothers Incorporation, or as it was renamed later Furstenberg Building Center.

At first I was hired to unload railroad boxcars. The task involved removing lumber of all dimensions stacked into the container piece by piece. The boards had to be removed piece by piece from the compartment while enduring the stuffy air and blistering heat. On days of rain we stacked the pine lumber in the warehouses.

After my high school graduation I returned to Furstenberg's business for another summer of employment. The second summer I had moved up the ranks in filling the customers' orders. In late summer I was considering college or working full time. I realized I lacked the goals, dedication, and funds needed for college.

In September, I continued working full time at Furstenberg Building Center (FBC). Over eleven years at FBC, I had adequate wages, first-shift hours, and health insurance benefits. I accumulated a retirement plan, personal days, and vacation days. I drove forklifts, loaded materials in vehicles, and unloaded semi-trucks. My final years at FBC I was promoted to the lumberyard's foreman position.

While at FBC many of my coworkers and I competed in the local softball league. After one of the games Jill and I reintroduced ourselves. In junior high school, Jill had been a grade behind me and seven years had passed since we had seen each other. During that time period I was at high school in Saginaw. Jill and I began dating, and we were married six months later at Mt. Sinai Lutheran Church in Montrose.

My first occupations brought me participation in the business world by providing a service and being paid a modest compensation. The employments at the horse farm and tree farm taught me the importance of transportation, work ethics, and a paycheck. My years at FBC provided me with benefits and an agreeable wage, which provided me the opportunity to purchase a house and start a family.

One of my experiences at Furstenberg Building Center I would recall one day to my students in the classroom for many years. The story was a favorite scoop of the students as they have mentioned the narrative twenty years later.

The account is a whopper of a tale, but true.

Chapter 9
THE MAGGOTS

On Friday evenings, after our work hours at Furstenberg Building Center, the employees would have competitions of tossing horseshoes. During the contests we loaded up with aiming juice, while also drowning our weekly sorrows with adult beverages. The happy hour and horseshoe tossing matches were held on the backside of our work shed in the lumberyard.

The yellow aluminum sliding shed during work hours was a place to warm ourselves, dry our gloves, and eat our lunches. The useful shack was convenient for storing numerous pieces of equipment and work supplies. On breaks we played cribbage at the work table in the shed.

Our days off from the business were aligned so that we worked every other weekend. Thus, being short-handed we vigorously worked the Saturdays and Sundays to have every other weekend off from work.

Due to the ambush of weekend warriors, the owners normally provided lunch for us on Saturdays. We would have a revolving menu of pizza, McDonald's, Coney-Island hotdogs, or sub sandwiches. We grabbed the grub on the run and hurriedly gulp down the food while filling customers' orders. The succeeding days we would eat the leftovers placed in the store's break-room's refrigerator.

On Sundays at FBC, the hardware store and lumber division was open from noon to 3 PM. One Sunday as Brad and I were laboring we found ourselves in the shed catching up on our paperwork. Brad noticed the leftover pizza carton on the work table, and he opened the lid exposing the pizza with its thin crust and assorted toppings.

"How long do you think the pizza has been here?" Brad asked me point blank as he stood over the carton like a dog on point over a covey of birds.

I replied, "I have no clue, Brad. How would I know?"

Never shifting his eyes off the pizza, Brad asked, "Do you think the pizza is alright to eat?"

Becoming a little annoyed I replied, "How would I know? I have no clue, Brad." I sarcastically added, "Try it, you'll like it."

As he spied up the pizza and wiped his drool, Brad replied, "Well, I'm hungry and I'm going to eat a slice. Do want a piece?"

"No, I'm fine. I'm not hungry," I said. My reply was unusual since turning down free food was not a specialty of mine back then or now.

Brad slid the carton closer to the work table's edge and grabbed a piece of pizza. Through my peripheral vision I viewed Brad showing an unbelievable engulfing of a slice of pizza into his digestive system in one single bite.

In prior fall seasons, Brad had been a running back on a high school football team. Under the Friday's lights, Brad had dashed by defenders and plowed over would be tacklers.

At Furstenberg's business, Brad was callous in most matters and he would have a stab at anything to prove his sovereignty. Once on a dare Brad took it upon himself to become the exterminator of the annoying nuisances in one of the storage buildings.

Brad was raised up into the rafters by a forklift and he grabbed the baby sparrows out of their nest. His means of annihilation of the hatchlings was performed by biting their peeping heads off. He finished the termination by heaving as hand grenades the unattached little downy bodies and severed heads into the nearby trash bin.

On this Sunday afternoon Brad was darting his way around the obstacles in the shed. Brad had determination in his eye and a body language asserting he was willing to smash through anything.

Chewing on the pizza, Brad executed a mad rush from the table to the exterior door without uttering a word. His hostility was carried out as he nearly yanked the wooden door from its hinges.

Instead of stumbling on the concrete steps outside the shed, Brad soared over the hurdle. To avoid the forklift, Brad twisted and landed with a slide in a cloud of dust in the dirt.

Brad dashed along the side of the building, a balanced sprinter running with one arm expended in his pumping motion. The other arm and hand were masking his mouth shut.

At the shed's corner he made a sharp right turn with his hips leading the way. As Brad reached the horseshoe pit he was halting the running play, but he was leaning forward for that one extra yard. My co-worker took two stumbling steps while falling behind the shed.

I overheard vomiting and gagging, and after several rounds of the commotion there was a silence from behind the shed. I had fretful considerations of me performing the Heimlich maneuver. But the silence was broken by another bout of gagging, and now an added spitting attack.

The weary Brad surfaced from the corner of the shed wobbling towards me. His frowning face had raised eyebrows, squirting eyes, and the corners of his mouth held the answer. The evidence was also sprinkled on his chin, shoulders, and stomach. Concluding a minor dry spitting session, Brad verbalized the solution to the brainteaser and delivered the features involving his predicament.

While sampling the pizza the callous worker noticed a squirming sensation between his teeth and along his cheeks. Brad did not stop his chewing until he detected something scooting across his tongue. Stopping his swallowing action, Brad began investigating the matter.

The confused young man rubbed his hand across his mouth and witnessed squirming critters among his fingers. Brad ceased his devouring of the thin crust pizza as the organisms were prominent on his lips attempting to escape. Dozens of the invaders had been slithering down his throat. His reflexes kicked in and out the door the ex-football player went in an effort to dispose of the assailants.

Brad had been devouring a hearty assembly of maggots colonizing the pizza. Brad, the self-reliant rough and tough guy, was defeated by a handful of wiggling maggots.

When Brad finished his account, I went over to the pizza to dissect the context. At first sight I didn't notice any unauthorized bugs. When I lifted the cheese layer of the pizza, I observed hundreds of fidgeting white maggots. The creepy-crawlies were scurrying around their exposed environment seeking another private place to hide.

After the occurrence I did not look at pizza for two years. When I did summon the courage to face pizza, I thoroughly scouted several seconds for any foreigners. Thirty years later, I occasionally perform a pre-examination ritual. Taking only refrigerated leftovers, I will inspect under the cheese and microwave the pizza until the cheese bubbles.

After eleven years at FBC, I made a decision to change my occupation and life's goals. I was thankful for my job at the lumberyard, though I craved for more in a lifetime occupation. Being away from a classroom for over a decade, Jill, our daughter Jenny, and I relocated to New Ulm, Minnesota to begin my college education.

As a twenty-eight-year-old married student with a six-year-old daughter, I was responsible for my tuition, housing, and living expenses. In order to support our finances and living provisions I was employed at Kraft Foods and New Ulm Building Center (NUBC).

While working at Kraft Foods, I executed six months on the Friday night sanitation shift. In the summer months I was on the assembly line, in the cook room, and unloaded whey in the receiving room.

My Kraft's sanitation outfit began with the company's pants, shirt, hairnet, and hard hat. Over the uniform I sported a yellow waterproof apron, elbow-length rubber gloves, and rubber boots.

I prevailed in the cook room at a stainless-steel tank with steaming water and hydrochloric acid. I removed the burnt cheese from the cooking pans, pots, and utensils with the water being swapped out hourly and the night's patrol spent scrubbing the items.

My promotion in the summer was cleaning the twenty foot stainless-steel cookers. My exuberance in the promotion was found in removing the nuts, bolts, and auger from the cooker. I disassembled and reassembled the cooker three times. At the end of the shift the cook room was powered-sprayed with everything being immaculate.

Earlier on Friday mornings, I was at college, while in the afternoon I worked at NUBC. After a late dinner I would be at Kraft for the Friday night sanitation shift. On Saturday morning, I would take a shower and head back to work at NUBC. At the building center I cleaned the store's floors, windows, and bathrooms. I stocked the shelves and worked the sales counter. Even with my color deficiency, I was able to prepare custom paint colors using the mixing machine.

After college I was a teacher with the added duties of principal, athletic director, and coach. I taught twenty-one years in the multi-grade classroom of grades five through eight. I taught reading, science, math, social studies, language arts, music, gym, health, computers, and art. I coached football, volleyball, basketball, softball, and track.

While a full time teacher I had summer employment at a magazine binding factory, installing shingles, and officiating basketball games. Currently, I substitute teach at four school systems with students and subjects ranging from kindergarten through twelfth grade.

An anonymous saying states, "I will make up my mind what I want to do with my life when I grow up."

Here's my twelve buckle list occupations in twelve months.

-Gold Mining in Alaska	-Subway Restaurant in Arizona
-Short Order Cook or Chef	-Cowboy/Ranch Hand
-Golf Caddie PGA Tour	-Hunting/Fishing Guide
-Secret Service Agent	-Song Writer/Author
-Independent Cameraman	-Teacher in Costa Rica
-College Football Coach	-Maggot Rancher/Farmer

Chapter 10
THE MILLERISMS

My choice of occupations through the years has been persuaded through my dad's influences. My dad, Davey Lee Miller, was born in Gary, South Dakota. He was raised in his early years on a farm near Clear Lake, South Dakota.

In the 1930s, when my dad was around five years old, his family moved to the vicinity of Flint, Michigan. During the Depression Era my grandfather and my great uncles pursued employment in the steadily growing auto manufacturing industry.

My dad's family settled into a farmhouse in rural Montrose, Michigan. After high school my dad enlisted in the United States Army and served in the 45th Division. Davey Lee was deployed to Korea spending his tour of duty in the United Nations Military Police Action between North Korea and South Korea.

At our cabin in the Upper Peninsula my dad would discuss with me his time of service in the Army. Serving in Korea my dad began his military service as a corporal in the Army and initially he was in charge of mid-range military mortars.

Obtaining a faint hearing loss Private Miller became the cook's assistant. Dad did not merely peel potatoes, serve meals, or wash dishes as he was involved with the preparations and the creating of the meals. Dad would continue his love for cooking throughout his lifetime.

My dad recounted the extreme winters in Korea in which he was confident his heavy rubber boots had protected his toes from frostbite and possible amputation. In his final days in the Army, Dad served as a military policeman (MP). Dad's accountabilities as a MP included escorting troops and individuals to various undisclosed locations.

Vibrantly, Davey Lee shared the story with me of two eight-year-old Korean orphan boys who would tag along with his company. Dad investigated the adoption process to provide the boys a life in the USA, but the paper work was never processed. According to my dad's recollection, days later the two boys vanished within the war.

In Korea my dad pheasant hunted whenever possible and I can envision my dad pulling off the odd diversion as he was a resourceful person and avid hunter.

Dad offered to me the abnormal details of his return trip to the USA. On the prolonged ship's voyage in the turbulent ocean my dad did not experience seasickness as he often avoided sleep in his assigned area on the ship. Instead of sleep, my dad spent extensive time periods playing cards with the other GIs and thus earning extra currency to assist him with his new civilian life in California.

During this time frame my mom, Nancy, bought a train ticket to California as a nineteen-year-old gal in love and in the persistent pursuit of my dad. On September 14, 1951 my parents, Nancy Joan Dowell and Davey Lee Miller, were married in a small church in Oakland, California.

While living in California, Dad still yearned for a rural life in the Midwest. After one year living in California, my parents shuffled back to Michigan. My dad found work in the city of Flint driving a cement truck, and he performed carpentry work during the seasonal layoff periods.

In the summer of 1960, two incidents would alter my parents' lives. The first incident was during one of Dad's layoffs from driving truck. While as a laborer in the construction of the new high school gym in Montrose, the provisional laborer applied for and was hired by the Montrose School District as a full-time custodian. After ninety days on the job Dad would receive valuable health insurance benefits.

The second incident was the birth of a third child to my parents' family. The medical benefits from Dad's employment would cover the hospital bills of the unscheduled arrival in November.

The growing family moved five miles to the northeast side of Montrose Township. My parents were closer to family and friends as they were within a mile away of their childhood farms. On the rural farmland they constructed their ranch style house, which would be their residence for over twenty years.

Due to their limited income they had to conceive the dwelling within a tight budget and time constraints. The tactic meant they would reside in the cement block basement for the first winter. The infant born in November was kept warm by placing his crib close to the dwellings only source of heat, the basement's fireplace. My parents heard predictions from family members and friends that the infant baby boy would be ill in the winter months due to the vicious living conditions.

With a certain charisma, my mother every so often would divulge I did not suffer a single ailment the entire winter. I did not suffer a common cold, cough, or flu symptoms. I was fortunate to avoid any ear or throat infections the first winter of my life. Perhaps those living conditions explain why I despise the Midwest's winters.

Finances were a strain for our young family, although, Mom and Dad provided sufficient clothes, food, and warm beds. My mom was known by her three children to be frugal when shopping for our clothes or for our family's groceries.

On one of the rare times we patronized a fast food establishment, the dining occasion left an everlasting impression on me. At a Burger King restaurant during a family vacation, I ordered a Whopper, French fries, and a chocolate shake. I was engrossed with the spellbinding food when I lifted my head from my feast and viewed Mike's scowl.

I strained to consume my meal as I developed a bewildered blending of guilt and confusion. Later, Mike delivered a big brother tongue lashing while relaying our parents worked hard and on a limited budget. Mike corroborated me as selfish in my actions and I should make sure in the future I was more considerate.

On my dad's driver's license his name was printed as David, and his birth certificate states Davey. Most people referred to him as Dave or Davey. My friend, Tim, and I began good-naturedly dubbing my dad as Davey Lee when we would work on the retirement home, or what was referred to at the beginning stages as "the cabin."

One of Davey Lee's life ambitions was to retire to the Upper Peninsula of Michigan. Dad longed for a home on the water where he could view the waves splashing on the shoreline while tracking the sun's daily and yearly path. Dad desired to step out his dwelling's door and scuttle into his boat to fish in the body of water before him.

To obtain his dream my dad wore a mixture of occupational hats. Besides working as a school custodian, my dad worked part time as a carpenter. One of his major developments was when he purchased a twelve acre plot bordering our one-mile square neighborhood. The parcel was a mixture of farm fields and woodlots at the start.

Dad would produce one saleable home per calendar year. The house's basement was dug in early spring and the building process would continue through the summer. Dad, Mike, and I performed the procedures and sub-contracted certain procedures not within our talents. Working on a strict timeline and with serious financial investments, the summer months of work were complex, intense, and time consuming.

When all the rural lots on the plot were established with homes in about ten years, Dad turned to flipping houses before the act had become a popular reality show. Dad had a knack for finding homes restorable, marketable, and profitable.

Another disposition displayed by Dad was the art of collecting materials for recycling. He was a lucrative junk collector. Over the years Dad had amassed and sold scrap aluminum, copper, steel, and iron. Dad moreover would snatch up the empty drink containers in parking lots, ditches, and parks to be exchanged for the vacated Michigan refund deposit of five or ten cents.

The uncommon salvaging acts of discarded cans and bottles was one of several *Millerisms* publicized by Davey Lee for years.

Dad welcomed walleye fishing in his fourteen-foot aluminum boat with his sure-starting 9.9 Johnson outboard motor. In his modest boat with three wooden benched seats, Dad cultivated the knowledge and patience to be a prosperous fisherman.

Equally, Dad liked to hunt upland birds and waterfowl. For Dad and his two sons duck hunting was achieved in the marshes, rivers, fields, and flooded timbers in Michigan.

On one wet day waterfowl hunting in the Saginaw Bay, we had a wretched outing. Dad, Mike, and I rose from our warm beds at 3 AM, and we hitched up the trailer and boat to Dad's truck. In the darkness we loaded our camouflaged blind, decoys, and guns, and drove forty-five minutes to our launch site. We had complications launching the boat due to icy conditions on the concrete boat ramp, but we made it unharmed through the first challenge of the day.

Motoring our heavy boat in the canal leading to the bay we struck a large rock under the water's surface causing a damaged shear pin on the motor's propeller. Changing the pin was a complicated hassle due to the cold and darkness. After securing a new shear pin, we discovered the wind and waves had awakened on the open water. The boating expedition to our hunting destination was however achieved in the unsafe conditions.

With tingling hands, we untangled the plastic duck decoys and released three dozen of the decoys' ropes and anchors in the hostile water. After mounting the heavy blind to the boat, we instantly had shooting action. The drawback was the targets were coots and mergansers, which are not suitable for table consumption. Besides being sportsmen and better managers of the wildlife, we vowed not to waste our shells or time on the uninvited birds.

Dad, Mike, and I would wait for the preferred bluebills, redheads, or mallards. Bouncing around in the boat, we sharpened our eyes and we grew imposing at identifying our desired targets. We permitted the unwanted species to fly over or flop within our decoys unharmed.

The weather conditions had become further detestable as we sipped hot chocolate and coffee from our Thermos to bring us temporary comfort. When Mike and I discerned birds we associated as anticipated targets Dad did not agree with our hurried analysis. Mike and I were begging to shoot. As brothers Mike and I rarely agreed on matters, but we were positive of this recognition and we were hotheaded about the subject. We wanted permission to shoot.

Dad said, "No boys, let's make sure. Keep your heads down, and don't let the birds see your faces. I will tell you when to shoot."

Mike and I obeyed Dad's orders and postponed our action, but we snuck a quick glance out the holes in the canvas blind at the birds. Seven sought-after bluebills winged over our set up and swiftly continued out of range. The escaping ducks made two young boys roll their eyes in exasperation. Mike and I presented to Dad our teenagers' silent act as we had spent frigid hours of the morning with nothing rewarding in our boat.

As if to add insult Dad turned to us, and with an Elmer Fudd animation stated, "Well, boys, we missed out on some good shooting. Plus you know what? Those weren't coots or fish ducks. My goodness, those were bluebill ducks. Ha! Go figure."

"Duh! That's right, those were bluebills," we sarcastically retorted.

For the rest of my dad's life, we would refer to a missed opportunity in any aspect of our life as "Those were bluebills." A Millerism.

I pray I have inherited the attributes I admired in my dad. I hope I have received his business sense, work ethic, and dedication. My aspiration in my life is to foster my dad's sense of humor, humility and his Christian faith.

For years people have implied I do have similar mannerisms as my dad. Dad loved to tease those he liked, and he would lovingly refer to children at school as a gang, pal, bucko, kiddo, young whipper snapper, or sport. I tend to have my Millerism of referring to students as yahoos, rum-dums, munchkins, and varmints.

When I seek to enter a busy street while driving a vehicle, I hear the Millerism's phrase in my mind, "Pete says, shoot."

Pete was a retired elderly farmer who Davey Lee had befriended while playing cards, discussing the stock market, and appraising their respective coin collections.

In Pete's final years on this earth, my dad would drive Pete for his errands to the medical clinic, to pay bills, and to buy groceries. Pete was a person with a lust for control of his surroundings and Pete maintained through his words and behaviors that he was the boss in all situations.

Riding as a passenger with Dad, Pete felt obliged to inform Davey Lee when it was clear to enter a busy roadway. In a brash voice Pete would decree a "Shoot!" when he figured it was clear to make the entrance. Dad would appease Pete's command with a pacifying "Ok."

Even when Pete sustained the rapid declining loss of his sight and hearing Dad would reply with a compassionate "Ok" to Pete's command concerning traffic.

"Shoot, says Pete," became our way of signifying when the coast is clear at a road's intersection. Over the years we have recycled the phrase as a battle cry while contemplating a dramatic life changing situation. When the route is clear for a personal revolution we announce, "Shoot."

My dad could easily place written in the wrong order or speak words in a confusing manner. Once again I have inherited a similar trait.

One of my personal Millerism came about as I was beginning to enter the online dating scene after my divorce from Jill. Replying to a potential date in a hurry, and instead of concluding the email with From Brian, I signed off with the twisted mixed up phrase Form Brain.

I never heard back from the prospective date, and I am still teased among family and friends about my creative typing. When I make an error in emailing, texting, or speaking, I call it my form brain or fb.

Millerisms abound everywhere in my life.

Chapter 11
THE TAJ MAHAL

Commissioned in 1632 by the Mughal emperor Shah Jahan to house the remains of his cherished wife, the Taj Mahal stands on the southern bank of the Yamuna River in Agra, India. The famed mausoleum complex, built over more than 20 years, is one of the most outstanding examples of Mughal architecture, which combined Indian, Persian and Islamic influences. At its center is the Taj Mahal itself, built of shimmering white marble that seems to change color depending on the sunlight or moonlight hitting its surface. Designated a UNESCO World Heritage site in 1983, it remains one of the world's most celebrated structures and a stunning symbol of India's rich history. *1*

I was privileged to contribute to one of my dad's lifetime goals. My dad's vacation cabin and retirement home, his Taj Mahal, is located on the St. Mary's River near DeTour Village in the Upper Peninsula of Michigan. The house has been our family retreat for over forty years.

In the late winter months of 1976, the foursome of Dad, Mom, Grandma Miller, and I trudged along in two feet of snow on a wooden lot four miles northwest of the Village of DeTour. The lot has a mixture of birch, cedar, and fir trees on the rocky landscape.

Prior to this day my dad had spent years searching out businesses to purchase in the eastern portion of Michigan's Upper Peninsula. He had considered acquisitions of resorts, bait/tackle stores, restaurants, and taverns. At one point Dad came close to obtaining a resort with rental cabins, but the deal fell through due to disagreements on the purchase price of the property and business.

We had vacationed in the eastern Upper Peninsula (UP) region as a family in the 1960s and 1970s. After my grandparents on the Miller side of the family retired, they lived year round on Drummond Island on the far eastern end of the UP. Because of those past involvements, my dad was biased in seeking prospects in the region.

The St. Mary's River is a body of water approximately seventy-five miles in length between Lake Superior and Lake Huron. The body of water is labeled a river due to the current in the system. The river appears and feels like a lake at the location of our cabin. The river is as much as thirty miles wide in that section and the international border of USA and Canada tracks its entire length. The waterway is dotted with islands and the larger well-known Michigan islands being Drummond Island, Neebish Island, and Sugar Island.

My mother was not thrilled concerning the tract of land purchased for a building site due to the isolation of the land and the commitment ahead in construction of the dwelling. My Grandma Dowell was still alive and living on the family farm 275 miles south in Montrose. My mother was apprehensive about sacrificing her attention and care for Grandma Dowell in her elderly years.

My parents purchased the building lot in April and began construction of the cabin and their retirement home in the same month. During the first summer we excavated the driveway, poured the foundation, and framed the exterior structure of the house. Industriously, we worked to enclose the structure with windows and doors before the winter season.

While being busy with all the tasks at the cabin we still found time to take a break and gaze at the freighters passing along the river. The Edmund Fitzgerald type of freighters range from a couple hundred feet long up to 1,014 feet in length. There are the fresh water cargo haulers and the salties. The salties are foreign countries' ocean-going vessels transporting cargo within the Great Lakes. Both types of freighters are large, powerful marine crafts carrying raw goods such as grain, dolomite, iron ore, coal, and cement.

Shippers was the adopted Millerism term Dad used to nickname the working vessels. The majestic freighters pass three-quarters of a mile in front of the cabin in the shipping lane as the watercrafts grant a striking view from the shore. The two foot waves from the freighters reach our rocky shoreline about ten minutes after passing our stretch of river. Ships heading towards Sault St. Marie and the Soo Locks are referred to as up bound, and ships heading south to Lake Huron and Lake Michigan are denoted as down bound.

Canada's St. Joseph Island is two miles north of the cabin across the river, so we are privileged to view and hear two separate sets of Independence Day fireworks. One display appears on July 1st on St. Joseph's Island, and the other spectacle is on July 4th in the village of DeTour and on Drummond Island.

Guessing the freighters' length as they muscle along on the river has become a competition we wrangle with as the shippers pass the cabin. The rumble of the diesel engines is an alert in our inland bay to stop our routines and take a minute to bask in the romantic scenery. Even with their constant growl, one or two shippers succeed in sneaking by us.

The nighttime view of the freighters is appealing with the glowing lights calling up images of the early twentieth-century Titanic.

From early on Mom and Dad referred to our trips to the Upper Peninsula as up north. Michiganders tend to use the phrase up north when signifying traveling anywhere north in the state. Where up north exactly begins, and what is inclusive in the phrase is debated. In the Midwest, up north tends to be an area of a less population, an abundant tree growth, and abounding recreational water opportunities.

Early on when we traveled the four-hour trip up north to the cabin our bathroom facility was a wooden outhouse we built and placed in the patch of cedar trees near the garage.

At the unfinished cabin we would snooze in sleeping bags on the plywood floor, and we would cook using the fireplace or a charcoal grill outside. Cooking and bathing water came from the outdoor well pump or from the cold river.

When the plumbing, refrigerator, and gas stove were installed, we were becoming civilized Yoopers. The term Yooper is comically exercised to describe residents of the UP of Michigan.

The construction process of the cabin was finished in a span of about three years. The cabin's elaborations were completed according to financial assets or as building materials were transferred to the cabin from down state, the term used by Yoopers for the Lower Peninsula.

Dad was famed in mounting resources to assist with the escalating projects as he combined cabin activities and recreational opportunities. In the midst of hanging the fourteen-foot drywall on the ceiling of the open-concept dwelling, the walleyes were said to be biting hot and furious. Family friends, Alf and Barry, helped us hang drywall for eight hours. We did manage to fish a meager one hour.

My cousin Paul, my brother Mike, my friend Tim, and I found it amusing that firewood splitting coincided with duck season. During a prime perch bite Dad just happened to schedule the building of the garage. Even the assembly of the front deck overlapped with the parade, cookout and fireworks of the July 4th celebration.

Fortunately, the masonry work of the fireplace came in early November, so we had no cabin projects the opening weekend of gun deer season.

Our neighborhood family friend, Tim, journeyed with Dad and me on weekends in the spring, summer, and fall months to work on assorted developments. One weekend in the early spring season, the three of us went to the Taj to install the six-panel interior doors. We had sanded and stained in Montrose as flatlanders (another term used by Yoopers).

Due to the snowdrift across the private road leading to the cabin we had to manhandle the doors through seventy-five yards of deep snow. Tim alleged the task was minor and he was prepared to carry two doors at one time. Dad and I tried unsuccessfully to convince Tim that it was a pompous idea. We tried to convince Tim that this was a marathon endeavor needed to be confronted at a simple, steady pace.

Dad and I chuckled as Tim took two steps and fell face-first into the wet snow. Each attempt by persistent Tim brought hoots from Dad and me. Ultimately, Tim threw up the surrender flag and carried the doors one at a time to the cabin.

Tim's dad, Emerson Belill, and I were with my dad one weekend in August applying the interior wood trim in the Taj. In the mid-morning hours we accepted a break from the drudgery as we clambered into Dad's fourteen foot aluminum boat for a round of walleye fishing. We motored out near the channel buoy in the shipping lane and easily found our secret fishing hole.

Fishing in the anchored boat, we were unproductive with our yellow colored jigs and night crawlers. Being a bored teenager, I was impatient and I switched over to a two-inch long rusty lure I dug out from the bottom deep corner of my tackle box.

While viewing Dad's rolling eyes, I embarked on casting the lucky lure while fishing for Northern Pike. Dad was a diehard walleye fisherman and he harshly referred to Pike as slimmies or snakes. The aggressive fish are very much edible and tasty, but dignified Davey Lee refused to fish for Northern Pike in his boat.

On my second cast with my vintage tackle, I produced a fighting northern pike properly netted by Emerson. Within minutes Emerson and I had engaged in a full-blown mutiny as we were catching one lengthy fish every third or fourth cast. After making a few inaudible grunts, Dad submitted and switched over to pike fishing. During the outing we caught twelve large fish for a shore lunch and future meals.

Frequently, Davey Lee had one-liners to express his feelings and depict his opinions within various circumstances. If while working on carpentry campaigns we were taking too long on a task, Dad would interrogate us by asking, "What do you think this is, the Taj Mahal? It doesn't have to be perfect, as I can assure you that we aren't building the Taj Mahal." The subtle phrase from Dad could be overheard at least once on almost every job site.

In the early stages of our cabin's construction we would shake our heads in disbelief in Dad's newfangled demand of precision. At junctions of the building's maturity we manipulated extra time for minor adjustments to guarantee the optimum achievement of each individual project. As we worked on the cabin, we would tease Dad concerning his new attentiveness to specific precision which was a contrast to his past attitude to construction jobs.

At the door of the cabin near the driveway, a person enters the room utilized to store coats, shoes, and firewood. Back in the day the room stored thousands of different individual cans of Dad's beer can collection. Now among the shelves hanging on the wall there is a five inch by seven inch black and white picture of the Taj Mahal in India. Likewise, engraved on the handcrafted stained firewood box in the living room are the words of Dad's grandchildren and the words Taj Mahal.

Another significant spot inside the Taj is the stone fireplace. The fireplace was fabricated one weekend using large rocks from the shoreline in front of the cabin. From the shore a perfectly fitted piece of drift wood was used as the mantel.

While viewing the fireplace there is one black stone in the center that stands out from the other gray, brown, red, and white rocks. The black stone was the fireplace's lone object retrieved from another area. The unusual rock was retrieved by Davey Lee years earlier on our family trip to the farm he had lived on in South Dakota.

Here are two of my dad's corny stories I recall from when I was an eleven-year-old child. I remember the stories because I heard him repeat the jokes over and over to people. There is something to be said about observing people's reactions as Dad would tell the story to avid gardeners, fishermen, and anyone willing to listen.

"I received a bucket of fish harvested during the March sucker spearing season and I recycled them as plant fertilizer in my garden. Throughout the season the tomato plants vigorously grew with healthy green leaves and countless blossoms. In late summer the tomatoes ripened, and I was fixated on consuming the tomatoes raw, as a sauce or tomato juice, and on sandwiches. The juicy tomatoes were delicious as the fish worked gallantly as a fertilizer. There was one problem as the eating of the tomatoes was overshadowed by having to remove the large number of fish bones in the tomatoes."

That was Dad's odd sense of humor. My dad would likewise tell the story of the not-so-smart friend who needed help with his intelligence.

"My neighbor Bob expressed he wished he was smarter. I told Bob I had special tablets to assist with a person's overall intelligence. Bob was doubtful but he bought a week's supply of the money back guaranteed smart pills. After a week Bob voiced a concern that the pills were not working, contending he was not wiser. The refund was transitioning between us when Bob declared the brown oval-shaped medication with its chewing texture was disgusting to swallow. Bob professed the pills smelled and appeared to be nothing more than rabbit pellets. I pulled back my hand with the money and I informed Bob there would be no refund as the pills were working fantastically."

If you didn't understand the joke, I will be happy to sell you a year's dose of the smart pills on behalf of Davey Lee.

Dad retired from his occupation at Montrose Schools in 1991 and spent five years of doing construction work in the DeTour area. Then Davey Lee bought a log structure within the village of DeTour.

The village has a residential census population of slightly over 300 people. In the summer months the population marginally swells in connection with the regions summer cabins, resorts, campgrounds, fishing opportunities, and a state of the art DNR marina.

Dad remodeled the vacation cabin and opened his shop, Log Cabin Antiques. He stocked the store with hidden treasures captured at flea markets, rummage sales, estate sales, and auctions. My dad was occupied buying and selling oak furniture, signs, slot machines, guns, and coins. In the shop Mom organized and marketed dishes, jewelry, knickknacks, and books. Dad was ambitious in his work efforts of restoring items and selling them as an entrepreneur at flea markets and events across Michigan and Arizona.

The Taj was Dad's paradise and he relished time with Mom at their little slice of heaven on earth. He treasured relaxing on the Taj's front deck with a beer in his hand and keeping an eye on the shippers navigating the river during the shipping season.

Dad's retirement itinerary included business hours at the antique shop, hitting up local garage sales, attending church on Sundays twenty-three miles away in Cedarville, and fishing in his boat when the weather permitted it. During the weekdays after working at his shop, Dad chatted with his buddies and the gang at the Village Inn.

Forty years later, moments at the Taj Mahal on the St. Mary's River continue to be relaxing, gratifying, and reflective.

Chapter 12
THE BOY HUNTER

Our family's Daisy BB gun belonged to my dad as he had received it as a boyhood birthday present. The pathetic gun could not slow down a hopping rabbit, and its shooting projection was unpredictable. However, the rusty object was highly sought after by me as a six-year-old boy.

My brother Mike first inherited the lever action BB gun and he stashed it away under his bed. Mike also kept the weapon in his camp, and he would stand on top of the third level target practicing on his little brother while I sulked along the fence row.

The firearm didn't deliver a detectable sting on bare skin even though the straying BB could have taken an eye out. Later in my childhood, I opposed Mike and the BB gun by throwing rotten tomatoes or apples at his impermeable fort.

Mike, the middle child in our family, spent his life's employment at the Buick Assembly Plant in Flint, Michigan. Mike could have had a livelihood in the carpentry trade with his skill in woodworking. His detailed work was commonly publicized in his extravagant childhood hideouts with trap doors, multiple levels, and built in bunk beds.

After Mike had tired of the BB gun and moved on to lethal weapons such as our family's 410 shotgun, the hand-me-down BB gun became all mine. Thankfully, as Mike's weapons amplified he moved on to different targets besides his younger brother.

On receiving the BB gun my practice targets were constructed from cardboard and a marker. I seasoned myself by climbing up the trees on our three-acre country lot, shooting from various heights and angles. Another artificial hunt was placing the cardboard targets along the creek and wading in the water while firing on the strategically placed objects in the adjoining brushes.

The round shot had a wavering track and a lack of meaningful power. The volley might come to rest twelve inches off the mark after traveling as little as ten feet. The unpredictable error could be left, right, up, or down. There was no way to compensate for the BB's flight.

On my first stalk I tracked the prey, made wind calculations while taking aim, and squeezed the trigger. As the proposed lethal shot drifted by our cat; the feline lifted its head, yawned, and returned to its afternoon siesta. Our two domesticated cats knew I wasn't a threat to their survival and they humiliated me by wandering under the trees and along the creek daring me to fling a shot at them. Therefore, I felt obliged to take my share of lob shots at them which I did with no confirmed hits.

At the age of eleven years old I received a Crossman air rifle. For years I appreciated the photo with my Beatles haircut and wire-rim eyeglasses as I'm holding my air rifle while standing in front of our Christmas tree.

With my Crossman air rifle I had advanced further up in the food chain. The air rifle came in an unopened box signifying it was no hand-me-down. The gun fired projectiles accurately and straight with a significant increase in velocity.

The most emphasized rule with the weapon was no pointing or shooting the gun at any humans or domesticated animals. Another accented regulation was whatever I shot and killed I had to eat. That meant field dressing, cooking, and consuming the slayed quarry.

The first adventure with the gun came around innocently. Our house had a large number of evergreen bushes next to it, which provided a nice hideaway for songbirds, rabbits, and squirrels.

On January 16, 1972 the Super Bowl featured the Dallas Cowboys and the Miami Dolphins. The Detroit Lions were difficult to watch in that era, so the Cowboys had become my favorite NFL team. At halftime I was in my bedroom assessing the birds in our shrubs.

Within seconds, the bedroom window screen was removed and my first shot was barely off the bull's eye on the white, gray, and black bird. The second shot hit the target as there was no last gasping breaths or theatrical climax as the chickadee fell dead to the ground.

The thrill of the gun's influence and my sharp shooting skill was overshadowed by my abrupt penetrating sadness. I struggled with convincing myself it was a fair contest since I was not baiting with bird seed and I was not concealed by camouflage. But after a range of shots with the tranquil birds revisiting the shrubs, I was disheartened with the wicked hunt. I could not raise the gun to my shoulders any more.

When halftime was done, I surrendered the carnage and returned to the game on TV. Midway in the third quarter of the game, our mixed breed Pekingese-Cocker Spaniel dog, Babe, roamed in front of the living room window. With a chickadee dangling in her mouth, I knew my safari would be exposed and identified. When Babe strode by a second time with another victim, my mom was airborne and scurrying to the garage. Following Babe's paw prints in the snow, my mom was led to the massacre. In the brushes Mom divulged three more lifeless birds.

My mom's probe steered straight to me. When I confessed the hunt's facts, I learned I had two angry parents. I was not forced to eat the tiny birds, yet I had to dishearteningly dispose of them in our burning barrel. I suffered the loss of my air rifle for three months while wallowing around the house in mourning for several days. I had disobeyed my parents, heedlessly killed God's creatures, and improperly used my gun.

During my air rifle retention period, I was introduced to our family's modern wrist-slingshot. This style of weaponry was not confusing to me, because I had a military involvement with slingshots in the seventh grade. Taking my cornet musical instrument apart, I attached a thick rubber band to one of the brass u-shaped section. My inventive armament was capable of firing a spitball across the large study hall classroom.

While in Miss Woddell's civics class, my calling as a missile launcher came to a hasty termination. I received two swats from Miss Woddell's paddle and two whacks from Dad's belt at home that evening.

With our family's wrist slingshot my hunting tactic was to sit on a pile of stumps and discarded branches in the fence row behind our house. In the morning hours I was exposed to dazzling sunrises, cows requesting breakfast, and distant cars transporting workers. I fell asleep by the sun's warmth and awakened by the local crow convention.

On the late afternoon hunts, I would sit on top of the wood pile long after the hours of daylight. I studied the fading day through sunsets and the moon became my reassuring glow. My eyes wandered up to the night's vast stars as I walked home in the darkness.

Eventually, I moved on to our single shot 410 shotgun. My rabbit hunting in the winter involved rooting a rabbit out from its hideout. I would discharge a shot at the darting rabbit and no matter how I calculated the scurrying rabbit's path I was all thumbs and a scatterbrain. Continued misses occurred and the gun barrel's straightness was questioned. On our makeshift backyard shooting range, my practice shots proved the barrel was true.

The process of raising the firearm to my shoulder and placing the open sights on the target was complicated. I could not master the art of swinging the gun while squeezing the trigger. Over time I obtained the techniques to be effective, but it did not arrive from reading hunting magazines or conversations with veteran hunters. Hands on experience was the tool used for the steps toward success.

Babe and I went together on my hunting journeys, and we learned the rascally varmints could be driven out by Babe weaving through the cavities of brush piles. Being better prepared for the bolting rabbit, my big break came with Babe burrowing and yelping in the brush.

One day as I was into my trampoline act on the brush pile, a cottontail rabbit dashed into the woods. I raised the gun to my shoulder in rhythm as I descended to a stationary position. I clicked the safety off and pulled the trigger while swinging the gun. At that moment the darting rabbit veered to the left in line with my pattern of BBs.

Within a flash it was a dash to the slayed rabbit, and I arrived in second place with Babe positioned in a sitting stance guarding our prize. Babe was rewarded with a boy's hugs and tears.

With my knife I field dressed the rabbit on the spot, and in the process Babe snatched up the entails. Her gastric releases later in bed caused an alteration of field dressing our quarry in the future.

The bonus attribute of the hunt was when I arrived home and my Grandpa Miller's white Ford pick-up was in the driveway. My grandpa lived a quarter of mile down the road and often stopped at our house on his way home from work. Virgil regularly brought his grandchildren doughnuts marshaled from a bakery next to his workplace in Flint.

Wearing my orange hat, I strutted into our house decked out with my wool pants and camouflaged coat. I received a smiling, "Hi, Burr!" from my grandpa. As I dragged my Grandpa Virgil into the garage, I managed a man-size pat when he saw my gun and my first rabbit.

A few fall seasons later on a duck hunting outing, the three generations of Millers, my dad, my grandpa, and me, were in a blind as a flock of ducks zoomed by us. My grandpa leaned forward and fired a shot while Dad and I withdrew from shooting. When we glanced towards my grandpa, he had evaporated into thin air. Actually, he had collapsed backwards with his hat off his head and his eyeglasses smashed. He was unharmed, but Dad and I teased him all that day and for months afterwards.

In October of 1976, my mom tracked down Dad and me while we were pheasant hunting. Mom conveyed that Grandpa Miller suffered a heart attack and had died. Being in my parents' presence at the time, endowed me with a distinct closeness.

Throughout the years I was introduced by my dad and many other people to the love and respect of hunting wildlife. I am honored and humbled as a manager of God's creatures.

Chapter 13
THE STALK

In my years of archery and gun deer hunting, the Lord provided me the blessings of obtaining food, celebrated camaraderie, and safe memorable incidents. Disappointingly, I did have failed opportunities due to mechanical errors or my blunders.

The first buck I squandered away was on our neighbor's forty acres. On the hunting excursion the property owner was cutting firewood in his woodlot, so I made a minor adjustment and went to the back portion of the section of woods.

Slowly walking through the trees, I eyed up the detailed movement of deer traveling from right to left in front of me. I spied five whitetail deer with the final animal in the line was a legal buck. I brought my twelve gauge shotgun to my shoulder for the thirty-yard broadside shot. While the herd of deer strolled along, I discharged four shotgun slugs at the young buck.

The gunshot echoed in the mature woods as I had magnificently shooed all five of the deer safely out my sight. When I approached the target area I disclosed one shot made a clean kill on a small poplar tree, and two other shots had wounded two living maple trees. The last round was never resurrected as I wretchedly resolved it was a complete miss. I unearthed no deer hair or blood in my massive search at the spot.

The miserable old tactics of questioning the gun's standards and accuracy were contemplated. The tale of my dreadful four missed shots was shared with my hunting buddies. Their good-natured ribbing of me was rousing entertainment for everyone.

I planned another negotiation with the hunting spot two days later as I wanted to thoroughly investigate the location. At my debatable buck fever zone, I meditated on my misses while settling into a seat on a fallen log. I theorized the unlikely odds of the buck reappearing in the identical spot after the previous day's annoying blasts and I comfortably relaxed, not expecting to observe any deer that afternoon or evening.

My eyes grew heavy and I was caught up in a refreshing late-afternoon nap. Once in a while I would open my eyes a tad to scan the environment for any bothersome deer. In one of those skirmishes to open my eyelids, I clearly differentiated two things. One, I had advanced to an early-evening nap as it was almost dark. Second, there was a deer with antlers standing twenty yards broadside in front of me.

Carefully, I removed my hands out of my pockets and I was diligent to avoid any quick movements while lifting the shotgun. While positioning the shotgun, I muffled the clicking sound as I slipped the safety to off. I steadily placed the open sights on the front shoulder and squeezed the trigger. There was a startling explosion with me losing sight of the deer during the commotion.

Five minutes later I began my probe with my flashlight where the deer was last seen and heard. I promised myself over and over I would not distribute the inexcusable missed shot with anyone. Raking the area by walking a large circle, I investigated the darken horizon and came upon a massive blob. In my beam of light, I recognized my whitetail deer only a few yards away from my napping log.

The modest buck was bagged on acreage near my childhood home and in a woods I requested permission to hunt. The deer hunt was wacky because I had squandered the harvesting of the buck two days earlier. The persistent teasing by my peers concerning my previous miss was laid to rest for a while.

My testimony of a buck I stumbled upon as I was rabbit hunting with Babe along the Flint River was another odd hunting account. On the peninsula along the meandering river I observed Babe, with her massive height of ten inches and length of sixteen inches, standing poised on a steady point. At first I didn't see the buck as it was bedded down, but then the buck magically appeared in front of me at thirty yards. Having only my irrelevant 410 shotgun with birdshot, Babe and I appraised the majestic buck as it paraded away seeking another bedding spot.

On an October archery hunting jaunt I was sitting twelve feet up in a maple tree using my portable tree stand. I was mixed in with a full array of the maple trees showing off their recently transpired bright yellow, orange, and red leaves.

While scouting the area I selected a location with two active buck scrapes. I disclosed the third scrape in plain sight after a buck came charging in and pawed the scrape directly below me. The buck with unswervingly nerve progressed to lick the very branch I was perched on in the tree.

The deer moved and stopped to check the next scrape as I released what should have been a flawless, broadside shot. My attempt failed reaching the buck as the broadhead's tip hit a small unidentified twig. The arrow went whirling off into the sky away from the alleged target.

The mature deer did not hear the carbon shaft clunking through the trees and leaves, and the buck proceeded to situate itself in a better position for a shot. Notching the next arrow to the bow's string, my last projectile was dropped by my lumbering hands as it unconcernedly floated to the ground. I had three scenarios to shoot at the buck within minutes. I had successfully botched all three chances.

The most exhilarating deer hunt I encountered was on Black Friday over Thanksgiving vacation. In Paul's woodlot, he manages his property and the adjoining land for quality deer control. Targeted bucks must have at least 8 points on their antlers to be harvested.

After the morning hunt on Paul's property in Michigan, I was drifting my way back to Paul's meat packing plant due to a combination of hunger and boredom. The gray sky matched the barren structure of the November trees. On my return I was deviating from certain regions due to the mud, ankle high water, and the fallen trees.

I had a calm disposition to observe features over the next hill or in this case behind the next tree. On a ridge to my right a dozen orange objects stood out in abnormal clutter. The noted plot was private inaccessible land, but I progressed closer for an improved overview.

Foolishness crept in my mind when I marked the orange modules as pumpkins disposed by the owner. The rotting pumpkins from the neighbor's garden were being used as deer bait, which now assisted my stalking through the woods with a reassurance of the neighbor's perimeter.

Leaning against a maple tree, I was daydreaming and vaguely scheming my next steps. As I was peeking around the tree, I noticed two female deer sauntering through the woods towards me. During the next minute I resisted touching the does as they slinked past me within inches.

The incident with the does provided me with confidence to stalk the area, yet my footsteps were taxing as the mud and branches presented a tricky obstacle. The course was slow as I had repositioned a skimpy thirty feet in thirty minutes. Kneeling on a log resting, I observed curved branches suspended in midair. I plodded three more steps changing my angle while keeping watch on the strange item swaying back and forth.

I focused my eyes while critiquing the outline of an oval sphere on the ground. The ghostly tree branches were the antlers of a buck and the immobile element was the deer's resting body.

The stretch of my imagination had exotic ideas ranging from a wounded deer to the complete opposite of a domesticated deer. I envisioned the possibility of a remote control decoy deer, or a sick chronic waste disease deer. My potential buck fever was securing the best of me as I was pondering if there was a deer there at all.

Taking deep breaths I analyzed the wind was in my favor blowing my scent away from the deer. Even though the buck was glaring in my direction, the downed trees blocked his view. I was knee-deep in stagnant mud with my adrenaline pumping. My face was confronting a cool breeze, yet I was on fire inside my clothes.

The past week delivered complex deer hunting results by Paul and his hunting partners. Due to their complications, I was advised to make a meticulous shot and use follow-up behaviors to avoid losing a wounded deer. From my location I viewed no hindrances existing in my shooting lane. I clearly marked my target with the deer being at least an eight-point buck. I took aim and shot.

I brought the gun down to eject the used shotgun shell and the buck was standing up. Trying to stay on the same page with the buck, I stood up while racking in another shell into the gun's chamber.

The buck made a quick rotation, and had his tail in the air while bouncing through the woods in the opposite direction. In my mind I was going to continue to imitate the deer's movements.

In my rush at the deer, I made one stride and flopped face-first in the boggy mud. I did not brace my fall with my arms, instead my obedient hands were the tools to keep the shotgun out of the muck. My drenching head first flop was a perfect score of ten.

From my thudding decent I emerged from the filth, stumbling and rushing my way to the last observed spot of the buck's flag. The forty yard dash was ceased as I became depleted and fatigued with exhaustion.

Having no indication of where the buck was in the woodlot, I swallowed air and adjusted my mental GPS bearings. I checked left and right. The buck was on the right side of me, standing broadside at twenty yards.

I distinguished his eye, nose, and ear, while his vital organs were concealed behind the trees. I directed the gun barrel at his head and touched the trigger. I was anticipating him to tumble like a dwindling domino, when instead I questioned my saneness.

The gallant buck was facing south when I first fired the head shot. The creature had now rotated and was standing in the same posture, but was unbelievably facing north. The deer's direction changed within the miniature time frame that I discharged the spent casing and slammed in a new slug.

My chronological and historical pessimistic attitude with a gun's proficiency went for another round of conflict due to the odd outcome. I placed the iron sights on the strands of hair I documented as the heart region, and I focused on the bulls-eye while squeezing the trigger for the third time on the stubborn buck.

I ejected the shells in and out of the chamber while maintaining a prying eye on the buck. I watched him every second of my exchanging shells in my gun. Nothing shifted in the deer's appearance or position. The ghost buck did not blink an eye, twitch a muscle, or wrinkle his nose as he stood upright and remained stationary.

I was beside myself as I doubted if the buck was real. I contemplated heaving my hunting knife at the phantom. I would have stormed my counterpart while bidding to wrestle him to the ground had I heard the trumpeted command of "Charge!" I had one option left, I would again fire my last shell at the beast's heart behind the front shoulder.

After the gun's blast, the blunt force of the impact caused the deer to be lifted off its hooves, and he was vaulted sideways in mid-air. The aftermath of the collision with the saturated ground was a rainbow of water sprayed within the gray landscape.

Making my way to the deer in the water I was repelled at the sight of no apparent antlers on the deer's skull. With shaking hands I reached down to the deer's front feet and I began to pull the configuration out of the water. I then eyed on the back side of the head the one remaining antler.

Relieved it was a buck, I stood admiring the unorthodox antlered deer. Digesting the wild adventure I glanced to the left of the buck. Six feet away in the water a peculiar article was catching my attention. Wading in the rude muck, I shockingly snatched up the matching antlers.

I had disconnected one half of the buck's antlers when I touched off the rushed head shot. The shotgun slug struck the antler's base and splintered it near the skull. Besides creating a massive headache for the deer, the extreme jolt must have caused the buck to spin the eerie, reversed 180 degrees.

Later when examining the deer, it was obvious my initial shot at the bedded down buck had penetrated into his spine partially paralyzing the deer. That would explain why I was able to shag the whitetail down in the nasty terrain, with my lack of speed, and challenging the usual agile speed of the four legged mammal.

My shot in which he was standing motionless did breach into the deer's flesh and the slug barely missed his heart. The deer was in all probability bewildered and in a state of shock like me as he didn't physically react.

I was beaming at my successful hunt. I wanted to field dress and drag the deer into Paul's business about a half-mile away. Dragging the whitetail deer five exhausting footsteps, my feeble attempt was deserted.

I trudged through the woods without my deer and arrived at the slaughterhouse in thirty minutes. At the meat processing plant Paul, Dan, and Joe teased me about being back at the store. They enjoyed announcing it was past lunchtime and I was now missing the prime hunting hours. Mockingly, they asked me if I was cold or if I gave up out of boredom. My buddies were willing to roll their eyes and label Brian Miller a city-slicker.

Then the question was jokingly asked by Joe, "Where's the buck?"

I hung my head and avoided making eye contact with my mocking mentors and because of my humble reaction they became mute. I reached inside my hunting coat and brought out the rescued shot off antler. I delivered it a sideways fling towards the tabletop on which they were cutting meat.

The antler rattled across the table and I soberly replied, "That's what I received from my day's hunt. I shot four times at a buck and there's my reward for dragging myself through the disgusting filthy woods."

Peeking beneath my cap's brim I checked out their sullen faces and I wanted to bathe in the rare moment. My exhilaration didn't linger self-contained as I rapidly unfastened my tale about my unique hunting pursuit.

The stalk was exposed with countless high fives and energetic wallops on my back. Paul's retail business was closed for the day and we jockeyed on the four-wheelers to the remote area to retrieve my eight point buck.

The Black Friday stalk was a hunt of a lifetime in my misfit mind. On a gray November day in the muck I stalked up to a bedded down buck, ran the whitetail deer down, shot off one side of its antlers, and spun it around. The distinctive hunt had drama, a display of skill with some luck, and personal emotions unlikely ever duplicated.

Chapter 14
THE PIERCING HUNTS

At twenty-two-years-old, I was on a gun deer hunt in the neighborhood of my youth and about to eat my morning snack of popcorn and a chocolate chip cookie. While sitting on the ground leaning against a tree a mature doe came strolling alongside within ten yards.

Without turning her head she halted her steps and executed the normal deer tactics when suspecting danger. The doe stomped her hoof, flagged her warning tail, and jerked her head up and down. Lacking any advanced notification the doe then moseyed away in the direction opposite me.

I began to breathe normal again and the doe suddenly twisted back around furnishing me a piercing glare with her brown eyes. After a few seconds the doe began charging at me in an all-out sprint. My first impulse was to fire a shot from my shotgun in self-defense, but due to my delayed reflexes and astonishment I didn't lift the gun.

The doe came to a sliding halt within inches of my boots and I was wondering if she was going to head-butt me or stomp me to death. One blink of my eyes and she bounded three large leaps to the left. After a sniffle of my nose the irritated doe was sneaking through the woods out of my sight.

On a breezy afternoon in a standing cornfield near the Flint River, I had a massive buck bolt across my vision while just two rows of corn over from my reach. I certified the monster's breathing from its blazing nostrils, when the panicked creature was stretched out in an all-out sprint. The colossal buck with the prevalent antlers appeared to be on steroids. I was suspicious of cornfields from childhood forays and I am even more spooked as an adult after the incident with the unnerving beast.

Though not a true hunting story, a stupendous feat was undertaken by our household cat. Our male cat, Purr, was momentarily let out of our house. When I looked out the kitchen window Purr was in hot pursuit of a whitetail doe. The chase was twenty yards across the grassy section of our urban property and Purr was a meager two strides behind the deer. Purr was perhaps protecting his domain or pursuing an enormous mouse for his dinner's eating.

While bow hunting in tree stands, I have had countless squirrels obnoxiously chatter at me for being in their favorite tree. My preferred method of exchange is to ignore their racket until my adversaries are on the ground. I then say hello to them by sending my practice arrows their way. Currently, the squirrels and I have a truce and the unsigned treaty states we will leave each other alone if everyone behaves.

For two decades I was present at a deer camp near Rapid River in the Upper Peninsula of Michigan. For the first decade the hunting gang lodged in an army tent with a potbelly stove. During the last decade in the remote woods, the young guys stayed in a popup camper, and the old men resided in a modern recreational vehicle.

At the week-long deer camp, we had no running water or indoor facilities. As family and friends, we had a great deer camp playing cards, sharing celebrations, and bagging a decent quantity of bucks. We wolfed down camp food, slept in our deer stands, saluted our successes, and sat around campfires while relaying our tall tales.

The other hunters had success in killing bucks, but I had no success throughout the entire twenty years at deer camp. I spied plenty of does never having the opportunity at a legal buck. I do have solace I had no faulty deer rifle as I did not miss a buck or any target practicing stumps. I have thoroughly missed the days preparing for and surviving the week of the November Belill's deer camps in the UP.

Paul and I as hunters in our twenties spent our spare time throughout the seasons in the quest of wildlife or fish. After the waterfowl and deer hunting seasons, the winter months were spent in quest of cottontail rabbits with our beagles, Sam and Bo. The brothers were AKC beagles, and I opted for Sam from the litter of pups because the adorable mutt had removed himself from the safety of the pack. The six-week-old puppy explored on his own the area outside his kennel.

Veteran dog handlers have one protocol in selecting a hound pup, the tip of the dog's ear should be able to touch the tip of its own nose. Sam's ears definitely fulfilled the traditional requirement.

My days of stomping brush piles were no comparison to our modern method. The beagles would find a trail left by a rabbit, or they would inaugurate a chase by bush whacking an unsuspecting rabbit. Using their strong scent of smell the brothers would cling to the rabbit's path howling after the cottontail. The rabbit generally circled back around providing us a manageable shot.

Sam was intent on rabbit hunting one day as he ejected himself out of the backseat of Paul's car. The vehicle was traveling 25 mph and Sam rolled twice before landing in the ditch. Unharmed in the breakout, Sam shook himself off and loitered towards the nearby woods for his freelance hunt.

On multiple instances we would leave our hunting coats when we exited the woods since our dedicated mutts would not desert their relentless tracking. When the floppy-eared brothers did relinquish the chase the fatigued beagles were found curled up sleeping on our coats.

In January of 1981, Paul and I started the morning with our black coffee as we yakked about past hunts and the day's possibilities. The day was too frigid, except the dogs painstakingly performed their hunting duties as the rabbits remained in their warm dens.

Around lunchtime we stumbled our way to our grandparents' farmhouse. Our Grandma Dowell (Vera) was eighty-two years old and had returned home after a recent stay in the hospital.

Grandma had a reputation as an independent gal driving her sporty blue Chevy Impala to town spending the mornings jawing with her crew at the coffee shop and bakery. Vera was known in Montrose for her spunk, being talkative, and having great vegetables and flowers at her residence.

As a child, I occasionally assisted grandma with errands around her farmhouse. I weeded flower beds, mowed her lawn, cleaned the chicken coop's storage area, and shoveled snow. My payment was receiving one of her famous butterscotch pies. They were the envy of the Millers, Dowells, Belills, and anyone acquainted with Grandma.

Paul and I stopped at Grandma's farmhouse that frigid Saturday morning and we came upon a posse of relatives at the house. Paul's sister Teri was at the farmhouse cleaning and cooking, and she had an outburst as we trounced in the house wearing our hunting boots. Teri was the firstborn of nine kids, so we silently ignored her rift.

Grandma Dowell was in her favorite chair in the farmhouse. The location of the reclining chair was in line with the television set and to the left of the recliner there were the intriguing sights out the window of the bird feeder, farm equipment, passing cars, and beautiful sunsets. To the right was a close up view of the non-stop kitchen's activities.

Grandma recognized us and inquired of the activities we were performing on the winter day. When we told her we had been rabbit hunting with no success, our opinionated Grandma Dowell started lecturing us as two greenhorns. She asserted if our Grandpa Don was alive he would teach us a thing or two about rabbit hunting. At our visit with our Grandma, who was a certified gabber, she fluently went from parleying about past glory days to present topics.

When Paul and I were children, we would sometimes shoot to town with Grandma Dowell for an ice cream cone or travel to the neighboring town of Chesaning to swim at the public pool. Whenever we were with grandma we made certain we used the phrases of please, thank you, and you're welcome. We were always expected to open every door for all females, and if we didn't strictly follow all of the rules there would be consequences to endure from Grandma Dowell.

On a summer afternoon Paul and I were egotistical as we received the privilege of joining our dynamic Grandma Dowell at a sit-down restaurant. Desiring to be an exhibitionist, I snatched up the drinking straw lying next to my water glass. With my fingers I pushed the plastic straw through the thin wrapper and slipped the paper down to the far end. The missile's countdown was thus activated.

Inhaling a large breath I elevated the straw to my mouth. During this phase I exhaled the built-up air through the plastic straw. The result was the elongated piece of paper floating across the dining room and settling on the far table near the window. The paper coasted to the landing strip on top of a man's newly arrived plate of cuisine.

The middle-aged man sitting in the booth barely blinked as the missile imposed itself in his territory. Paul and I were dumbfounded at the flight. Grandma, who was returning from the restroom, followed the path of our wayward eyes and spotted the wrapper. The piercing eyes of our grandma were fixed on us. Without any urging, I stood up and made eye contact and confessed my folly.

After my declaration to our grandmother, I made my way to the booth and the wayward aircraft. I stated to the man my apologies for disturbing him with the paper wrapper. The man listened and replied everything was okay as I observed a smile on the forgiving face.

I returned to our table and Grandma replied she was positive I wouldn't behave like that again. She moved on to her meal as I made an inner vow never to disrespect my grandmother again.

On the freezing day of our failed rabbit hunt, we left Grandma's farmhouse feeling happy sharing our hunt with her. In spite of the dismal health report from my mom, we perceived Grandma Dowell was in excellent spirits. She was witty, inquisitive, and focused.

The next Saturday the cold weather had subsided and had Paul and me out rabbit hunting again. Warmer temperatures, fresh snow, and a different hunting location meant improved results. The two cousins had a great day with our dogs trailing rabbits and since we were scrupulous with our marksmanship we had four rabbits in our pouches.

By mid-morning we were at Grandma Dowell's farmhouse hoping to heap on her a few mischievous digs. Even though there was a large crowd at grandma's house, the duteous motions filling the house the previous Saturday were absent. In the living room there was a coldness as our grandma slept in her recliner. When she awoke she closely evaluated us. We shrugged off the odd mood as Paul and I dully discussed the politics, sports, and weather with her.

Our grandmother sat in her recliner and she began to identify us. We proudly showed her the bloody rabbits we had shot. Intently focusing on us she replied with a smile, "Good job, boys."

The visit continued with modest conversations and we left after thirty minutes. I was downcast at the obvious change and three days later my Grandma Dowell was with the Lord in heaven. As one of her pall bearers I reflected on all of my grandparents who instilled in me the values of respect, manners, and unconditional love.

Another piercing hunt happened while I was working at FBC. Due to my years of employment I arranged most of my vacation for October and November. Paul and I duck hunted or deer hunted during the time span and we became relatively successful waterfowl hunters.

In order to consume all of our attained waterfowl I ceaselessly feasted on ducks. The chef in me urbanized duck stew, pulled duck barbeque, duck breast sandwiches, roasted ducks wrapped in bacon, duck shish kebabs on the grill, and deep-fried duck nuggets.

Months prior to the hunting season Paul and I honed our skills by shooting skeet, training our dogs, and painting our camouflage flat-bottom boat. In the process we tuned up our outboard engine, cleaned our guns, repaired leaky waders, and untangled our decoys. Our final preparation was practicing with our wooden duck calls.

During my duck hunts, the sunsets and sunrises grasped while in a marsh, flooded timbers, or a harvested grain field were gorgeous. The fresh air on a wind-burned face or being mesmerized by falling leaves was pleasing. The twisting waterfowl reconnecting to the ground or water was whimsical when their landing gear collapsed. The marvel of flight was fostered when the gliding birds use their fixed wings to cup the air, and their necks bent scanning their arrival zones.

The sensitive old man in me has been transformed and I would be miserable shooting ducks now. I am not anti-hunting as I simply achieve joy in viewing waterfowl at the Taj or fishing on a lake.

My most piercing hunting expedition was on October 21, 1982 which was a day Paul and I both had a taken off from work. The foolish duck-hunting cousins conceived this day in light of the presented data of Jill's pregnancy and her estimated due date.

Paul arrived at my house at 3:30 AM, and we were scheduled to hunt in the Shiawassee State Waterfowl Area. Prior to leaving Jill mentioned feeling ill. Through the means of a phone call, Jill's mom arrived at our house and the future grandmother confirmed she would stay with Jill for the day. Jill directed us to continue with the hunt and she suggested I could hurry back for the delivery if she began labor.

With the day's insurances fortified, Paul and I went to the registration site, launched the boat, and set up at our hunting location. After first light we had decent decoying of birds and notable shots. But then we heard hollering from the dike around eight o'clock, and we quickly diagnosed the shouts were for us. Gathering the decoys in a flurry, we operated the boat full throttle back to the launch site.

After loading the boat and equipment, the speed limit was ignored the twenty-five miles to my house. My shower with a change of clothes was a well-executed pit stop. Driving twenty more miles to the hospital, I again had a heavy uncontrollable foot on the gas pedal. Of course in the parking lot the nearest open space was a farfetched distance from the entrance.

I went to the front desk, maternity ward, and nurse's station receiving no direct answers concerning Jill's condition. The employees did point me to the elevators and through the hallways. Arriving in the recovery room Jill relayed the news we were blessed with a healthy daughter. Within minutes, Jenny Lee was in my arms. I praised the Lord for the miracle of life, and for a healthy mother and child.

I am thrilled Jenny has the middle name of Lee. My dad was named by my grandparents in connection with the frontiersman Davy Crockett, his grandfather Albert Simonton, and his uncle Lee Miller. Our family's ancestry order is Albert Lee, Uncle Lee, Davey Lee, Brian Lee, Jenny Lee, and my granddaughter, Leah Lee.

Jenny's first minutes of her life were missed by her dad, but I thank God for granting me a lifetime to share with Jenny my love, friendship, and faith. I have cherished our moments together and the extreme joy in being her dad. I love her with all my heart, soul, and mind.

I thank the Lord for richly blessing Jenny's life with a fantastic husband and two wonderful children. May Jenny and her family find peace and joy in worshiping our loving Savior, Jesus.

My past piercing hunts have given me cherished memories.

Chapter 15
THE OTHER SIDE

In the summer after I turned eighteen, due to a disagreement with my dad, I decided to transfer out of my parents' house. I didn't plan my new start well, and I ended up living out of my 1972 Chevy pick-up truck for a few months.

My readjusted schedule included working the day at Furstenberg Building Center, eating evening meals at restaurants, and washing my clothes at the local laundromat. I would retrieve a shower at a friend's apartment, at my brother's house, at camp grounds, or by sneaking back into my parent's house after they left for work in the morning. Concluding the day's activities, I attempted to conceal my greenish-gold color truck on a secluded road as I slept away the night.

After two days spending a hefty amount of money eating at restaurants, I developed the system of preserving my groceries in a dry cooler and in a cooler with ice. I stored the blue coolers inside the cab of my truck during the day or in the truck bed during sleeping hours.

Nearly a month after beginning my new lifestyle as a homeless person in my truck, I was curtly interrupted by a police officer. The stern officer informed me that I was not permitted to reside in a vehicle by drifting from place to place. The policemen specified the next time I showed up camping out in my truck, I would be issued a citation with a monetary fee.

The officer's chorus of words led me to arrange dwelling with a coworker at his apartment. After two weeks at the shabby apartment, the coworker transferred to another friend's apartment. Trying to secure the contract of the vacant apartment, I was ineffective in my attempt.

I was back on the streets and my truck's vinyl bench seat, a pillow, and a blanket served as my bed. After several weeks of evading a confrontation with an officer and practicing primitive techniques, I bargained for temporary refuge at my brother's house. At Mike's house with his wife and two young children, I was smarting through rigorous growing pains.

I tried to seize command of my life by telephoning apartment complexes in the area. In my teenage mutiny I could not secure an apartment to rent. My dad even owned an apartment complex and he had no available openings. I may have been wet behind the ears at this stage in my life, but I was quickly drying out.

My dad came to the rescue of the lost, prodigal son. Davey Lee arranged for me to meet with a realtor whom he had had multiple transactions with over the years. I would invest my entire savings as a down payment on a fixer-upper house. I toured a number of structures and within two days I placed an acceptable offer on a two-story house in the city of Montrose. The dwelling had a stone basement, screened-in porch, and white slate siding. The residence with its five bedrooms was once a boarding house in the early twentieth century.

Montrose has an approximate population of 1,600 people and is by all accounts a typical Midwest rural town. There is one traffic light within the downtown businesses on Main Street and another traffic light on the edge of town near the Flint River. Montrose's high school is known in Michigan for its prosperous football and wrestling programs, and the small town comes alive celebrating its Blueberry Festival the third weekend in August.

My purchased house was over one hundred years old and there was a vacant lot attached to the back of the property. In the structure I tore out the old plaster and wood lath, and I reinstated new electrical wiring and plumbing. I insulated the walls and attic, hung fresh drywall, and mounted modern bathroom and kitchen cabinets. Being employed at FBC allowed me to obtain discounted building materials and slightly impaired accessories.

The furniture in my home was a store-bought living room set consisting of two by six wood frame couch, loveseat, chair, rocker, end tables, and coffee table. The furniture was purchased by frugal bachelors and newlyweds in the 1970s, and the complete ensemble with removable flowered designed cushions was purchased at a discount furniture store for $400. Generally, I am not proficient at the bargaining table, but in this transaction I was competent to swindle two cheap lamps as I paid cash for the items.

For leisure necessities I invested $200 toward the purchase of a stereo through a catalog at the hardware store, which verifies the dubious quality of the eight track player and turntable. My television viewing was accomplished through a twelve-inch black and white portable television set my mother endorsed me to snitch from our family's home. My entertainment center was fabricated utilizing red bricks stacked as columns and two stained pine boards stationed within the pillars as shelves.

I was an eighteen-year-old bachelor with a decent-paying job and a house. I was content with turning my life around in four months. There were eggs, butter, and beer in my refrigerator. The freezer had ice cubes and TV dinners. Life was good with my cupboards containing cereal, bread, and peanut butter. Plus, I had a hefty supply of popcorn, soup, and crackers stashed away and my cooking was accomplished on my rummage sale stove with one operating burner.

I existed in the house for three years as a young bachelor. Two years after Jill and I were married, we sold the renovated house. Jill, Jenny, and I shifted to a rural house two miles outside the city of Montrose. Again I performed home improvements at the ranch style house remodeling the kitchen with new cabinets and flooring, building a two-car attached garage, planting 300 tree seedlings, and installing a wooden privacy fence.

Even in conjunction with the home improvements and being involved in an eventful lifestyle, I had an aspiration for a different lifetime vocation. I was satisfied with my family, friends, and work, except I was missing something. My intellect took eleven years to figure out a goal and plan for my life.

One of my interests was working with children in educational and athletic environments. In a sporadic revelation, Jill, Jenny, and I relocated 750 miles from Montrose, Michigan to New Ulm, Minnesota, and I enrolled at Dr. Martin Luther College.

New Ulm was a city I evaluated on my senior trip as being positioned on the other side of the world. Journeying out of New Ulm as a seventeen-year-old, I prophesied I would never return there for college courses.

Heading west and crossing the Mississippi River with a U-Haul and all of our belongings I was absorbed in the notion of exploring the other side. But I was concerned about separating us from our family members and a host of close friends. I heard strong opinions from my relatives and friends that I was crazy leaving our well-paying jobs and an ample residence in Michigan. In our new adventure it was difficult to leave a transformed house sitting on five acres of wooded land.

Dr. Martin Luther College (DMLC) was a college maintained by the Wisconsin Evangelical Lutheran Synod (WELS) to prepare teachers for service in the elementary schools and high schools in the WELS system. DMLC is now Martin Luther College (MLC) after amalgamating with Northwestern College (NWC) of Watertown, Wisconsin. MLC still grooms future teachers, but the college equally trains pastors and staff ministers for callings in the WELS churches and schools.

Jill, Jenny, and I wheeled our U-Haul into the city of New Ulm and began settling into the rental house by sorting through the boxes, arranging furniture, and preparing for the first day of school. Jenny was a kindergartener and I was a college freshman at twenty-eight years old.

Neither Jill nor I had a paying job, and we had rent payments in Minnesota plus a mortgage in Michigan. We had bills and insurance premiums at both places, and the yearly taxes were coming up due in Michigan. Added in were the expenses of the U-Haul and my college tuition fee.

After making final arrangements at college, I began surveying for a job. I acquired employment at the first place I applied and within one week I was working at New Ulm Building Center (NUBC). On the Thursday of the second week I had stomach cramps and sharp pains in my abdomen at NUBC. My coworkers mentioned my irritation was probably caused by the recent flu affecting people in the area.

After work I reached home and started on my evening homework. My college courses were at a crucial crossroad as the first round of homework, quizzes, and tests were forthcoming. I was loading up on coffee and the discomfort in my stomach was increasing. I blamed the symptoms on the local flu while adding liability on the coffee and the stress of my studies. Through the evening hours I made four marches to the bathroom, but my stomach did not improve.

At 1:30 AM, I could no longer tolerate the pain. I made the five city block journey to the hospital and after a short examination by the physician, he connected my problem to my appendix.

The physician reassured me the procedure was a minor surgery, and I would be home the next day relaxing in my recliner. The ER doctor pointed out it was advantageous I had traveled to the hospital so the appendix could be removed before it ruptured inside me. All I remember upon entering the operating room was counting backwards from one hundred and making it to ninety-eight.

When I awoke in the recovery room, the surgeon informed me the good news of my appendix being removed. The bad news was the appendix had burst as it was being escorted out of my body. The toxic liquid had leached into my abdomen cavity and the revised situation now required me to remain in the hospital longer than expected for the recovery phrase.

I theorized it would be a couple of days and I would swagger out of the hospital. The first day I was unable to climb out of the bed. The second day I treaded the four tender steps and used the bathroom in my hospital room. The third day I tolerated ten petite steps down the hallway for a change of scenery besides my hospital room.

One of my nurse's duty was protecting my lungs from being congested and the process involved daily breathing exercises. The breathing apparatus required me to blow into a tube and raise five round colorful spheres. The process was dreadful and I was in tears three times a day. The attractive nurse tending to the exercise had no compassion for life and offered no sympathy towards my circumstance. In fact I don't think the nurse had cracked a genuine smile for years.

During one treatment the monitoring nurse christened me as a wimp and I was infuriated. I took my frustration out on the plastic tube of the gadget as the result was all five foam balls inside the machine went to the top level of the contraption.

I was proud of my accomplishment as the snippy gal exited the room. I was left behind with a wounded dignity for being called a wimp, but I had clear-functioning lungs.

Relaying the story to my dad, he attained a large chuckle from the innocent incident. For years if I mentioned a task was too difficult, my grim appearing dad would imitate the sassy nurse and label me a wimp. Another Millerism.

The discomfort from the contamination in my system was affecting my daily sleep habits in the hospital. For relief and as a sleeping aid, I was prescribed a prescription for morphine.

In the middle of one night I quietly stalked my way to the seventh floor, opened a window, and proceeded to stand on the outside window ledge. After scanning the widespread view, I jumped off the perch.

My hallucination continued as I floated around the city monitoring the residences, parks, and industries. Yet, there were many troubling features with the delusions. First, there was no seventh floor in the hospital. Second, it was a perspiring experience in mind on the unsafe window ledge. Third, I was straining to stay afloat in the dreams. Most disturbingly, I was having a difficult time separating reality and fantasy.

Wanting the delusions terminated, my medication was altered and I returned to a certain normalcy at night. The new medication was slightly adulterated as the method of application was an injection on my swollen backside.

My appendix affliction has amplified my empathy for individuals who undergo surgery of any type. I am conscious and aware of those who have surgeries and are progressing through their recovery stages. I think the recuperation is grueling while God's chosen healing route and timetable is astounding to experience or witness in person.

By the fifth day after the operation, I was gingerly walking down the hospital hallway. My mom and dad had come from Michigan to

Minnesota to visit us and assist us in any way possible. On the sixth day I was cruising up and down the hallway eager to get home.

To add to the complications, our household refrigerator had ceased functioning. Our circumstances three weeks into residing in New Ulm had advanced within the glacial weather to the point of witnessing our life's savings fading away, being 750 miles away from the security of our friends and family, and the strong possibility of ditching my college classes and my fees. I will admit I had meaningful considerations and prayers of abandoning college and returning to Michigan.

The Lord knows our limitations within all of our trials. I had college professors who understood my situation as the instructors assisted me to establish time lines to make up my schoolwork. The owners at NUBC allowed me to take time off from work to heal and focus on my studies, and Jill received a job at a local nursing home.

The medical bills for my appendicitis were taken care of through a blessing from the Lord, and after several infections with the incision also ripping open numerous times, my body did heal in five months.

In due time we settled into our jobs, developed friendships, and dug into our studies. The first summer in New Ulm I worked full time and had a needed break from my academics. In late summer we sold our house in Michigan as we aborted the burdens of mortgage payment, taxes, utility bills, and insurance premiums with it. The monetary situation was stabilizing, and in September we were better prepared for our school and work paths.

In my sophomore year of college I was required to do an Early Field Experience (EFE) in an elementary school. I was in a fourth grade classroom for one week observing, tutoring, and performing limited teaching duties. The following year I was again required to do an EFE week and I arranged to be in a classroom in Houston, Texas. After both of the EFEs, I was confident we had made the right decision move to New Ulm to seek out for me a new career path.

In New Ulm we made friends through college, Jenny's school, and our work places. We had a full plate in the summer with softball games, camping, and swimming. In the winter we went ice skating, sledding, and attended sporting events. Through the years we were blessed to entertain family members and friends as they visited from Michigan.

My schedule was hectic with work at the Kraft Cheese Factory and at New Ulm Building Center and I embraced being content in being a husband, father, and a college student. I was fortunate my junior and senior year of college to participate on the college football team.

At DMLC in my senior year I was assigned to perform my student teaching at St. Paul's Lutheran Elementary School in New Ulm. I would be in Mr. Blauert's fifth-grade classroom and Fritz was an excellent role model for student teachers. His love, compassion, and dedication for the teaching ministry were commendable services.

With the conclusion of my student teaching I was evaluated by a college supervisor and I received acceptable feedback as a teacher. The evaluation was laid in the remote region of my brain because of my fast approaching graduation day. I was remembering the struggles at New Ulm during our first month. I was contemplating the hardships with finances, health, jobs, and college while also reminiscing of God's protection and guidance in my life.

After completing my student teaching I had no other commitments at college before my graduation and possible assignment. Therefore, I substituted taught in Mr. Blauert's classroom and at the end of the second day I received a phone call from the college's office.

Jill and I met with Pastor Krueger as he presented us a stimulating divine call to ponder. Jill and I prayed about the opportunity, and we accepted the offer that evening. I would be assigned as teacher/coach/principal in Peridot, Arizona on the San Carlos Apache Reservation.

New Ulm, Minnesota was my first address outside the state of Michigan after residing twenty-eight years in the Wolverine State. The new locale in New Ulm opened my mindset to the possibilities of a second career, forming new relationships, and intriguing scenarios. Jill, Jenny, and I formed memorable relationships with the residents of New Ulm through college, our employments, and recreational activities.

New Ulm is rich in German heritage and it was a terrific place for us to live. Jill, Jenny, and I enjoyed the churches, schools, and people, and we were gratified with the restaurants and shopping. In our three years we took full advantage of the state park and available family activities.

The nearby towns of Sleepy Eye and Walnut Grove, location of several Laura Ingalls Wilder's stories and *Little House on the Prairie,* added intriguing possibilities to the region.

Trips as a family or with friends to the Twin Cities of Minneapolis and St. Paul's for tailgating as spectators at the Twins, Vikings, or Gophers were on our agenda frequently.

During our stay in Minnesota the Twins won the World Series and the Super Bowl was held in the Metrodome in Minneapolis. For me the Metrodome would be the location of two memorable moments.

One experience was being introduced to Terry Steinbach. Terry was born and raised in New Ulm playing his professional baseball years playing with the Oakland A's and the Minnesota Twins. Terry's fourteen year career was monitored by New Ulm's residents through the New Ulm Journal's daily box scores.

I had come to know Terry's sister and his mom through a mutual friend. After an Oakland A's and Minnesota Twin's baseball game in the Metrodome the four of us walked with Terry from the concourse to his vehicle in the parking lot. Terry chitchatted about the baseball game and he asked his family members questions in regards to their lives.

I was euphoric when Terry's mom introduced me to the all-star catcher. I inquired several questions of him, which Terry candidly answered. Flipping the conversation, Terry asked about my background, college, and family.

Terry Steinbach, a World Series champion in the prime of his career was conversing with me. I was privileged to have met the talented, successful, and humble Terry Steinbach.

At DMLC the oddity of being a married student could have provoked my misfit feeling, but that wasn't the case during those years. My college professors were encouraging and entrenched in me the knowledge and strong will to serve our Lord.

I considered another year earning a degree in Secondary Education at DMLC, though I had to get busy as a teacher and I was looking forward to continuing my life as a husband, dad, and teacher.

At my graduation ceremony and celebration at our house I was privileged to have in attendance many friends and family members who had made the trip to Minnesota. My life-changing adventure in New Ulm was gratifying even though I had once rudely referred to as the other side of the world.

Chapter 16
THE ATHLETICS

Athletics have been an epic part of my life. My first memory of a televised sporting event is the Detroit Tigers' victory in the 1968 World Series. My next nostalgic incident I can recall watching was Bo Schembechler's University of Michigan Wolverines upset of Woody Hayes' Ohio State Buckeyes in 1969.

Through the years a referee's call against the Wolverines or a heartbreaking last second lost would lurch me into flinging objects across the room. Watching U of M football games in solitude has been a self-imposed rule due to my pouting and temper tantrums.

That is not to say I was limited to existing only as a buffoon while a fan, I could be just as atrocious as a player. My style of dribbling and passing a basketball fetched me taunts claiming I was a show-off.

In my logic, if I was chided as a hot dog I might as well confirm the decree. I desired and exasperated to perform in the showman's style of Pistol Pete Maravich.

My aptitude of playing basketball may have been adopted as my dad and I had trailed exciting athletes and contests in the Michigan cities of Flint and Saginaw. In the three decades we tallied basketball games while checking out great teams from Flint Beecher, Flint Northwestern, Saginaw High, and Saginaw Buena Vista. We shadowed the star athletes of Magic Johnson, Glen Rice, Roy Marble, and even a crossover in football and baseball, Flint Central's Jim Abbott.

In grade school and middle school I had played on the school's organized sports' teams. In high school I continued to participate in football, basketball, and baseball. In each sport I was an average player at best, and I had to ardently practice to obtain that modest status.

In my junior year of high school I was on the varsity football team as the third-string quarterback. I was an unconvincing signal caller as I labored learning to call out the cadence, receive the snapped football, and read the defense while operating the veer offense. I was a terrible passer and as a ball carrier I despised cuddling the ball and being tackled my forbidding opposing players.

The days of my masquerading as a high school quarterback came to an abrupt end during the first inter-squad scrimmage of the season. On the play I retained ownership of the football only because I missed handing the ball off to our star and stud running back.

Getting out of harm's way by running towards the sideline I then ran along the sideline towards the other end of the field. I was amazed to interpret a wide-open field void of any painful defenders.

Running for ten-yards the goal line was in my obvious view, yet I didn't notice the defender dashing his way to me. The defender drove his shoulder pads into my knees with me falling hard to the ground sideways. My big no-no was positioning my left arm and hand toward the ground to brace the upcoming collision.

At the medical clinic across town, my wrist was X-rayed with the results leading to my first plaster cast on my arm. The unwelcomed obstruction extended from my left elbow to my fingertips. After three weeks I sulked back to the clinic and the nurse removed the cast. I was enthusiastic about finishing the football season on the gridiron. Facing multiple X-rays and two additional plaster casts, my wrist did heal until after the conclusion of the football season.

The fractured wrist mended in time for our school's basketball tryouts. At the tryouts I did not bring much for height or athletic ability even though I had experience on the freshman and junior varsity basketball teams the previous two years. I went through the November basketball practices and I had obvious concerns about surviving the cuts and making the varsity basketball team.

Before the roster was set, I was presented by the basketball coaches with the prospect of playing down a level as a member on the junior varsity team. My initial sentiment was feeling like a misfit junior student intertwining with the sophomores. I did throw my ego out of the gym and I joined the junior varsity basketball team rather than be cut from the organized high school basketball teams.

Coach Toepel, my teammates, and the games that year of junior varsity basketball were exceptionally pleasing. I was selected as a captain and I had decent numbers in assists and steals with minimum turnovers. I was never a true offensive threat, but I did score some points and I played solid defense.

My attitude on and off the court was appropriate and there was no showing off on my part. I encouraged others, accepted criticism, and wore a happy face on a regular basis. Due to enrolling in kindergarten as a four-year-old this was my true peers I reflected I should have been contending with according to our ages.

The next fall in my senior year of football I was comfortable to be employed as a defensive back and wide receiver on offense. At wide receiver I caught only two passes during the season as I was used to run the offensive plays in from the sidelines.

On the defensive side I did make tackles and my highlight as a run-of-the-mill competitor was my seasons' interceptions. One interception was on a rainy Friday night between two evenly matched teams with similar records. The temperature was mild and it had been raining all day. The football field at Freeland High School was saturated and we were waddling around in a mud puddle.

Before the game I decided to avoid wearing my contact lenses and I wore my wire rimmed eyeglasses. The game was played on the drenched field and I was attracting slime and chunks of grass on my lenses. It was alluring rolling around in the sludge yet frustrating attempting to wipe off the grunge with my jersey. My effort in between the plays was only making the blurred condition worse.

On one specific defensive play I heard our sideline players yell "pass," which caused me to aimlessly hunt around for the receiver in his route. When my teammates continued with the shout of "ball," the saturated leather object smacked my chest with a thump. I squeezed the slippery object to my stomach while I procured one step forward in the sludge.

I collapsed in the slop and this wouldn't be the only time in my life I would descend face first in mud. I had an interception because of being in the right place at the right time. My interception was not caused by my ability or tactical maneuvers as I never did visually locate the football while pulling off the unlikely interception.

After my high school graduation I fulfilled my competitive spirit with athletic contests available to a seventeen-year-old not attending college. The next winters I braved three basketball seasons in a city league with most of my prevailing time participating in recreational softball leagues and tournaments in Michigan, Minnesota, Arizona, and Wisconsin.

Years later I was at DMLC with the opportunity to attempt to participate in my chosen college sport's program. Along with family requirements, college studies, and work obligations, I was able to join one DMLC athletic team.

Baseball was an option due to my past participation and experience on prosperous teams. I was on softball teams as a thirteen-year-old boy until I was a fifty-three-year-old man. At New Ulm I participated on four different softball teams in the area. One summer I tracked my at bats during the games and I finished the season with about 600 at bats. After playing so much softball I was not interested for college baseball during the unstable spring weather.

Basketball was the sport that I spent hours as a youngster dribbling a ball on our tiled basement floor. Similarly, I had my everyday shoot arounds in our turnaround area practicing my jump shots, layups, and free throws. In the winter I shoveled snow from our concrete turnaround area and I would suspiciously avoid the driveway's remaining sections. At DMLC basketball was not an option due to my insufficient talent.

Football was the sport in which I would find fulfillment as a player and coach in my life. At DMLC there were no tryouts or cuts in connection with the football program. A student with a certified physical, attended classes, and present at the football practices would be welcomed on the team due to our small enrollment.

In my sophomore year at college I showed up at the home football games and checked out the football field, team, and coaches. I liked watching the games, but I was also examining my potential as a member of the football team the ensuing season.

The next spring I spoke to the head coach and Coach Gronholz was acceptable to my attendance at the football practices. The spring practices were stress free and without wearing pads we executed warm up drills, stretches, and reviewed various playing positions' responsibilities. The coaches and players operated as separate teams of defense and offense, and we ended the practices with a scrimmage of two hand touch.

That summer I struggled to follow a training routine for my conditioning as I slacked in my weight lifting at the college's exercise room and my sprint training outdoors either at home or on the practice field. I was distracted from my workouts by softball games, work, family activities, and the traps of the laidback summer months.

The first practice of the fall football season came in August and after thirteen years away from a locker room the smell and the sounds of the enclosed room hadn't been rehabilitated. I was ready for the football practice surrendering the fact I had forgotten how to wear shoulder pads. Even forming my mouthpiece guard was a refocusing chore on my part. When my reality was interviewed by myself, I knew I was in significant trouble among the real football players.

In the first full-pad practice I was marginally traumatized when we switched into full-blown blocking and tackling. The team steadily propelled into a live contact scrimmage with the offensive unit going against the defensive unit. Due to the low number of players on the team I was on the field even though I was not a potential first string player.

Since the time I was on my high school football team I had an increase in my body weight and I had lost a step or two or three in any questionable speed I may have had in the past. Consequently, I was assigned and work my apprenticeship as an outside linebacker.

Linebacker is a football position for hard hitters and great tacklers. I had neither of those qualifications as I understood the need to hide me or manage me as a live, blocking dummy.

The first play from scrimmage was a run to my side of the field. With the running back swinging around the line of scrimmage, I was concocting my tackling technique. Shuffling forward, I was contemplating aiming for his waist and I would be possibly assured of slipping down to his ankles during the process. I may have been naïve about certain facets of this novel concoction, but I was honest with myself about my tackling abilities.

Coming around the end with the running back was a steam-puffing freight train. The locomotive was clothed in football gear and the disguised offensive lineman was bearing down on me. I had no eye contact with him even though he made bone-jarring contact with me.

I did not expect the particular following result as I endured the full attack. I soared in the air backwards with my feet completely off the ground. The flight was magical as I settled flat on my back five feet behind the spot of the initial hit.

Lying on my rump, I didn't perceive who made the tackle or where it was made. The coaches and other players weren't excited or upset about the play. This was football. In spite of being pancaked by a forbidding pulling guard, I was having a nifty start. Misfits acquire bliss in the oddest ways.

As we broke from our huddle, I had a sense of relief as I was confident they would run the next play to the other side of the field. When the ball was snapped I understood I was in for a windfall of additional torture.

The quarterback rolled to my side of the line of scrimmage for the second straight time. The real ball carrier became evident as the quarterback pitched the football. The unwavering lineman was again steamrolling his way to me and I didn't have the viable option to scurry off the field in an outright treason.

No one had even remotely conveyed my duty to me and I was out on an island by myself. I considered taking on the blocker and perhaps then a genuine stud on the defensive side of the ball would tackle the ball carrier. Even though I had lots of doubts, this time I wasn't going to be a pushover.

I was preparing to stand my ground. To avoid another unwanted liftoff I stationed my legs shoulder width apart for a stable stance. I planted my spikes in the practice field's grass turf and I leaned forward to plunge my shoulder pads into the opposing pads.

The force of the clash was as fierce as the first contact. The result of me planting my feet was minimal. Even with my counter blow I again sailed backwards and this time I sailed two feet backwards.

By some bizarre standard, I guess I had obtained partial success. But the hit on the hard ground was another serious jolt. The wallop directed shock waves to my back, shoulders, and head.

My purposed journey from the horizontal stage on the grass to the vertical stance back in the huddle would be a taxing endeavor. I stalled for a second or two and the steam-rolling freight train extended his hand out to me. I would love to say he assisted me up, but in truth he pulled me up with my contribution to the maneuver negligible.

As Justin dragged me up he said, "Hang in there, old man."

While wobbly standing on the shifting ground I could only reply, "Thanks."

My pride was dented and I was sizing it all up while considering the inaugural day of my college football affiliation. I was banging away with young athletics. I was in my own exclusive federation concerning my age, size, and athletic ability.

Justin had promisingly breathed the phrase to me and it was true I was an old man trying to play football at twenty-nine years old. I had last suited up with football pads thirteen years ago.

But I was part of the team and I was in this no matter the outcome. I was planning to savor every second of the awesome adventure.

Chapter 17
THE FOURTH DOWN

For two years I was a Lancer as a member of the football team at Dr. Martin Luther College. I was listed in the official program and played defensive outside linebacker. In the first game of the 1990 season I did not participate in a single play in the first quarter. The upcoming fall days looked as though they would mold me as a sideline motionless statue. Nonetheless, I was determined to make the football season a positive experience by encouraging my teammates, faithfully practicing, and persevering with a positive attitude.

After the first quarter in the first game, I contributed in at least one play in every quarter of the game over the next two seasons. Within the two football seasons, I was never on the starting unit, yet I played on the special teams of kickoff, kick return, punt return, and punt team.

Once in a while I played a defensive play if the situation was right. I was not a factor on the football field, but I never missed a game or practice. I was decked out in my smelly practice duds or in my snappy game attire and loving it all.

On game day there was an air of tension and it was an adrenaline-charged pressure. The team traveled on coach buses for away games and it was an eye-catching examination observing the different college campuses, football fields, and scenery from New Ulm to our destination.

Saturday nights I devoted the evenings on my living room couch wrapped up in ice packs. I was aching with an assortment of bruises and cramped muscles, and I forfeited more ice packs after those football games than I ever coerced the rest of my lifetime combined.

The extended trips to contests in South Dakota and North Dakota had us being provided lodging accommodations at homes of members of our synod's churches. In a designated city a group of two to five members of the football team would be embraced by a household. We would have dinner with the hosts while spending the evening watching TV or becoming acquainted with our sponsors.

On one evening in North Dakota, three teammates and I were surveying the downtown region of the small city. We came upon students from a nearby Baptist college and we had a riveting discussion about theological teachings. The debate between the Lutherans and Baptists on that Friday night was fiercely contested, though we did not have a startling epiphany or solve any world problems.

DMLC's biggest rivalry in football was Northwestern College (NWC) in Watertown, Wisconsin. On a sunny October morning our coach bus motored on Highway 14 east to Watertown. After the 400-mile trip, we spent Friday night in the campus' dormitories, and played NWC on Saturday afternoon.

My daughter, Jenny, and Coach Gronholz's daughter, Sarah, were on the trip. The eight-year-old girls were in the same classroom at St. Paul's, and they jabbered, giggled, and slept as they sat in the front bus seat during the seven hour ride.

Jenny and I toured the campus while eating our Friday evening dinner and our Saturday morning breakfast in the college's cafeteria with the football team.

I am amazed at the run-of-the-mill baggage that gets romanticized by our human minds. I recall none of the particulars of the game except we lost. On the other hand I do recall the buffet after the football game. As a color-deficient misfit I can summon up memories of the green farm fields and the woodlots splashed with yellow leaves.

One of my fond memories of a football game was held on our campus. The football field at DMLC is a picturesque setting with the configuration being recessed below the ground level. The bowl has inclined slopes on the end zones and on the home side of the field. The opponent's sideline has a flat ground surface stretching to the mature oak trees in the foreground.

In the morning hours before the game, an October wintery storm dumped four inches of slushy snow on the ground. The maintenance crew cleared a three foot wide path on the five-yard markers from one sideline to the other.

Supposed experts will state such conditions level out the playing field competition. As a low to the ground player with a chubby frame I can't decree I had any highlights worthy of ESPN. Though, I was pumped up for the game and I think I played well.

The biggest snow game I could have participated in was when Minnesota received a huge accumulation of snow beginning on Halloween in connection with the Perfect Storm.

The Halloween Blizzard was a period of heavy snowfall and ice accumulation that affected parts of the Upper Midwest of the United States, from October 31 to November 3, 1991. Over the last week of

October 1991 a large storm system over the Atlantic Ocean (1991 Perfect Storm, which inspired the book and movie, **The Perfect Storm***) blocked most of the weather patterns over the eastern half of the United States, and in turn moisture from the Gulf of Mexico was funneled straight northward over the affected region. By the time the precipitation stopped falling, many cities in the eastern half of Minnesota and northwestern Wisconsin had witnessed record early-season snowfall accumulations. *2*

We were scheduled to play Concordia College of St. Paul's, Minnesota as our last game of the season. Neither organization could host the game on their football fields due to the storm's snowfall. The agreement to play the game at the Metrodome in Minneapolis was organized. The Metrodome was the home of the Minnesota Vikings and Minnesota Twins and could seat over 64,000 fans for college and professional football games.

At DMLC we continued our football practices in our gym and despite a season filled with adversities the team's mood was jovial. In our season we surrendered five out of our seven losses by more than twenty points and we were involved with one horrendous beating. After a lengthy bus trip to Mt. Senario College in northern Wisconsin we received our worst whipping of the season by the score of 14-60.

Going into Metrodome game we had a record of 0-7. Besides the winless record, the season had been frustrating because we had a troublesome incident in a close game.

During the home game against Northwestern College of Roseville, Minnesota, both teams demonstrated flashes of flourishing moments. At one point we were driving down the field with a mixture of running and passing plays. On the drive we had avoided costly penalties and a deflating turnover and a score of either a touchdown or field goal appeared perceivable.

Calling out signals, our quarterback received the snapped ball and presented a fake to the running back. He took three quick steps as he rolled out of the passing pocket. The quarterback was eyeing up our receiver who was on a five yard passing route to the right sideline.

From my view I saw the defensive cornerback jump the throwing lane connecting our passer and our receiver. The d-back snagged the ball in its flight and without changing his stride he was galloping towards an unchallenged score down the open field of play.

As I leaned forward and twisted my head, I studied the opposing player coasting by me and toward his goal line. Glaring down the sideline in the fall sunshine, I noticed a figure stepping onto the field. The defender rotated his body and placed himself in an athletic position facing the opposing player.

The erratic stumbling and falling by the opposing player signified he was going down. The dishonest tackler barely wrestled the ball carrier to the ground. During the duration of the fraudulent confrontation, it was the only time in my life I was rooting against a teammate of mine.

There was a deep groan from the fans and our sideline was lacerated by the scene. The opposing team stormed the field with their coaches demanding nothing less than the rightful touchdown and six points. They were livid in connection with the ejection of the illegal participant from our sideline bench area.

After a brief discussion the officials did award the touchdown to Northwestern and the officials did eject the illegal player. Ultimately, we lost the game 6-12 in overtime. After the game our locker room was silent with embarrassment and despair. The drama of the frustrating season was beginning to surface.

Generally, our Monday practices were relaxing as we would perform minor stretching, a round of light weightlifting, and a fun-run manipulating abnormal corners of the college campus. After the jog we would be back in the athletic complex reviewing the videotape of the previous game, and discussing of our past personal and team goals. The final portion of the Monday practice was used for the scouting report and establishing our new goals for the upcoming game.

Entering the locker room on the Monday after the painful overtime loss, we understood practice was already tarnished as we read the hand written chalkboard announcement. We were to assemble on the game field in the bowl wearing our full practice uniform.

On our game field we were informed to line up on the goal line. Our coach's whistle blew and we sprinted a one hundred-yard dash to the other end of the field. I was expecting two or three sprints as we would then resume our customary Monday practice agenda.

We plunged into each dash after the whistle with the team becoming subdued. The pursuits became an affliction with a series of coughing and vomiting by players. I have no official count of the routes back and forth on the field, but our team definitely received the coaching staff's objective. The coaches conversed with us for a few minutes and we were dismissed with no other requirements for the day's practice.

Weeks later, on the day that we traveled on the coach buses to the rescheduled football game in the Metrodome, our football team had a full bucket of defeats, turmoil, and heartache. We funneled into the empty Metrodome and one of our players shouted "Hickory!" emulating the echoing scene in the movie *Hoosiers.*

Even at game time the Metrodome was far from a sell-out as there were a few hundred people supporting the teams. My mind was busy taking it all in. During the warm ups my feet were confused by the energetic responsiveness brought on by the artificial turf.

In the game we blocked, tackled, and avoided turnovers. We eluded penalties, and avoided being overly hyped when elements were prosperous or too downcast when matters turned weighty.

Our defense was bending, yet didn't break as we kept Concordia from scoring on numerous occasions. Our offense picked up first downs and had decent drives. In between swapping the football on fourth down punts the defense had time on the sideline to re-energize.

Concordia had the ball late in the fourth quarter and needed a touchdown to avoid a loss. At midfield and with only minutes to play, Concordia's running back broke through our defensive line on the left side of their formation.

The running back was on his way to a large gain on the play as our outside linebacker was able to smack at the football in the opposing player's grasp. The ball carrier had way too much daylight between the ball and his grasp. The ball slid, jiggled, and was tumbled to the turf out of his custody. The pigskin bounded a few feet in front of the running back and the scenario was preposterous. Our defensive safety appeared in the area and he easily had the fumbled ball in his control.

Our team, both on the field and on the sidelines, erupted with shouts of elation, fist pumps, and high fives. I was excited though I was computing the yards and plays we needed to run out the clock. Our jubilation was devastated as the referee closest to the play ruled it to still be the other team's possession.

The official had not seen the obvious turnover and had called the player down by contact, even though the player never hit the ground. There were no red flag challenges or instant replays in this primitive age of sports. The ruling official stood by his initial decision and the sanctioned call was no fumble on the play. Serious disagreements resonated in the dome as the game continued with Concordia having possession of the football.

Concordia's offense lined up over the ball as the sparring match continued. Concordia moved the ball in a timely manner to inside our ten-yard line and they had enough time left to run four plays using their remaining time-outs. The game would hinge on us keeping them out of the end zone or they in all likelihood could win the game on a touchdown and extra point.

On first down they operated a run for a minimal gain. On second down I was sent in for the defensive play as we went into our goal line formation. We had fostered the defense throughout the season, while modifying it with different personnel. We had been using an extra linebacker, me, and subbing out one of our defensive backs.

On pass plays I simply rushed the quarterback and was to keep him inside the pocket. During a run play on my side of the line of scrimmage, I was to make sure the ball carrier did not get outside of me. I had to steer the ball carrier back to my interior teammates so they could pursue the ball carrier and tackle him.

At the time I didn't allow myself a flashback to my first inter-squad scrimmage at DMLC. Sixteen months earlier Justin had nailed me with two crushing blocks and he had horizontally flattened in the live scrimmage. As an old man I still wasn't a notorious athlete, and I could definitely perceive the negative results returning.

Concordia snapped the ball and ran a sweep to my defensive side of the field. I was anticipating the ball carrier to pursue the path heartlessly right through me or over me. I prayed and attempted to make a stand as the running back turned inside. The opponent was tackled for no gain by our defensive tackle and inside linebacker.

Concordia used one of their time outs in order to discuss their next play. My emotions were ludicrous as I was having the time of my life. Yet, there was a part of me frightened I would blow my assignment as I had in past crucial athletics moments in my life.

On third down, Concordia's quarterback took the snap and dispensed the ball off to the running back. This time the ball carrier was bouncing the play outside. Our defensive tackle's task was to attack the runner, with our defensive tackle and me meeting together while compressing the ball carrier to the ground.

My rendering the tackle had at best a fifty/fifty chance of succeeding with my eyes open. Thank you, Lord, because with our defensive tackle, inside linebacker, and myself, the trio tackled the ball carrier after the running back obtained a minimal gain of maybe a yard marking the ball inside the five yard line.

There was no time to rejoice in the minor triumph as we had one final defensive play to undertake. The situation was fourth down and goal to go for a score with the balance of the game on the line.

During Concordia's last time out I browsed the sideline towards our bench. I spotted my replacement hastening back onto the field heading toward our huddle. With him returning to the playing field, I would be replaced for the crucial fourth down. I was heartbroken as I was the discarded player on the decisive play in Metrodome.

Trotting off the field I was dejected, and our defensive coordinator replied to me he had decided to use a different defense. He was anticipating a different play from our opponents on fourth down. I respected his decision and his revised plan of attack, and my attention returned to encouraging my teammates.

On fourth down Concordia ran again to their left side. The running back crossed the goal line into the end zone for a touchdown. For all practical purposes the game was over. After the remaining time expired we lost 14-15. We finished the season with a 0-8 record.

We shook hands with the opposing players and we had a team picture taken on the field soaking up the last memories in the Metrodome. On the sideline near the fifty yard line Nine-year-old Jenny created a remarkable hug for her dad as I concluded my meek association with college football.

In our post-game locker room in the Metrodome we received two revelations. After our team prayer we were thanked for our effort. Coach Gronholz then sullenly announced he was stepping down as head coach of the football program at DMLC. The season had been enthralling for me, but it was an undecorated burden for Coach Gronholz. My head hung in remorse feeling a huge responsibility as a player. I should have done more for my coach on and off the field.

Throughout the years Professor Gronholz faithfully served our Lord as a fantastic teacher, coach, leader, Christian mentor, and person.

The rigid mood continued as the second announcement from Coach Gronholz was in connection with the recent *Sports Illustrated (SI)* edition. The magazine had produced for years the top ten college football teams in their issues and they had printed their opinionated view of the ten worst college football teams in the nation.

The *SI* article had the DMLC Lancers ranked 677 out of 677 teams. A teammate pointed out the Lancers could now, through the common tournament seeding, take on the top ranked Florida State. *SI* even went on to rationale their rankings because of our league.

There was no mention of our school's tiny enrollment with two thirds of the students being females. There was no high praise or declaration of our graduation rate, academic standards, or non-existing recruitment outside of our WELS. There was no remark of DMLC as a private ministerial institution not offering scholarships, free living provisions for athletes, or reduced book fees/tuition.

As football players we didn't seek headlines or a transfer to a Division I program. Certainly, dreams of being drafted by the NFL were inaccessible. We attended our classes for future callings in serving the Lord and we played football for the love of the game.

The final setback before my thirty-first birthday was the breaking news I heard while falling to sleep on the bus ride back to New Ulm. Through my headphones I was smitten with the news that Irvin "Magic" Johnson publicly announced his diagnosis of HIV.

As a teenager I was in line to play a three-on-three basketball game against Magic on a playground in East Lansing. Things did not transpire as I only watched him through the chain link fence. I did cheer for Magic in his championships at Lansing Evertt High School, Michigan State University, and with the Los Angeles Lakers.

Unlike other adventures of mine I do have pictures of the Metrodome experience. In the photos I am wearing number twenty-nine which was my age when I first wore my college jersey.

When I entered the teaching ministry I coached flag football for five years and for nine years I was the head football coach of the Junior Vikings seventh- and eighth-grade tackle football team.

During my years as a football coach, I was privileged with great assistants, supporting parents, and talented players. We were blessed with winning records, exciting games, and opportunities for fostering our faith and lives. My years of coaching football were gratifying as many of the players stay in contact with me through weddings, athletic events, and church services.

Of all my involvement in sports my football years at DMLC were the most memorable and rewarding. I was injury free and thankful for every second I was able to participate. The 1991 football season taught me life lessons about adversities and challenges.

As I observe teams undergo a losing streak or winless record, I am severely punctured with empathy for their condition. I pray they find blessings in their adverse state of affairs.

There are setbacks in this sinful world that God uses for our good. Our Lord is guiding our life's steps that are planned out in all aspects. The Lord knows what is best for us, even during the fourth downs.

BRIAN LEE MILLER,
1962

FIRST PERCH
LAKE GOGEBIC, 1967

BRIAN AND AIR RIFLE
CHRISTMAS 1971

UNCLE DICK, 1974
CALIFORNIA TO MICHIGAN

BRIAN & PAUL
FIRST SALMON, 1975

THE TAJ MAHAL
SPRING 1977

FIRST CAR, 68' CAMARO
1978

SENIOR YEAR, MLS
1977-1978

BRIAN'S BROTHER MIKE
SUMMER 1981

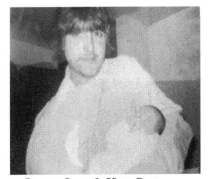

JENNY LEE & HER DAD
OCTOBER 1982

DMLC FOOTBALL
1990

RARE ASSIST TACKLE
METRODOME, 1991

114

DAVEY LEE & BRIAN
NEW ULM, MN 1992

PERIDOT CHURCH/SCHOOL
PERIDOT, AZ 1992

BRIAN & JENNY
PERIDOT, AZ 1992

ST. LUKE'S, OAKFIELD, WI
JULY 18, 1996

JOSH, KRIS, BRIAN, JENNY
MARCH 12, 2010

RON KRAMER & BRIAN
2010

115

BRIAN & KRIS, 2011
GOLDEN GATE BRIDGE

KRIS & THE TAJ
2012

DOWN BOUND SHIPPER
2013

FIRST MARATHON
EVANSVILLE, IN 2013

GRANDMA AND LEAH LEE
ST. MARY'S RIVER, 2014

ST. LUKE'S, OAKFIELD, WI
2015

Chapter 18
THE APACHE REZ

After graduation day at DMLC, my divine call to teach at Peridot Lutheran School in Arizona was officially announced.

As moving day arrived, we spent the entire day packing the U-Haul. In our operation an inherited player piano was the toughest obstacle due to its uncooperative size and considerable weight. The piano had been a resource for Jenny and me to practice piano lessons at home versus spending practice time at our schools.

Our foursome of Jill, Jenny, me and the piano was embarking on a journey. We would be determining the features on the other side of really large opposing hills, the Rocky Mountains.

The twenty-six-foot U-Haul truck contained all of our belongings as we towed our red and black S-10 pickup truck on a car trailer behind the rental truck. We were eager to push across America, but it was difficult to leave our New Ulm friends and move even farther from our Michigan connections.

The radio was on in the truck cab and there were background noises of sniffles. As the day progressed on I-80 the mood improved and we completed the first day in North Platte, Nebraska.

Along the 1,600-mile journey from Minnesota to Arizona I made two observations. We were averaging about four miles per gallon with the diesel truck and the size of the truck was often a factor in deciding our probable paths. I had to be observant of locations we entered to avoid being boxed in, running over a curb, swiping the side of a vehicle, or crumbling the top of the U-Haul truck on low overhangs.

On the second day of the journey, we motored south on I-25 as I scheduled our crossing of the Rocky Mountains and the Colorado/New Mexico border by way of Raton Pass. The plan was to conclude the day's driving while snatching up a hotel in New Mexico.

At Raton Pass, I gambled on not filling up our fuel tank before the ascent of over 7,000 feet. In essence I was a headstrong male and I was going to push the fuel consumption to the maximum. Driving through Raton Pass the fuel gauge was on a rapid pace to the empty mark and I became fearful of running out of fuel.

I had enough common sense of diesel engines to recognize it would be difficult to restart an engine after exhausting it of fuel. The process is time consuming and not easily pulled off. Besides not every gas station sells diesel fuel, finding proper fuel can be challenging.

Toiling up Raton Pass with the truck and trailer the mountain tops contained a stunning view, but no exit signs. Therefore, we brought out our paper bound Rand McNally Road Atlas. Two exits within the next sixty miles and to conserve fuel I coasted down the southwest side of the pass. Miles down the road we entered the first exit after the mountains and observed three abandoned buildings, four residences, a post office, and a library, but no gas station.

Pulling the rig to the side of the road and feeling desperate I walked into the library. I introduced myself to the middle age librarian and I explained our situation to the astute woman. Her calm face brightened with an enlightened proposal.

Our first guardian angel of the day telephoned a local rancher and arranged the purchase of our needed diesel fuel. The rancher had the fuel in his pick-up truck box in a large metal barrel with an attached pump. We didn't have to drive the fifteen miles to his ranch as he would meet us two miles south on the frontage road.

While transporting to the fueling summit I'm unsure of the trigger for my uneasiness. My edginess may have been because the two people dearest to me were in the truck, and I had no way to reveal our predicament to friends or relatives. My paranoia may have been activated due to a horror movie I had foolishly viewed in the past.

In my befuddled mind I had visions of the isolated road and the incident not turning out well. My prophecy contained a pole building swallowing up our U-Haul truck and trailer while my family and I would be victimized by a mutated man and his tormenting sons. This was the end for the Millers and our disappearance would be a lifetime unsolved case for friends, relatives, and law officers.

Jill and Jenny perceived my stress and I was scolding myself for not obtaining fuel earlier. I now had no control of the appointment with the sinister rancher. I admit, we occasionally need a random act to validate that our destiny is in God's protecting hand. Maneuvering on the road in the middle of nowhere with all of my belongings, I was hoping the Lord's lesson would be reviewed with me at a different time and safer place.

We met the gray whiskered man and we made introductions. My fears of a mishap were seen as nonsense as a tragedy did not transpire. The rancher was a pleasant man and not out to plunder us. He was pleasantly providing assistance to the traveling nomads in spite of his hectic schedule.

Our Good Samaritan inquired where we were heading, and boastfully I disclosed we were traveling to Arizona for my first teaching job after my recent college graduation.

The middle-aged Marlboro cowboy mentioned he served on the local school district's board of education and our new companion conveyed the school district was in the process of hiring a teacher for the fifth-grade classroom. Graciously, he offered me the job. On this day I had lots of choices to make in a matter of seconds and in reply to the rancher I politely passed on the offer.

After the purchase of the fuel, we liberally thanked him for coming to our aid in our dilemma. On the road again I hadn't completely set adrift my diesel fuel issues. We returned to the interstate attempting to conserve every drop possible and after a series of anxious miles we made it to a gas station. Thankfully, the business did have diesel fuel and I topped-off our fuel tank.

By the time we reached Santa Fe, I had a choice to end early or continue driving. In hindsight my testosterone level must have been off the charts and we should have remained in quaint Santa Fe.

The gloomy drive from Santa Fe to Albuquerque took longer than expected and arriving in Albuquerque the hotels were booked full for the night. To heap on an extra concern, I maneuvered the truck in a hotel's driveway in which the canopy's height was inadequate to drive through. I struggled to back out I jackknifed the rig thus producing a solid barrier blocking all the traffic in and out of the hotel.

We were exhausted as we had a nerve-racking day with diesel fuel, driving hefty chunks of miles, and skipping dinner. Jenny had tears on her cheeks and a pivoting turmoil in her stomach.

The receptionist at my no-vacancy hotel saved us an obstruction by phoning area hotels. She secured a reasonably priced hotel room with a parking lot we could adequately maneuver.

Our three guardian angels, a librarian, rancher, and hotel clerk had rectified my day's choices. After a late meal and night of sleep, the next day we clocked the lowest miles on the entire expedition. We terminated the third day's driving by stopping outside the city of El Paso, Texas. We stayed at a respectable mom and pop motel while indulging ourselves in a peaceful afternoon, evening, and night.

At the San Carlos Reservation, the church members were somewhat disappointed we did not arrive on our journey's third day. Pastor Pontel and the church members had planned a surprise reception party. Fortunately, our dinner was rescheduled for the next day.

One of the first interactions I had with an Apache person was the day at the pot-luck dinner. An elderly man named Mr. Dude introduced himself and broadcasted he was not a direct descendant of Geronimo. Mr. Dude did moreover declare many of his fellow tribal members on the Apache Reservation (Rez) were direct descendants of the Apache war-chief feared by the United States government in the 1800s.

"We Apache people aren't quite like the Indians in the Hollywood movies," Mr. Dude asserted. "John Wayne fought the Apaches who carried only bow and arrows, we have improved and more lethal weapons today."

The elderly man followed the statement with a blank stare, but the smiling reactions from the other Apaches told me that my first friend on the Rez had made an attempt to rile me up.

My obligations at Peridot Lutheran School were principal, athletic director, and teacher of grades five through eight. I was leader of the youth group and coached football, basketball, and softball. In my first year of teaching I was shocked at my attendance booklet smeared with tardys by the students. In my second year of instruction I had a perplexing, yet blessed classroom numbering thirty-nine students.

The compound's buildings at Peridot Lutheran Church and School contain exteriors made from a lightweight tufa stone. The steel bars on the windows and steel gates over the doors are there for the protection of the inside belongings. The called workers are typically from the Midwest and there are days in the summer or during the holidays when the compound is barren of personnel.

One of my possessions making the trip to the Rez was my Midwest metal snow shovel. There is no need for the implement in Peridot as the semi-arid desert weather makes it basically a snow-free location.

Living on the Rez I immediately initiated desert hikes for my recreation, and I was made aware by people that everything in the desert either pokes, scratches, pricks, stings, or bites.

Rain on the Rez would turn our clay-sand surface on the compound's parking lot into a sloppy mess. Operating a vehicle on the slimy surface was a complex undertaking with even the task of walking between the buildings impractical. The sticky clay was stubborn and would be carried around by remaining on the bottom of shoes.

The Arizona sun rapidly dries everything while developing layers of agonizing dust in the separate buildings used for the classrooms, the cafeteria, offices, and church. Outdoors on windy days the dust would sting your bare skin and eyes. But the dust was the least of the trepidations.

On a fishing outing to the San Carlos Lake, I parked my truck a hundred yards from the shoreline as we were seeking out the coveted twenty-inch southwest crappies. My fishing partners for the day were Deano and Monster, and their children. Mr. Dude's sons had become good friends of mine as the three of us had hunted together while also being on the same softball and baseball teams.

Hiking to the shore of San Carlos Reservoir, the two brothers veered off in an odd direction. I continued my straight path and arrived at the shoreline. Before long the brothers and their children began fishing alongside me. Twenty minutes and five fish later I persuaded Deano to explain their wandering loop. Deano briefed me concerning a rattlesnake track perpendicular to our original path.

At first I presumed he was enlightening me of an Apache characteristic in tracking snakes for consumption, safety concerns, or trophy hunting. They were disturbed with the snake track, though not for the reasons I was discerning.

Based on their Apache belief, they considered it bad luck to cross over the track. Non-Apache people would label it a superstition. Learning to identify a snake's trail in the desert I had a difficult time letting go of my theory of the Apache's expert tracking skills.

I had been informed that once you witness the sound of a rattlesnake's pulsating tail the particular noise will not be forgotten. One day in the fall of my second year on the Rez, I found myself at school working late into the dark hours. After completing my school tasks I mindlessly gallivanted to my compound's residence. The distance was seventy-five yards between school and the tufa stone dwelling.

With the hair rising on my neck and my body shivering, I heard the distinct rattle sound. I broke into a tiptoe sprint down the grade as I was convinced my running style would provide me added protection. At my residence I dialed-up Pastor Pontel, who lived on the other side of the compound, and we planned a hurried hunt. Within seconds we met at the location for the eradication of the trespassing rattlesnake.

Pastor Pontel, standing over six feet tall, appeared with his shaggy beard and sporting a grungy cowboy hat. His clothes consisted of a tank top exposing his outcropped belly and his lower section was exhibiting tight blue jean shorts. For footwear he had slip-on rubber boots that in a different time period was used for milking cows in Wisconsin. In Pastor's leathered gloved hands were a radiant beaming flashlight and a muddy, spade shovel.

The other snake slayer wore a blue Michigan baseball cap, a gray cotton T-shirt, and the extremely short athletic shorts. I had changed out of my unprotecting sandals and wormed my gray cowboy boots on my feet. In one hand I had a dim operating flashlight with a clean spade shovel slung over my shoulder. I had forgotten my gloves.

Our Midwest hunting outfits were adjusted for the desert quest and we had emerged as nerds on a safari in the Southwest's clear moonlight. We weren't pursuing a trophy or probing for food. We were men on a mission to establish a safe school environment for the next day.

Part of me was wanting the snake to slither away and skedaddle into the wilderness, with no butchering process taking place. Hidden in my thoughts, I was projecting if I did have a confrontation with the brute, I at least wanted to garner the serpent's rattles as a souvenir.

Pastor Pontel and I trailed the snake being lead to the far backside of the compound. Loitering in the dark the ground had transformed from effective tracking sand to non-tracing gravel. The sneaky snake had safely slithered into the arid region. As I stood near a Mesquite tree I bewilderingly gazed up at the identical sparkling stars I viewed as a child years ago in Michigan.

Besides the spontaneous snake hunting in Arizona, I also hunted Gambel's quail. My treks in the canyons and on the plateaus prying out the quail were outstanding. When the quail took flight under my footsteps, their explosive takeoffs were rather startling. Their low flight is erratic, short, with a gentle cruise back to the desert floor. When the birds glide over the sides of a steep embankment or coast over the walls of a canyon, the sight is astonishing.

The quail themselves are small in stature yet attractive in their color and vocal sounds. The males are more colorful while the male and female birds both having a plumed topknot on their head.

Many hunters consider it unsporting to bag a running bird. While I take neither side in the debate, the Gambel's quail is a skilled renegade with their zig-zag escape patterns. The odds of survival are in the quails' favor when they scatter within the bushes of their landscape.

My Labrador retriever, Cisco, and I turned our heads while marking the birds' mocking us with their cooing of, "We fooled you, we fooled you…we fooled you." If you have the pleasure to hear a Gambel's quail, the silly comparison will then make sense.

Hunting the quail using up a box of twenty-five shells, and having three quail on the dinner table, is humbling to a hunter's smugness. The birds are tasty, and I was fortunate to hunt the quail and relish a quail feast with my Uncle Ward and my cousin Paul on the Rez.

Walking on the Rez's terrain requires being alert for prickly pears, Cholas, organ pipes, and grand saguaros. The scenery similarly has plants of yuccas, creosote bushes, ocotillos, and poppies with the canyons home for javelinas, cottontail rabbits, jackrabbits, coyotes, road runners, lizards, bats, eagles, hawks, doves, and owls.

The distinctive plateaus with their flat top surface are first-rate for a views of the countryside. The sloping sides were inspiring climbs for a former misfit transformed into a conquistador.

My first glimpse of the noble mule deer bouncing up the side of a ridge brought me a smirk. I was accustomed to the whitetail deer escaping danger with a sprinting motion. The mule deer appears more like a hopping kangaroo with its head is held high like a proud king. The mule deer antlers grow larger than the whitetails, and there is a smaller whitetail deer in Arizona the Coues deer.

The upper reservation, which is about an hour drive north of Peridot, supports mature pine trees, a trophy elk herd, and snow in the winter. Visitors to the Rez can conceivably snow-ski in the White Mountains on the upper reservation, and drive two hours and water-ski on the lower reservation's San Carlos Reservoir.

Both portions of the Rez have open range practices with livestock. I learned a valuable lesson when managing a curve in the road and I came within inches of a half-ton beast. Hiking in the desert and coming nose to nose with free roaming cattle, I'm not sure who was more alarmed-the partially domesticated animal or me.

One morning at my residence, I peeked out the kitchen window and five horses were embezzling my green grass. The mare and colt were brown in color, one horse was black, the largest horse was white, and the wariest horse was a flashy palomino. I once tallied nineteen jackrabbits foraging on the same grass. The animal's ears and body are a noticeable ridiculous dimension and the wily coyote has an enormous feast when claiming an Arizona jackrabbit.

Another intriguing desert wildlife is the protected Gila monster lizard. The approximately ten to twenty-inch lizard is sluggish and little threat to humans when left alone. The Gila monster has a fearful reputation of biting in a hurried manner by moving its head sideways while emitting a toxic venom through its unrelenting bite.

Our students were presented a spring field trip to my dwelling as a Gila monster was removed from my kitchen window screen. Pastor Pontel and I exposed no goofy outfits as we wore khaki shorts and polo shirts. With a spade shovel we led the lizard into a bucket and we then transported the reptile into the remote desert.

Speaking with the elder Apaches, I tried to absorb as much as I could in regards to their language, history, and customs. I was charmed by the myth behind the black stone branded as the Apache Tear.

The legend states Apache women in the 1800's mourned for their braves who were killed by the US military or had jumped off a deadly cliff to avoid being captured. The women on the mountains scanned the horizon for their lost warriors with the women's tears flowed down the slope gathering dirt particles along the way. When the rolling mass reached the hill's base it solidified forming a black rock as it cooled.

In my excursions in Arizona, I did not discover any nuggets of the glassy obsidian. Thankfully, I was bestowed pebbles of Apache Tear from individuals on the Rez.

The community of Peridot has a population of about 1,200 people. The mineral Peridot is found in isolated locations in the world with one area being in the hills between the communities of Globe and Peridot. The olive-green gemstone, which is the birthstone for August, is one of the few gemstones found in one color.

Before arriving on the Rez, I was informed we would experience culture shock due to the high percentages of tribal members embroiled with unemployment, alcoholism, and poverty. Another weary feature would be litter on the Rez. I envisioned the 1970's public service announcement with Iron Eyes Cody viewing garbage, water pollution, and smoke while shedding tears of sadness.

The Apache people are generally reserved in their conversations and very respectful to the called workers. Most Apache youngsters have little awareness of their native language and culture. But their parents are able to speak their Apache dialect and they recognize most of their Apache customs. The grandparents' generation tends to hold resilient to the native dialect and they are well versed in their traditional ways.

On the Rez, I did not feel culture shock as my days were centered on my family and the Apache people's souls. I grasped the beauty in the natural features and I was immersed in the love showed by the people. Among the Apaches on the Rez, I had numerous pleasant experiences. However, I was anxious and concerned about being scalped during one occasion.

Chapter 19
THE SCALPING

One of numerous connections I had in Arizona was with my Aunt Judy and Uncle Roger. During my years in Arizona they lived north of Phoenix in Peoria. Jill, Jenny, and I cherished traveling to Aunt Judy's and Uncle Roger's house. As an eleven-year-old, Jenny, adored being near their horses and swimming for hours in their in-ground pool.

We had terrific conversations and meals during our retreats on holidays and some weekends with our aunt and uncle. As our most frequently visited family members in Arizona, Aunt Judy and Uncle Roger provided us a boost with their love, support, and encouragement.

On the Rez we had our fair share of challenges, diversions, and adventures with the desert's wildlife and the Apache culture. Even though there were many differences environmentally and socially, only once did I question my personal safety.

About a stone's throw away from our dwelling we could hear the beating of the drums at the sunrise dances for young girls. Due to differences in the Apache's traditional beliefs and Christian theology the dances are disputed between the Apaches and the Christian missionaries.

During the monsoon season we had sudden flash floods and rock slides across several roads on the Rez due to the downpours. Driving on the hazardous roads after rain storms was often avoided.

Prior to Good Friday, an art application for my students was stepping into the terrain behind the compound's buildings. Using plants on the small mound we crafted individual crowns of thorns resembling the painful crown placed on Jesus' head at his crucifixion.

I respected the Apache's style of food, nevertheless I never could eat the bitter-tasting acorn soup. The homemade fry bread was one of my favorite foods on the Rez and I would never turn down a delicious mouth-watering tamale at a church function.

My most distinctive eating opportunity on the Rez was mountain lion meat. I tenderized and grilled the steaks, and still found the red meat to be gamey and snarly to chew.

Finding a scorpion in my shoe seconds before I slipped it on my foot was disrupting, and the near calamity taught me to always check the inside of shoes before I placed them on my feet.

Watching a tarantula spider crawling down our home's hallway brought me a grasp of the insect kingdom. Jenny and I herded the furry creation through the kitchen and ushered it out the exterior door.

Being awakened in the night by an intoxicated male person panhandling for money was scary. My future similar encounters with a homemade sandwich and glass of water became opportunities to converse and console the individuals in their time of trouble.

The first week occupying the Principal's dwellings I trapped thirty mice from our house. The house had sat idle the previous weeks. In that same week I viewed my first road runner. The birds depicted in cartoons are large and the actual road runners are smaller, yet super quick.

The students would say a horny toad made a cut on them when the lizards were handled. Actually, the horned lizard squirts a harmless stream of blood from its own eyes as a defense mechanism.

Tolerating a stench for a week, I hunted out the despicable odor and discovered the source on the side of the road in front of our house. I came upon a decaying dog in the one hundred degree Arizona heat. With my snow shovel, a wheelbarrow, and a handkerchief filtering my breathing, I went on a mission to dispose of the carcass.

I was scraping the remains off the gravel and laboring to lift the corpse to the wheelbarrow. Halfway to removing the lifeless shell, the lump of flesh slipped off my shovel and buckled upside down on the ground. Exposed to my eyes were thousands and thousands of maggots. I was reminded of Brad and his doomed slice of pizza at FBC.

On the Rez, receiving a visit from Harlem Globetrotter star Meadowlark Lemon was unexpected as the acclaimed basketball player visited our school promoting a basketball game being held at the community center. He displayed a curiosity of the reservation, our school, and the Apache people. At the game I was captivated when Meadowlark shared with me the joys of his Christian life.

One common hobby in Arizona due to the weather conditions was competing in men's baseball games and co-ed softball games. I participated with friends on a baseball team which played against other teams on the Rez.

My teammates sought my participation in an upcoming baseball tournament sponsored by the Rez. The hardball teams had traveled to

Arizona from all over the United States for the All Native-American Baseball Tournament.

I was willing to occupy myself in the tourney until I was apprised the competitors needed proof of processing at least a quarter Native American ancestry. My teammates assured me I would have no hindrance in the tournament due to my dark hair, eyes, and skin. As for documentations denying my German and Irish genealogy the strategy was to snub out any request from the director or opposing team.

I knew it was wrong performing the act contrary to the principles I was endorsing in the classroom even though I went along with the arrangement.

At the first baseball game of the tournament, the wooden grandstands behind home plate contained numerous fans. A larger collection of spectators lined-up along the foul lines with the region containing haciendas, tailgating scenarios, and operating fire pits. Even beyond the outfield there was a wealth of fans in their lawn chairs.

Due to our ace pitcher's unavailability and a lack of anyone else volunteering to pitch the first game, I was elected to be on the pitching mound. Besides being well past the prime of throwing a baseball, I was nervous. My first worry was not having the credentials to be on the ball diamond. My second concern was being the only Caucasian within gunshot of the festive event. On the elevated dirt mound, I was surrounded by hundreds of Native Americans.

At one time my pitching of a baseball did have adequate speed and movement. After years of abuse of my arm I had lost considerable velocity. I was resorting to throwing a fastball only to set up the batters for my unorthodox off-speed pitches of sliders, curveballs, and screw balls. Similar to my years of playing quarterback in high school football I was not qualified as a valid pitcher.

After the tournament announcements and the national anthem, I completed my warm-ups. For the first pitch I wound up and hurled the white leather baseball to the catcher. The baseball skidded through the dusty surface twelve inches short of home plate. My pathetic first pitch made the count 1-0, and my throw did nothing to fire up my already low level of confidence.

My second pitch was a slow curve ball and it didn't curve. I struck the lead-off batter squarely in his left thigh. The unsuspecting batter flicked his bat toward his dugout while trotting to first base. Watching the player jog next to the chalked line, I re-questioned this nonsense of pitching as I could be relaxed and safe in the outfield.

As I was preparing for the next pitch I was on pins and needles on the mound. I forgot the signs with the catcher, so I had to call a time out. The catcher trotted to the pitching mound and reviewed the signals with me. Our shortstop, Deano, and our third baseman, Monster joined our little pow-wow.

My two friends whispered to me a shot of encouragement with their limited support noticeable through their obvious smirks and snickering. They were being entertained by the white man who was their children's teacher and principal. They found it hilarious I was a wreck.

As the next batsman stepped up to the plate my outward appearance was no different than normal. The Arizona heat wasn't affecting me because as everyone knows it's a dry heat. Inside my tense body my heart was punching my chest cavity to observe first-hand the happenings on the field of play.

For my first pitch to the second batter I compensated for the drumming of the first batter. My inside pitching policy was forsaken and I threw a slider which floated just a little outside by two feet. The wild pitch went cruising past the shocked, motionless catcher. Skating all the way to the chain-link backstop, the runner on first base now advanced to second base by means of a lethargic promenade.

My ultra-ego was begging to throw an old-fashioned strike over the plate. Whispering to the ball and God, my next throw to the catcher landed in his mit and was closer to a strike. The pitch was outside as the count had quickly become 2-0.

I decided to attempt a different strategy. I fruitlessly had been flinging my compliment of junk balls to the batters. I elected to let loose and throw a two fingered seamed fastball. I checked off all of the catcher's signs until he finally signaled a fastball.

I checked the runner on second and propelled the ball as hard as I could manage. Feeling the ball's stiches leave the release of my thumb and two fingers, I ranked the pitch as rather promising. I had forcefully chucked the ball and the round object had a surging movement as it slinked across the plate. When the hard ball smacked into the catcher's leather mit I heard the umpire bark out, "Strikeeee...one!"

The count was 2-1 and the next pitch was a no-brainer. I elected to throw the identical pitch for the ensuing assault. The catcher and I agreed and I checked the runner on second. With a whip of my arm and a kick of my leg I launched the ball with every ounce of energy in my frame. For a second time I tossed a hard, straight pitch. Only this time the batter turned sideways to avoid being smacked by the rock-solid ball. The rival was struck in his lower back.

Batter number two had likewise received a free pass to first base. I faced two batters, and two of my pitches to the batters concluded with minor impediments hitting their thigh and back. At this rate I would be off the pitcher's mound soon either shuffled to a new position in the field or eradicated from the premises by the agitated opponents.

As the second batter was trotting down the first baseline I heard a chant from the onlookers. The clamor began among the spectators in the canopies on the first base side with the hearty rumpus gaining momentum towards the wooden grandstands.

Before long the chant included the fans behind home plate and the racket now rotated to the third base side of the fan's section. All of the sovereign nations of North America's population attending the game, whether young, old, male, or female, were tangled up in the audible verses. The ruckus had my complete attention.

When Deano and Monster approached the mound I understood the crowd was not chanting Rudy…Rudy…Rudy. Because of ruckus I was prepared to surrender for the sake of my emotional stability and physical well-being. The mixture of tribes were reciting in unison, "Scalp the white boy…scalp the white boy…scalp the white boy."

Years of mistreatment of the Native Americans would be pacified through the human sacrifice of one white man daring to be an imposter. I was fit to be tied and massacred.

Observing the cheery faces and hearing the laughter from my teammates Deano and Monster, I doubted their upright friendly intentions. With nervous eyes, I scanned the horizon for an escape route, and I watched for any hostile natives entering the ball field.

I noticed the crowd with their extensive smiles and playful laughter. Flashing a sheepish look, I received the baseball from the catcher while being at ease that they recognized my ethnic background and true identity. The fans were not irritated as they accepted me for who I was before them. I had no misfit thoughts in my mind.

With my revised sentiments, I was ready to plunge into the ball game. I stepped on the mat and threw strikes. Throughout the game we were able to obtain the three outs required in the innings. The opposing batters did receive some base hits and scored a few runs. I avoided hitting any further batters as I pitched the entire game. Our team and I batted well, but in the end we lost the close game.

Claiming to be a Native American, I was proud and honored to be an Apache for a day. As a sovereign nation within the United States adjustments on the Rez can suddenly appear or slowly develop. The aspects of the Bureau of Indian Affairs, the operations of casinos, the fading of traditional ways, education, medical needs, and recreational prospects are serious topics.

The students at Peridot were delightful to lead. They presented me with respect and they industriously worked on their academics. The students were fun and a joy to motivate. Moreover, the parents provided encouragement in my ministry and I was blessed to share God's Word of salvation with them.

In the spring of 1995, I had the opportunity to take a comparable teaching, coaching, and principal position in Oakfield, Wisconsin. After prayerful consideration we concluded I could better serve the Lord at St. Luke's Lutheran Church and School.

I departed from a culture where I felt loved and less like a misfit. Leaving the San Carlos Apache Reservation, we traveled through the Salt River Canyon as I was not returning to Raton Pass. The Salt River Canyon was frightening enough with the trek up and down the canyon having hairpin turns with no guardrails.

Again in a twenty-six-foot diesel truck with my pick-up truck loaded on a trailer, I predicted the revised route would leave me with white knuckles and gray hairs. Breaching into the Salt River Canyon, my radical waltz in the scenic canyon went well.

The first indication I had acclimated to Arizona was viewed as we entered Texas. I had an abrupt realization that I had seldom observed over the last three years the now noticeable puffy clouds. In Arizona I rejoiced in the big yellow ball in the clear blue sky seeking out sunglasses stored in my house, truck, and classroom.

In Wisconsin a variation emerged within my daily wardrobe. My attire in Arizona was casual shorts, dress shorts, work shorts, and athletic shorts. In Oakfield, I returned to long pants with only six months of shorts. In the winter I resumed to hoodies, stocking hats, thick gloves, insulated boots, and heavy coats. The weather pattern threw me a curve ball when undergoing foggy mornings in Wisconsin. I was offensively claustrophobic from the disorder.

Back in the Midwest, I had a strange outlook at stores, church services, and school functions being engulfed by a dissimilar society. I experienced a reverse culture shock viewing myself as an Apache person removed from the surroundings of the Rez.

Living on the San Carlos Reservation, I confirmed my thoughts that each individual is special due to their upbringing and background. All people are shaped by their family, friends, and lifetime envelopments. Every person is wonderfully and marvelously created by God. We are diversely different, yet we are all sinners in need of a Savior. All nations have that Redeemer through Jesus.

Chapter 20
THE NEAR DEATHS

For years my friend Tim and I duck hunted at various settings near the Taj outside of DeTour. We had pursued waterfowl in front of the cabin on the big body of water in Dad's fourteen foot boat. On windy days we would pass shoot from a ground blind off the point of the cabin's peninsula. For other planned hunts, we set out decoys in the marsh or bay behind the cabin.

On a duck hunting excursion at a local beaver pond, Tim and I faced an unpredictable occurrence. Tim and I were twenty years old and we had been hunting together since we were twelve years old.

We had driven on a familiar township road three miles outside of DeTour and surmised a beaver pond was stationed nearby. We estimated the water's location by peeking through the trees at certain angles thus viewing a region void of trees. Over the past weeks we had validated an overflowing of ducks dive bombing into the area.

Tim and I drove near the secluded territory opting to conclusively investigate the duck factory on foot. Tim pulled off the road creating a parking spot in the woods, and we geared up for an appointment into the configuration of chaos by throwing on our hunting coats, slipping on our chest waders, and loading our shotguns.

The ramble to the edge of the beaver pond was finessed through tag alder brush and fallen cedar trees. At the edge of the water we became stationary on a few yards from the last bit of dry ground before the water. I figured we would ultimately be waist deep in the wet precincts shuffling around chasing the migrating birds.

We considered the scene in front of us with the silent view broadcasting its harshness, ruggedness, and uncanny characteristics. Around the pond's edges were dabs of cedar, birch, and poplar trees. Along the shoreline were pockets of marsh grass, crisscrossing logs, and the prevailing feature of dispersed rotting stumps poking out of the water. In the middle section of the uncluttered water were insignificant ripples developing on the greenish-blue surface.

Tim and I were browsing the sky, while scanning for ducks on the water surface. Tim strode two steps forward and descended downwards into the water. While he was plummeting into the stale water, my eyes validated his knees fading away and his waistline was next in line to be dissolved. By the time his shoulders were about to wane under the water's surface, I was rousing from my disbelief.

Tim was diminishing into the hole while swinging the loaded shotgun. Tim was battling to keep from dispersing into the cavity and he was yelling, "Help, Brian, help!"

Fearful of a wallop from Tim's gun barrel, likewise, I was concerned with the shell in the chamber. I maintained an eye on the gun with the primary strategy to remove the firearm from the equation.

Taking to heart Tim's yells, I positioned my shotgun behind me a short distance as I dropped down to my knees. I fastened one hand on Tim's shotgun and the other hand on Tim's arm. Tim clung to my arm while we were inches apart and face to face. His wobbly testimony was that he had not contacted the ground in the aquatic hollow.

"Tim, let go of the gun. I will hold onto you," I announced.

With our floundering hands and uncooperative arms we were able to stack Tim's weapon near my shotgun. Through all of this commotion his rubber waders were filling up with the heavy liquid. Between the intrusive waders and Tim pulling on my arm it wasn't farfetched to imagine two dreadful drownings in the beaver pond.

Using our leverage and being persistent, Tim and I proceeded to suspend his upper body on the mossy edge of the ground with his legs hovering over the bottomless pit. With us working together, Tim and I were less flustered and we had a rejuvenated attitude. We were defying death for the moment with Tim not sinking farther into the abyss.

While gathering our breath and thoughts, we collectively pulled three powerful heaves. Tim was dragged out of the water and we collapsed five feet from the hollow on the spongy, mossy area. In our conversation we declared no duck-billed bird was worth that kind of drama and suspense. Later, we conversed about the invisible life's perils and as young philosophers we reasoned the best that we can hope is the will to never quit the fight in life's battles.

A common excursion for Tim and I involved duck hunting in the bay behind the cabin. While hunting on the shore, we would wade in the water to enlist a dozen decoys or paddle our flat bottom boat in the water deploying the fake birds.

One fall Saturday morning Tim and I waded across the cattail bay wearing our chest waders as the mild quest was motivated by our mutual curiosity of exploring the other side of the inlet.

The two hunting buddies had a distinct view of the surface water, shoreline, and sky from their new perspective. Wading into the main channel, we had discovered the deepest potion of the bay. The wind's velocity had picked up and the increased waves were within an inch from the top of the loose-fitting waders. The larger waves splattered cold water into our waders while we were on our tiptoes.

Struggling to resist gravity's pull, we found the surface of the bay's bottom a mucky, stifling clay. The long march was menacing as we struggled with the amplified weight in the waders. Tim and I made slow progress.

On the shoreline we observed a middle age man tracking our dilemma. The solemn man didn't say a single word while glaring at us and shaking his head. The young adolescents were merely bothersome and disruptive to his morning.

Tim and I rallied to where the water was waist deep with the final steps being precarious due to the odd escalation of hidden boulders. Arriving at the shore, we avoided one more date with death.

On a different fall Saturday afternoon, Tim and I were hunting in the flat-bottom camouflage boat in the bay. I'm sure we were involved in a manly conversation solving all of the world's problems.

When the wind shifted and became a fierce headwind, we pulled on the anchor rope to escape the overbearing waves. During each tug, gallons of the water poured into the sinking boat while I had flashbacks of a homemade raft.

Without any indecision, the two duck hunters cut the rope and aborted the anchor. We rode the fierce waves to shore, with Tim and me not forfeiting our equipment or lives.

My best man at my wedding, Tim has been by my side in times of my life's most challenging tests. As best of friends, Tim and I have been there for each other. Even though I did not always need Tim or a partner for acquiring my own hazardous adventures.

Another incident I underwent was in Fife Lake, which is located in the northwest portion of Michigan's Lower Peninsula. The softball team I was a member on at the time was in a tournament and I was staying with relatives in the area. Playing baseball in the relatives' yard between the tournament games I was chasing down a long fly ball and framing myself to perform a back pedaling catch.

I had executed a similar feat in high school by means of intensely back pedaling while in pursuit of a high, long fly ball. In the varsity baseball game, I made the catch smacking into the chain-link fence and falling over the fence. Tumbling over the barrier, the waistline of my baseball pants caught on the top of the fence.

While I was hanging upside down looking up at the clouds, the fans received a good laugh. Even after arriving in the dugout, my teammates were chuckling up a storm about the incident. To add insult to my wounded ego, no one congratulated me on my remarkable catch.

At Fife Lake I did succeed in cradling the baseball in my glove while I was back pedaling. During my landing on the ground, my left foot disclosed a sunken divot. The clumsy step caused me to fall backwards on my neck in a bent position.

I laid motionless for about ten seconds passed out. When I regained my consciousness I was totally disorientated with everything in my world spinning and tilted. I turned on my side and vomited as a tingling and sharp pain shot through my body.

A relative's pick-up truck hustled across the lawn and I was lifted into the front seat, and throughout the process I wanted to drift away into a peaceful sleep. The truck growled fifteen miles to the clinic and I collapsed in a wheelchair brought to the truck at the clinic's front door.

In the urgent care unit I drifted in and out of coherency, yet I do recall the physician's conversation. My mind did not comprehend the medical jargon with respect to the spinal cord, vertebrae, and nerves, but I documented his emphasis on certain details. He declared I was fortunate to have avoided dying, and there was a one-in-a-million chance of my survival without being permanently paralyzed.

With a sour tone the attending physician appeared agitated, and he was inferring I was careless in my conduct. Contrary to the physician's thoughts I knew the episode was an accident as I was involved in a physical activity.

My guardian angels and the Lord has worked overtime surveillance as I have endured concussions, have escaped water tragedies, survived a burst appendicitis, and eluded a lifetime of paralysis. Most people can relate to dangerous and threatening times in their life.

God's grace and mercy have granted us time on this earth to nurture our faith and to proclaim God's saving message. As witnesses of God's love we can find comfort and peace in the words that we may not know the plans God has for us, but we know our plans are in His hands.

"I know the plans I have for you," declares the Lord, "plans to prosper you and not to harm you, and plans to give you hope and a future." Jeremiah 29:11 *3

Chapter 21
THE FUNERALS

Within the first twenty years of my existence, three of my grandparents journeyed from this earth to an eternity in heaven. During the next twenty years, I attended a limited number of funeral services. Over that second interlude of twenty years, I was only present at funerals of church members, casual acquaintances, and distant relatives. Nevertheless, I dismissed those years without attending a funeral service of an immediate family member or a close friend.

At thirty-nine years old, I mourned with my family as Davey Lee left this sinful world. However, we rejoiced as he began living in Heaven with his Savior, Jesus. Nine years later after my dad's funeral, I experienced the deaths of my Grandma Miller, my brother-in-law, my mother, and three precious friends within a five year span.

My close friends of Mike, Ed, and Janice died while in their fifties. The funerals left an impression on my concepts as I was entering the fifty year old bracket when the first friend died, and the last friend died when I was fifty-four years old.

At a Beach Boys concert at the Fond du Lac County Fair, I met Janice. At the concert we stood side by side among the crowd as we were in our separate worlds of tapping our feet and humming along with the 1960s surfing songs.

During the evening we began talking between the songs. Janice had been divorced for a number of years and I was in the process of going through my divorce proceedings with Jill. After months of turmoil between Jill and me, we attempted a period of living separate and we were officially divorced in 2005.

Because Janice was ten year my senior, she identified the Beach Boys' songs better than I did. Janice and I had many things in common and we were at ease conversing with each other. Over the next years we had spiritual discussions, attended church, hiked trails, and had every day conversations while establishing a sincere friendship.

A few years after my divorce Janice and I grew serious in our relationship taking a big step as divorcées becoming engaged. However, we had a realistic outlook on our future since Janice had spent several stressful years battling cancer through surgery, chemo, and radiation treatments. Janice's last years of living were a meshing of treatments, illnesses, and remission.

Janice was a great mother with two grown boys, and a caring grandmother to four grandchildren. She was fond of her grandkids, hiking, fishing, and yoga. As a nurse she was loving and dedicated to her profession.

I was humbled when I would accompany Janice during the excruciating cancer treatments as Janice was a brave, uncomplaining fighter. Janice, a dear Christian friend in my life, confessed her faith in Jesus as her Savior and is now pain-free in Heaven.

William (Ed) was a longtime childhood friend of our family. Ed had dated my sister Yvonne in their junior high school grades. As an eighth grader Ed hung out at our house, and I was eight years old and labeling Ed a nuisance in my life for stealing my sister's attention. Conflicting my adolescent mind was the fact I idolized Ed because of his athletic ability and his carefree demeanor.

In high school Ed had worked the summer months at Montrose schools helping with maintenance projects and mowing grass. Most of Ed's assignments were under my dad's supervision, so our childhood paths crossed often on the school grounds.

I was a rambunctious brat when Ed dated Yvonne, and Ed began referring to me as Tiger. My nickname of Tiger has stuck with me in certain circles of my life and it is a favorite nickname of mine. It is right up there with my Grandpa Miller's nickname for me of Burr.

Ed was married to Tim's sister, Sheri, as Ed and I became close friends hunting in the same deer camp for twenty years, cheering for the same sports' teams, and traveling on long and short road trips together. Ed and I were on the same softball teams until he dislocated his shoulder diving for a ball in the outfield.

For many years Ed savored in sharing interesting stories from our life's experiences. One favorite narrative was our eluding a near-death truck accident dubbed the Sheboygan Shuffle. Similarly, Ed delighted in retelling about our monetary payout at a horse track and his alarming experience at an Interstate rest area. After a heart attack my revered friend Ed went to heaven to live eternally.

My friend Mike and I became acquaintances within the last fifteen years by being introduced to each other through a mutual friend. Mike died from bone cancer at the age of fifty-nine years old. He was a Christian man with an appetite for life, a positive attitude, and contagious energy. I witnessed many times when Mike would rivet people with his original conversations and irresistible smile. Mike was a loving husband, devoted father, enthusiastic golfer, and an admirer of music. My dear friend Mike has joined the multitude of heavenly saints.

When I was in seventh grade, my mom rendered me a pair of dark brown pants and a corresponding leisure suit jacket. Mom's fashion statement included bell bottom pants having a button fly instead of the traditional zipper. The bulky leisure suit had unusual huge black buttons, a stout collar, and a straight bottom hem.

The cloth outfit was heavy and baggy on me, and I tolerated the get-up conceding the fact I had not marketed my growth spurt yet. As leisure suits went out of style I nippily buried mine in the darkest and remotest section of my closet.

Besides her full-time job at Montrose's school cafeteria, Mom loved being a housewife and mother. Nanny was a nickname our family derived because Mom behaved with her children like a dedicated, protective mother hen.

The closeness in spelling and pronunciation of the words Nanny and Nancy made the transaction uncomplicated for my speech mannerisms. When I teasingly called her Nanny, it was my way of expressing thanks for all the many blessings she instigated in my life.

I referred to my mother as Nanny often, though my preferred nickname was Nosey Rosy. The label was a heartfelt teasing that had an insight into her fixations. Mom would watch over our teenage gatherings by asking in depth questions related to our friends, dating, and hobbies. She kept a watch eye on our homework, bedrooms, and activities.

Mom had no qualms in being inquisitive of her children's lives and even in our adulthood she did not back down from her responsibility. Mom fostered the belief she had the loving and caring duty to be Nosey Rosy as God's representative and our devoted mother.

About four years after my dad died, my mother experienced medical concerns of her own. First came the onset of type II diabetes, which she was able to control through a strict diet while admitting her passion for sweets of all types.

Later in life, Mom would require daily insulin injections. In addition she had medical issues with stomach polyps, low iron levels, and being anemic. Mom was mentally astute through her lifetime until the end of her life she suffered from mild dementia.

Before the use of Internet came about, Mom was profoundly involved with our family's genealogy. She treasured her research in public libraries and within public government records. Mom was affectionate in discussing our family background and organizing the data in her notebook.

Nancy immersed herself in tending her flower gardens, being involved with the local Red Hats organization, and volunteering at DeTour's historical museum. Mom was especially partial to traveling, cooking, quilting, sewing, reading, and showering her family with love.

Nancy resided for twelve years on her own at the Taj in the Upper Peninsula. The feat was quite an accomplishment for a gal who never considered it a necessary act or a desired plan to be a Yooper. She endured winters of frigid temperatures, darkness, isolation, and accumulation of snow. After my divorce, Mom occupied three or four months of three separate winters at my house in Wisconsin.

As my mother resided at my house in Oakfield for three winters, I was embarking on the transition as a bachelor and converting into the role of caregiver. One trifling concession at my house I understood right away was the evening time schedule of one certain hour. The house's static time frame was reserved for Mom's viewing of *Jeopardy* and *Wheel of Fortune*.

My mom appreciated Oakfield because she was comfortable at St. Luke's Church and she cherished the companionship of her granddaughter, Jenny, and Jenny's husband, Josh. The meals I provided for Mom were a reprieve for her as I was on a serious health kick. Mom adapted well to the salads, fruits, and green veggies, but Nanny did keep her private stash of chocolates, cookies, and chips in her bedroom.

The nearest Walmart at the Taj in DeTour was fifty miles away in Sault Ste. Marie, Michigan. From my house in Oakfield the closet Walmart was nine miles away in Fond du Lac. Mom didn't crave to rove Walmart on a daily basis, just her weekly trips to Fond du Lac for browsing and shopping.

Mom was a people pleaser and she lived her life as a lifetime learner. One of my preferred imprints of my mom is her as a teenage woman raised on a Midwest farm who took the incentive in the summer of 1951 to travel across the United States by means of a train. She was on a lover's mission tracking down the man she desired as a lifetime partner.

Mom lived her earthly life as a loving wife, mother, grandmother, and a faithful child of God. On March 15, 2013, my mom began her eternal life at the foot of God's throne in heaven.

I have been encircled by a multitude of family and friends who now reside in heaven as saints. My utmost prevailing implication of losing a loved one was my temporary good-bye to my dad, Davey Lee.

Dad had been suffering complications for three months as he was formally diagnosed with colon cancer in September 1999. In that fall period Dad was tolerating the four-hour weekly trip across the Upper

Peninsula for cancer treatments at Northern Michigan University in Marquette, Michigan.

In November, Tim and I had driven three and a half hours from deer camp near Rapid River to my parents' residence in DeTour. The once-proclaimed seasonal cabin, the Taj Mahal, had been converted as their official retirement home. My eyes were adjusted during the visit as I realized my dad was in a serious clash with cancer.

Four months later my dad's treatment was switched to the University of Michigan hospital in Ann Arbor, Michigan. My dad would reside at Mike's house in Montrose and Dad would be transported the daily one-hour trip to Ann Arbor for his treatments. The change in the provider of health care was due to the cutting-edge facilities, specialized physicians, and innovative strategies at the hospital. Plus, in Montrose my parents would be among family and longtime friends.

For five months I traveled the seven hour trip as the lone occupant in my truck back and forth between Wisconsin and Michigan. Jill and Jenny would remain in Oakfield due to their work and school commitments. My weekend expresses would involve departing Friday afternoon for Michigan and returning to Wisconsin on Sunday night.

On the traveling carousel I replayed my life's episodes with Dad as I cried, laughed, and prayed. I wandered from fall pheasant hunts to attending high school March madness basketball games.

I reminisced of Davey Lee holding Jenny as a baby and I laughed out loud of fist pumps after winning a fourth of July raffle. I recalled Dad attending my college football games and I hung onto the memories of conversations Dad and I had while fishing. I had vivid visions of a shipper laboring down the St. Mary's River while we peacefully fished in his boat.

In the U of M Hospital in Ann Arbor I cherished Dad confessing to Mom and me his lifetime faith in Jesus as his Savior. I hold precious to my heart Dad's triumphant statement he was prepared and ready to be with Jesus in heaven.

In July of 2000, Jenny and I were in Eau Claire, Wisconsin. Jenny as an upcoming high school senior was participating in an AAU basketball tournament. Jenny's team played four games the previous day and Jenny and I were preparing for her first game that Sunday morning in a nearby community.

The phone in our hotel room rang and on the landline telephone was my sister Yvonne. She stated, "Brian, if you want to see Dad, you need to get back to Michigan today."

"I'm on my way," I replied.

Jenny and I hurriedly packed our belongings and we drove the four hours to Oakfield. At home we emptied out our travel bags and reloaded the pick-up truck with suitcases and clothes for the departure to Michigan. After the drive through Chicago and Lower Michigan Jenny and I arrived at Davey Lee's hospice room in Flint, Michigan around eight in the evening.

Earlier my parents' pastor had been visiting the facility while singing hymns and praying with my parents. When I entered the room Dad was conscious, but in excruciating pain while lying in the dim room. My dad responded to my presence as I sat alongside. After our greetings and a brief discussion, Mom, Dad, and I prayed together the Lord's Prayer.

I held my parents' hands with the evening hours being disbursed sitting at Dad's bedside with us sharing hugs and our love. As much as possible I reiterated Dad was my hero and he had always been a great father. As often as I could, I relayed my love and admiration for his guidance, influence, and love in my life.

Around nine o'clock, Dad and I expressed our good nights and Dad fell asleep. I stayed with Mom in the room until shortly before midnight. Growing extremely exhausted, Mom convinced me to ride with Yvonne to her apartment for a couple hours of sleep.

The day of driving had drained my mind, body, and eyelids. Yvonne and I stayed wake for a bit at her apartment sitting at the kitchen table conversing about life. The siblings were interrupted as Mom phoned us from the hospice's hallway.

Yvonne and I returned to the hospice facility to share our love and support with mom. Davey Lee entered God' kingdom in Heaven on July 25, 2000. Thank you, Lord, for allowing another sinner/saint to spend eternity in your presence through Jesus's redemption.

Davey Lee loved competitive games and silly quirks in perspective to life's moments. Using his wristwatch Dad would monitor and time a wedding ceremony. From the wedding party's entry until the finale of the couple sealing the deal with a kiss, Dad used his watch for his amusing ruse. Dad conveyed the confidential information a particular friend's wedding was witnessed his shortest-timed church ceremony at eight minutes.

When I was a youngster Davey Lee introduced his invention of a trifecta fishing contest which was contended by the persons in Dad's fishing boat. As we began the fishing, spree the winner of each category won a third of the pool of the monetary entry fees from each fishermen. The three categories were:

-The first fish of the day caught among the group.

-The most fish caught by anyone on the fishing outing.

-The biggest fish caught of the day.

Contestants in the trifecta fishing tournament were assured of the return of their entry fee or a third of the prize by catching the first fish on the fishing expedition. Winning two of three categories provided a fine monetary reward for the individual fishermen. The ultimate goal was to win all three categories, thus receiving the jackpot and the bragging rights as the champion fishermen of the day.

Dad had a way of making everything an entertaining competition. His oddities were quite interesting, helped pass time, and were sneakily learning tools. On most road trips Dad would have us guess the estimated time of our arrival at our desired destination. The winner of the contest would receive some type of a goofy prize.

After our family's meals we would play euchre or a hand of poker to figure out the disbursement of the duties of washing the dishes, taking out the garbage, or retrieving the newspaper. The physically skilled contests to determine the assignment of the chores were the longest baseball hit or the most free throws made.

Normally, the winner of the contests were presented the first choice of the household obligations, or in some cases be completely excused from the activities. In extreme cases due to a shortage of time or patience we would simply cut a deck of cards with the low card being assigned the most difficult job. Every now and then we would digress to rock, paper, and scissors.

Funerals were not excused from my Dad's notice. Dad light-heartedly trained me at my Grandpa Miller's funeral in categorizing prominent funerals. Dad's belief involved the procession to the gravesite after the church service. If the motorcade was continuing onto Highway M-57 from Mt. Sinai Church as the hearse entered the cemetery, the ceremony were deemed as prominent event.

As a thirteen-year-old boy, I turned around in my seat in the vehicle during my Grandpa Miller's funeral procession. From on top of the highway's hill my young eyes witnessed cars turning the far corner as the hearse entered the cemetery. Grandpa had a wonderful, well-attended funeral service with lot of friends and family present.

At Davey Lee's funeral my solemn eye-inspection authenticated a full cast of vehicles entering the highway when my father's hearse entered the cemetery. I had a good bye smile on my face remembering Dad's goofy Millerisms as my tears of sadness and joy were beginning to surface.

When "Amazing Grace" was sung at Dad's committal, I beamed outwardly and inwardly as the United States flag laid across his casket. In my serene mind I was re-constructing Dad as a Korean War Veteran and mulling over the special information he shared with me at the Taj.

I was immersed in an encompassing love as the flag was folded and handed to Mom. Then as we escorted Mom back to the vehicle I confirmed in my peaceful mind Dad's confession of being a sinner on this earth. Davey Lee was now a saint in Heaven though Jesus' life, death, and resurrection.

That day in July, remembering and saying my temporary good-bye to my dad, was extraordinary. Fifteen years later, I think of my dad every day. The departure of our loved ones is comforted through the reassurance of their presence in Heaven eternally praising and worshipping our Creator, Savior, and Counselor.

Chapter 22
THE CHANGES

Jury duty is a fascinating concept of our democratic process and I support our nation's judicial system and trials by jury. If I were accused of a crime I would fully implore to be judged by a group of my peers. Agreeing with the process of trial by jury I do strongly dislike being in the position where I'm judging someone else's deeds or lack of actions. I was summoned for jury duty twice, once in Michigan and once in Minnesota.

In January of 1986, I was selected for jury duty in Flint, Michigan. The first case I could have served on was a high-profile civil case involving a paralyzed teenage boy. The plaintiff and his attorneys were suing a motocross race track due to the teenager's injuries. I was in the courtroom for jury selection, but I was never called on as a potential juror. Eventually, the case was settled out of court.

Back in the jury's waiting room, I read through the newspaper and I was irrationally wishing I was at work. After wandering around the room, I did grab a cup of coffee and plopped myself down at a table that was organizing a card game.

I weaseled into the game and my partner was a man from Montrose, who had played cards with my dad. As we began our game of euchre, we were overshadowed by people in the busy room conversing about their families, jobs, and weather.

The television mounted high in the corner of the room was blaring out to no one in particular, but the attentiveness changed as individuals began examining the screen. The observers were witnessing a vertical line of smoke ascending upwards in the clear blue sky. The gray line split into two wider stretches of smoke which formed a Y pattern. Smaller streaks appeared on the sides and the zig-zagged lines were scattering in unpredictable directions.

The only notion I could conjure up in my mind was if anyone was alive after the upheaval as I said to myself, "Where are the parachutes?"

The lively chatter in the room was hushed sifting through the unfolding of the Challenger disaster. January 28, 1986 became a date when many people can recall their location and the activity they were performing at the precise moment. The NASA program and our lives were changed in a blink of an eye that January day.

On a September morning at St. Luke's Lutheran School in Oakfield, I was finishing up my Tuesday morning fifth and sixth grade Catechism lesson. After the lesson I went to the office to make copies for the students of a worksheet.

A parent entered our building to drop off a child's lunch and spotting me in the office he asked, "Mr. Miller, do you have a TV in the classroom?"

The question seemed odd, but I replied, "No, I don't, but I can have one in the room within a minute."

John then commented, "You should get to a TV in your classroom if you can, and turn on the news."

"What's up?" I asked.

"I'm not for sure, but something dramatic happened in New York City involving a plane," he replied. John said he had to get to work and he exited out the front doors of our building.

From the media room I rolled the TV cart to the classroom and the news report was on the first station displayed. The image appearing on the screen was a skyscraper with dark gray and black smoke billowing out of the windows high above the ground level. We observed a bundle of smoke coming from the other matching tower as the reporter stated two commercial jets had crashed into the World Trade Center Towers.

My first reaction was the aircrafts had gotten off track due to a technical glitch, and in my simple mind I didn't predict the incident as a terrorist act. The violent ambushes of terrorist actions were not as prevalent in our society at that time.

The students and I were shocked viewing the tormented buildings' fire, smoke, and debris. Nothing was said as we were taking it all in and processing it in our shaken minds.

The seventh and eighth graders returned from their Catechism lesson with Pastor Bitter and the talkative students came into the room after their walk down the hallway. The stunned pupils became mute when they viewed the action unfolding on the television.

Before our morning recess we watched live as the North Tower collapsed, and we remained speechless from the gigantic cloud of dust and devastation. I was praying all the people in the building had been evacuated from the structure. I was unwise to the total amount of destruction and certain deaths unfurling. The students and I discussed before our break the conceivable cause of the tragedy, praying for everyone involved in New York City.

We went outside for our recess and the uncomfortable emotions made the usually enthusiastic and boisterous break a low key, quiet time period. Granted, we did welcome the outdoor fresh air retreat as a temporary reprieve from the constant anxiety and drama playing out on our classroom's television screen.

The day continued with the students' fears increasing because of the nature of the surprised attacks and the possibilities of vicious assaults being committed in other places of the United States.

Reports of the Pentagon attack and the Pennsylvania field crash came through on news reports as we attempted to stay focused on our lessons. We disbursed most of our time discussing our anxieties while praying to the Lord for comfort, guidance, and protection.

The world was distorted forever that September day in 2001. The security at airports, sporting events, and government buildings has been reformed. The painful loss of lives and the ensuing military conflicts will probably always remain in our impressions.

That exclusive September day was the most traumatic occasion I encountered with students in an educational venue. Both the Challenger disaster and 9/11 terrorist attack depicts the fact that life can transform in a blink of the eye and without warning.

My cousin Paul and I have for a long time embraced the theory a person's life can change in a matter of minutes. We pointed out as evidence our incident with the opposing hill and the near drowning in the creek in our youth at twelve years old.

In reality a person's life can be transformed in a matter of a split second. Of course not all moments are so devastating or so globally dramatic as the Challenger disaster and 9/11.

Some life-changing procedures can be pleasing. For myself a pleasing stretch of time began when Jenny Lee entered this world as an infant. When I was Jenny's teacher I was thrilled to begin and conclude my days with her in my presence. Equally, I applauded her high school and college years, and all the ingredients connected with that busy duration of her life.

When Jenny and Josh were married and gave birth to their children I was bursting with joy. Jenny and I have shared our lives in many blessed distinctions with the moments being exuberant for me.

On the opposite end of the spectrum was the defining moment when I filed for divorce. Though the troubling instance didn't come about in a matter of minutes. I had been married for twenty-four years and there were signs through the years of things eroding between Jill and me.

Two people fall in love and create a life together in a marriage. Equally, an end to the marriage necessitates two people. A rocket scientist wasn't needed to point out to me our marriage was ending, but it did take marriage counseling for me to organize my perspective of the changing situation and my possible actions.

As a family in the called worker ministry, Jill, Jenny, and I had lived in four different states and in seven dwellings by the time Jenny was eighteen years old. Due to our nomadic lifestyle we emotionally leaned on each other. When as a family we settled into a stable life in Wisconsin we spent less time together.

For years as a principal/teacher/coach/athletic director I had dispersed considerable time removed from my family and our activities. When I did find time away from work, I applied time to Jenny's childhood needs and I unintentionally neglected Jill.

There were other footprints of vulnerability over the years. We were attending fewer family gatherings together and growing apart in our interests and friends. Maybe the most prominent item was Jill and I had dissimilar goals for our lives as empty nesters.

I had been dealing with my jumbled marriage since the first of the year and I was stressed out over completing the school year teaching in the classroom. My first anxiety attacks emerged over a span of two Saturdays in April. I was alone at our house and the madness of my crumbling marriage was forefront in my unsettling mind.

Everything seemed to be racing out of control according to my observance, but emotionally I would suddenly change and involuntarily everything felt alright. In the course of time I would circle back having a difficult time breathing, deeply depressed, and suffering an intense overwhelming grieving in conjunction with my hammering heart pounding away in my sweaty body.

Around noon on one Saturday an anxiety attack reared its ugly head. The first twenty minute attack was appalling and the outbreaks continued approximately every hour.

The occurrences were taxing emotionally and physically. My well-being was affected, and I made the decision to scamper out to my truck in the garage and drive myself to the hospital. The temporary treatment I received at the emergency room was medication to assist me in obtaining some much needed sleep.

Early the next week I made an appointment with my personal physician for a thorough examination and a discussion of my mental state. After the physical exam my physician explained the condition labeled obsessive-compulsive-disorder (OCD). I had no knowledge of OCD before our conversation and I was briefly enlightened in regards to my non-clinical case.

Due to my recent bouts of depression and my OCD, the doctor suggested a prescription for an anti-depressant to aid the symptoms of my anxiety and depression.

On the Saturday of Memorial Day weekend, I was on my way to fish for walleyes on the shore of Lake Winnebago in Oshkosh, Wisconsin. The last day of our school year was two days earlier and I was rewarding myself for completing my teaching duties.

On the way to Oshkosh I pulled over to the side of the road to phone by mother, and I disclosed to Nanny the certainties of my forthcoming divorce. I wasn't seeking sympathy or answers or advice. I was germinating an inner quest for an understanding of my circumstances. Beginning to map out alterations I would be confronting, I was taking one small step. My mom didn't offer any advice even though she stated she would pray for our faith and our decisions.

After the phone call a profound gloom flourished in me. I had similar bouts of the mood before, though not this type of extreme penetrating feeling of loss, hopelessness, and helplessness. This was the first time I tapped the phrase, I feel alone on an island.

For the past months there were good days and there were the terrible days. I was on an endless life's turnstile of emotions. On the good days my attitude was positive and the day's bearable routine was a welcome comfort. On the awful days everything was falling apart.

Whether linked to work, home oriented, or leisure matters, everything seemed meaningless. From my overall perspective I saw myself as a worthless human being. I did not want to be alive and I was rationalizing ways of ending my anguish.

Before I pulled away from the roadside I phoned a dear friend of mine. Steve and I had first became acquainted through officiating and other aspects of sports. Our families attended different churches and schools, but Steve and I were the same age with similar childhoods. Both of us had callings in the public ministry while spending a number of years coaching football together.

While I commenced my driving, I hinted to Steve about tagging along on the fishing trip with me. Steve had prior commitments, but he stated he had time for our phone call. I instantly jumped into the concerns with my mental state of mind and focused on the misgivings I was entertaining. While prodding Steve with questions in regards to obtaining psychological help our exchange was the first time I was willing to discuss the topic of suicide.

In my opinion I was a pitiful human being as I couldn't pull myself up by my bootstraps. I was stinging since I had inward thoughts God was punishing me for my misdeeds.

The taboo topic was difficult for me to discuss because of the consolidated shame I was embracing. My wobbly opinions were analyzing me as a depraved Christian with a weak faith and lacking a proper prayer life.

While talking with Steve, I vaulted into my main request, "Steve, I need help. I'm an emotional wreck. How do I go about getting help?"

Steve replied, "Drive to the hospital in Fond du Lac and park in the south parking lot behind the building. Walk in the emergency doors on the east side of the building. At the desk relay to the receptionist you are there to talk to someone regarding anxiety and depression."

Parking in the hospital's parking lot, Steve had mentioned I sat alone in the truck while Steve offered four times to come to the hospital and enter the doors with me. But I was determined to go through the admittance process on my own.

I remained in my truck speaking to Steve concerning the hospital's suicide prevention procedures. Without judgment Steve prayed, consoled, and provided me with guidance and we ended our phone call with me replying I would stay in touch.

Nonetheless, I did not enter the hospital and my proposal leaving the parking lot reverted back to my Oshkosh fishing diversion. Time at the familiar fishing spot would be a welcome distraction.

In Oshkosh I set up shop on the shore overlooking my familiar fishing hole. I began drowning night crawlers with the fishing conditions being excellent. Yet, I could not stop the splashing around in my thoughts the reflections of my life and I could not receive any satisfaction with the fishing engagement.

A shabby ten minutes passed and I returned to my parking spot. Storing away my gear in the pick-up truck, I began a short walk in Oshkosh. I ended up embarking on an eleven mile saunter through the downtown section, residential areas, and city parks.

I knew I was putting a Band-Aid on my emotional wound. I was closer to addressing the conundrum even though I preferred to flee from the oncoming transformations. As a temporary escape, I latched on to a partnership with a few alcoholic pints, which made me brave enough to express my thoughts.

At my house in Oakfield, I shared with Jill my displeasure concerning our current situation. I voiced my concern about the stress we were causing Jenny within our crumbling life style.

That evening I highlighted ideas out loud I had been considering for months. I was convinced God was letting me down and I ached for my control of things. I didn't seek God's input about my woes, despite the fact I was serving the Lord in the public ministry.

God didn't care about me, so in my pity party I was going to have a dance with a caring confidant. Somebody who would make me happy or at least assist me in burying my sorrows and pain. Dancing with the devil seemed like the right solution.

In my discussion with Jill, I stated not caring about our relationship or myself. After dispensing my views to Jill, my plan was to occupy the evening as far from her as possible at our residence.

I wasn't at the point I would hurt myself, but I had lost trust and faith in myself. While sitting in the garage, a firm knock was heard at the garage's service door and I greeted an officer from the sheriff's department standing at the door. Jill had reacted to my statements and she had called 911 with concerns about my mental state.

The officer interviewed me as I admitted to the earlier comments about not caring about myself. Turning to face the wall, I was handcuffed for my protection and placed in the sheriff's vehicle. The officer navigated to the hospital in Fond du Lac. The officer was professional and cordial as we discussed life's surroundings and problems during the drive.

At the hospital I went through the south doors with the officer—the entrance I had agonized over earlier in the morning. After admittance I was escorted to my hospital room. My life had been traumatic for months and filled with sleepless nights. When my head hit the pillow on the bed I slept like a rock late into the next morning.

My first day at the ward was a wide awakening revelation. I had a strict itinerary which included meals, group therapy, homework, and counseling. I was making a strong bid to absorb all the concepts and procedures while working through my confusing contemplations.

Fellow patients tugged at my heart as they were near the bottom with choices in their life or had reached rock bottom. The agony was palpable in the ward yet there was hope. The compassion and dedication of the staff was complementary with counselors, therapists, and nurses involved in the health industry performing outstanding work.

I found the information helpful and encouraging. Moreover, I am now disturbed with individuals insisting depression lingers because of a weak faith or the absence of a strong prayer life. They may even announce there might be a deficiency in the suffering person's fortitude. Shame on individuals or society for fostering a false contention.

I wish I could express, "I'm not going through this anymore" as everything becomes hunky dory. Depression/anxiety treatment involves support, therapy, and perhaps medication. Healing takes place through education, changes, and energy with big doses of affection, understanding, and patience required of people involved.

On the third day, I was released from the hospital and spent three additional days at home praying. I construed my marriage was not salvageable and a week later I filed for divorce. Over the next weeks I informed St. Luke's, relatives, and friends of the pending divorce. I informed my cousin Paul of my situation. After processing the newsflash Paul replied, "Life can change in five minutes."

My message had changed Paul's life and his perspective of mine even though my marriage had been unstable for months. I had accepted certain aspects of my upcoming changes and I was already leaning on my family, friends, and church members.

I was especially assisted by my daughter, Jenny. For a few long months, Jenny and I flipped flopped our responsibilities of leadership, guidance and managing. Jenny was the stable person, emotionally supporting her dad. My parenting role was put on hold with my focus centered on improving myself psychologically.

My divorce presented me with the task of facing personal life altering moments. Gone was a twenty-four year spouse, my in-laws, and selected friends. To adjust to the modifications my summer months were working at school while regrouping and recharging. I evoked the difficult stages of the grieving process involving denial, anger, bargaining, depression, and acceptance.

My perception of marriage and divorces has since been converted, and I take a compassionate notice of society's members who shuffle through the delicate junctures after a separation, break up, or divorce.

My restored stability emanated because of God's grace, accepting change, and an exhaustion of available resources. Changes do happen, and life does continue. After my divorce I became a forty-five-year-old bachelor and that was a big, weird change in my life.

Chapter 23
THE TRIP SOUTH

There is little doubt I have a fired up attitude towards outdoor activities and athletic contests. Also, I am at ease doing my own laundry, grocery shopping, and performing domestic tasks around my house. Being a newfangled bachelor at forty-five years old wasn't perplexing because of the daily required household duties. I had been performing the chores since I was twelve years old.

My test came in the form of dating, which I had not executed for twenty-five years. The twenty-first century online dating scene was an intrusive universe in my sheltered world. After I dispatched a mammoth amount of personal information through dating services and with prospective dates, I actually went on face-to-face dates.

My dates consisted of a theatrical play, a walk on a beach, and dinner at a casual restaurant. The ingenuous gatherings included a cookout at my house, breakfast at a tavern, and ballroom dancing lessons.

I understand certain intricacies about myself as I am a people pleaser, except I can't please others if I don't take care of myself first. I will make mistakes and the layer of scars from those sins may remain in my soul. Every so often I view myself as a misfit wearing a capital D. The letter is evidence I am a divorcé-a failure due to the conclusion of my first marriage. I know time does heal, and most importantly I knew I am a forgiven child of God through Jesus.

One of the turning points in my therapeutic route came on an unexpected trip. After attending our Easter's sunrise service and breakfast at St. Luke's, I had a week-long vacation from teaching. In the late morning hours I loaded my truck and I headed south to Tennessee for an escape from everyday life. I packed my camping gear, a duffel bag of clothes, and a provision of water and food.

I steered into Louisville, Kentucky in the evening hours, and I wasn't picky about my accommodations or the healthiness of my food.

I had a greasy pizza delivered to my cheap hotel room. My bed was clean, the shower worked, and day one of my adventure was a success.

The next day was a sunny spring day and I detoured to Bowling Green, Kentucky. I moseyed around the city and stationed myself on the buzzing grounds of Western Kentucky University as their men's basketball team was alive in the sweet sixteen round of the NCAA tournament. After exploring the campus for an hour I was back on the interstate heading to my first destination, Nashville, Tennessee.

In my childhood I was musically influenced by observing my Grandpa Miller strumming his guitar and singing his favorite country songs at the neighborhood's parties and family gatherings. I also observed my Grandma Miller's informal organ recitals at their house.

Falling asleep with the '60s and '70s top twenty tunes rocking and rolling through my bedside clock-radio was common. I even swayed along with the Motown music on my headphones attached to my portable transistor radio. Hanging out in our basement I was revved up by my sibling's eight-tracks and cassette tapes. By the same token I drummed along with the music blaring from the radio on our garage's workbench.

My mom presented a steady dose of country music on the turntable playing in our dining room. I grew up listening to my parents' choice of music resonating through Tammy Wynette, Patsy Cline, Merle Haggard, George Jones, Buck Owens, and Loretta Lynn. Out of the numerous country music voices I became fascinated with Johnny Cash.

As a seven-year-old lad my parents surprised me with tickets to the sold-out Saginaw Auditorium watching my favorite entertainer. By the time the man in black reached the stage I was snoozing on my mom's lap. My mom tried arousing me during the concert, except the result was minimal with it being well past my bedtime. I battled my grogginess monitoring three of Johnny's melodies.

My first effort as a country music star came about shortly thereafter. I manufactured a homemade guitar from cardboard boxes, glue, and rubber bands. The makeshift guitar crumbled after one gig as the provisions were too frail to hold up to my gibberish picking.

Musical Plan B involved raiding the scrap pile next to our garage. The resources were classified as rough building supplies and they were salvaged from Dad's past construction campaigns. I rummaged through the clutter amassing two pieces of wood.

The guitar's neck was fashioned from a crude two by four pine board and the guitar's body was molded from a piece of plywood. The plywood had peeling edges and on the back was a black ink stamp identifying it as the lowest grade of plywood. Not to be outdone the pine board had complex gouges and scratches.

The guitar's components had jagged cuts performed with a handsaw and I used siding nails to fasten the two parts together the best I could manage. I should have used an overabundance of glue while learning that screws are superior to nails in wood projects combinations.

For the guitar's tuners and bridge I hammered three large-headed galvanized roofing nails to each end of the instrument. For harmonious strings I installed three unrelated sizes of rubber bands.

The heavy instrument conveyed unforgiving jaunts in the construction trade and the device existed like the Frankenstein of musical apparatuses.

On days of performances, I decked out in any black clothing I could find in my closet or dresser. My stage was the basement's fireplace hearth, the same concrete slab that had shielded a newborn from the fire's blazes. Springing up on the platform, it wasn't large enough for prancing back and forth, though I did spiffy up the amateur production with a spotlight. The garage's trouble light with its silver aluminum shield was clipped to the nearby wood countertop bar.

I entertained myself with my pre-adolescent voice and my peculiar guitar. As a Johnny Cash imitator I sang my opening tunes of "I Walk the Line" and "Ring of Fire." I had a restricted audience of my mother in the basement's laundry room or our family dog, Babe.

Babe with her Pekingese mug and bulging black eyes was my one loyal fan. She didn't spend the entire performance wagging her tail, but she was respectful and remained seated through the unabridged concert. Babe never yelped criticism in response to my forfeiture of the correct lyrics and she didn't howl when I was having an off day with my pitch. My best friend, Babe, never asked for a refund.

In my routine I crossed over to Beatles' tunes, and later concerts concluded with my encore selection of "Build Me up Buttercup."

This was my background which directed me to Music City, Nashville, Tennessee. The city was one of my long-time desired destinations and was on my wish list for thirty years.

I wanted to wing my vacation in Tennessee. I wanted to wander, be schedule free, and thrive off my spontaneous interest. Arriving in Nashville at lunch time I did have one goal. I had to wet my whistle while lumbering up to a karaoke barstool. My tactic was to hunt out an appropriate platform in the Broadway Street area.

I parked in a downtown lot and I familiarized myself by taking a midday stroll along the Cumberland River. I mingled with the lunchtime crowd attesting to the frenzied metropolis of skyscrapers, government agencies, and traffic. The number of homeless people and panhandlers was staggering, as I hadn't expected Nashville to be equal to other large cities and their social plights.

Later in the afternoon, I did enter a karaoke bar as it was too early for any major raucous, jam-packed hoedowns. I was astonished with the singing possibilities in the city, but my heart and soul did not converge into the musical diversion.

I dawdled in Nashville for two days touring the Gaylord Opryland Resort, the Opry Mills Mall, the Grand Ole Opry, the Titans' LP Stadium, the Johnny Cash Museum, and the Country Music Hall of Fame. I spent the evenings and nights at my cousin's townhouse in Franklin. Angie and I had chats divvying up tales from our childhoods and recent dysfunctional marriages.

My hiking excursions in Franklin were spent monitoring the older southern brick-style homes with their white pillars. I was awestruck by the prosperous budding of trees and the flourishing flowers. Spring had marvelously arrived in the south.

After my second day in Nashville, I was primed for a more rustic adventure. Driving my truck east, I could not recall packing my tent in Oakfield. I had jokingly suggested if I had forgotten an item I would stroll into a retail store and make the needed purchase.

Shuffling into Walmart, I purchased the first tent I spotted. The blue nylon tent was listed for $49-a reasonable price for shelter in the wilderness. Not that it mattered one iota, the fancy tent could lodge up to six people.

After my camping supply buying collaboration, I stuffed my stomach at a KFC restaurant and the all-you-can-eat buffet. I was bulking up my reserve of body fat and taking advantage of my last hoorah in civilization.

The first Tennessee State Park I evaluated was impeccable. The campsites had asphalt-paved approaches, a regimented fire ring, and a painted picnic table. The park contained a celestial lake within its confine and the campground was a bit more civilized than I preferred. Consequently, I continued my journey by driving further east with my overall plan of camping near the Appalachian Mountains.

By means of brochures, I chose a particular park isolated from towns or major highways. From the campground I could rise the next morning and drive to the Smoky Mountains in a timely manner.

I was within a mile of my destination in the back country when I halted at a four-way stop sign. Nonchalantly, I glanced across the crossroads and comprehended a derelict wooden structure. The building was slanting hard to the west and the openings in its outer walls were perfect for critters to crawl in and set up residence. The sagging roof had a fifty/fifty arrangement with nature; it had 50 percent of its shingles missing and 50 percent attached.

There were two front rectangular windows probably two feet wide and three feet high with each unit consisting of six individual panes of glass. Every windowpane was essentially broken and there were tokens of jagged glass left in the corners.

The front porch had wooden four by four posts holding up its tin roof. The porch railing was not painted and it gave the impression of being sturdy. There were three wooden chairs which in my mind had to be rocking chairs, yet I did not stay mesmerized on the chairs.

My undivided attention was on the guys in the chairs. I don't mean to imply anything groundless, except I would never have introduced a single one of them to Mom. The approximately thirty-year-old men wore stained baseball caps and baggy overall denim bibs with the garments under their shoulder straps being short sleeve t-shirts.

Gesturing towards my direction two of the males were large and wore bushy untrimmed beards and both of the men had a limited amount of surviving teeth. The third remaining dude was rising from his chair and he was modeling a scowling face. The fit man was days into a five o'clock shadow on his jailhouse profile.

If any one of the three men would have licked his chops I would have soiled my pants on the spot. The drainage would have been a wide-awake wetting like the accident in my bed as a youngster.

Even more disturbing was my surveillance of a lack of vehicles. I hadn't seen an operational automobile for miles even though I had viewed broken-down autos in driveways, dumped alongside barns, and abandoned in the woods.

I tried my best to hide my presence, however my truck was not necessarily blending into the surroundings. My white Chevy truck with Wisconsin license plates was announcing, "Hey, I'm a stranger all by myself and not even my family or friends know my whereabouts."

My brain flashed into the movie *Deliverance* and the background music of the dueling banjos. I soared through the raw rape scene in the woods, and paused as the hunting arrow penetrated the villain. I frowned when the canoes crashed in the rapids, and my imagination went to slow-motion at the intense cliff panorama. I closed my movie trailer nostalgia with the hand rising out of the water and hearing the southern dialogue, "Squeal like a pig."

Back in my world, my choices were to turn left to the campsite down the road or turn right scooting off to a safer cultured location. I executed the left turn and my silent prayer was more intense than any prayer I had ever recited Sunday morning in church.

Leaving the intersection I was pleading with God to allow me to drive away without a flat tire, overheated radiator, or faulty alternator. Although I did have back up plans in case the mishaps appeared.

If a tire shattered, I would keep grinding down the road even as the wheel wore down to the bare metal rim. If there was steam oozing from the hood, I would continue blindly chugging along. If my truck stalled within the corner's eyesight, I was bailing out of the truck and sprinting away. With any luck I would collapse dead before the horrendous outlaws caught me.

I had no ambition to discover the aspects over the hill and my survival was the lone concept in my disarrayed brain. Out of sheer instinct I drove to the unattended state park entrance. With shaking hands I filled out the admittance envelope and in the permit box I edited I was the sole camper. Surprisedly, I had no qualms about camping even after my tomfooleries with the fellas at the shack.

My plan at the campground included setting up my tent, renting a rowboat, and wetting a fishing line. In the late evening I planned to cook a meal and enjoy a campfire. Before the daylight faded I rowed to the lake's isolated cove and caught three bass. I took my first selfie ever holding a bass in one hand and my flip phone in the other hand.

Jeepers, I could not relax as I had delusions of people lurking around in the surrounding woods eyeing me up as they slithered from tree to tree. After watching a striking Tennessee sunset I made my way back to the shore, returned the boat, and retired to my campsite.

The darkness came rapidly in the hills, and the weather conditions shifted due to an increased wind. The vegetation on the ground was exceedingly dry, and with thoughts of an out of control roaring blaze, I passed on a campfire. I could do without making national news for a major catastrophe in the countryside near a national forest.

After I set up my brand-new tent, I sat on a large rock and took in the solitude. Within seconds my privacy was broken as I singled out the thunderous roar of a muscle car. On the remote road a quarter of a mile outside the park, an automobile was bellowing back and forth. I assumed my buddies from the previous crossing were bantering me. I counted three obsessive passes before the vehicle departed, and I enjoyed two minutes of complete silence besides the hollering wind.

Now stirring my attention was the upheaval in the bushes next to my campsite. I substantiated by the intense racket it was either a black bear or a mountain lion and I was assured I was going to be devoured alive. In my deflated mood, the hectic clamor was the last straw as I resolved to quit the camping festivities and recede as far away as possible from the hill's nighttime disturbances.

First though as a mountain man surviving the rugged outdoors, I darted off to the nearby convenient and modern restroom. Finishing my time at the men's room I treaded back to my campsite equipped with my state-of-the-art weapon, a stick I had retrieved on the path.

I approached the underbrush where I had heard the noise and my flashlight's beam spotted the reflecting eyes of a yellow feral cat. The large feline came out with a desolate meow and I wanted to hang it in a tree by its tail. Avoiding any unnecessary confrontation, I merely stomped by foot and yelled, "Get out of here, you flea bag."

I wasn't in the mood for a companion and the fat cat didn't insist on a stare-down. The tom cat didn't waste any time as it darted off into the darkness. Wanting to leave the creature with my personalized manifestation I heaved a side-arm sling of the stick in the general direction of the animal. For a finishing touch I yelled in my stern playground voice, "And stay out of here you varmint."

Looking around, I re-examined the site and I decided to remain in my groundbreaking kingdom. I crawled into my sleeping bag and delivered a short prayer for my survival through the night.

In the middle of the night, I was rudely awoken by a suffocating presence with my body immobilized being entombed. I twisted my way out of the imprisonment, establishing that my blue tent had collapsed from the mountaintops' gusting wind.

The sleeping quarter was renewed with bungee cords securing the sides and I crawled back into my asylum being fully aware of the option of retreating to my truck. I was lying in my flimsy shelter listening to the wind while considering the feral cat, thundering car, and strange menfolk. I was at peace for the first time in a long, long time.

I slipped into a sleep conceding that, "God is in control of my life." I had ceased fighting and I accepted the truth God is in control of everything, even a seemingly insignificant misfit like me.

Early the next morning the wind had subsided. Peeking out of my tent, I spied a trail roaming farther into the hills. Hiking for ten minutes on the path I staggered upon a four-foot-high rock supervising a glorious mountain assessment. I parked my backside on the boulder and I prepared a bowl of cereal. An unbelievable sunrise touched my side of the mountain, and brought warmth to the springtime creations.

The day was mine to explore the gargantuan playground before me, but first I had a serious discourse with God. Up to this point I was rebellious for weeks in my relationship with the Lord. I had felt abandoned by God in regards to my divorce, depression, and my life's plans. I had been reasoning He was not listening to me.

But I had to admit the Lord had been with me and guided me through all of my heartache, change, and healing. God had answered my prayers in His time and in His way.

Later in the day I delved into the Great Smoky Mountains National Park, or more precisely, Cades Cove. The valley is circled by mountains and the park contains an eleven-mile auto tour traversing through the area. I hiked the trails, scrambled through the mountains' bald spots, and captured a nap against a fallen log.

Hours later I left Cades Cove and pulled off the road to eat lunch near a mountain stream. My picnic consisted of a ripe banana, a granola bar, a crunchy red apple, and a bottle of water.

When I had completed my lunch, I trailed the glistering stream up the mountainside while being saturated in the sunshine. Advancing for two vigorous hours I had a humble first in my endeavors. Panting my way up the forested mountain side I unintentionally loomed over the stream's origin on the hillside.

My reborn passion to climb a hill motived my curiosity as I continued upward discovering a secondary trail. The trail connected further above to the Appalachian Trail (AT) and I unexpectedly fulfilled another desired objective. I marched along my praised AT scrutinizing the trees, mountaintops, and valleys. My pace and the scenery were light hearted as I was floating with the clouds.

Dejectedly, I had to retreat from my utopia playground in the mountains and I was smacked by reality as I drove through the town of Gatlinburg. I proceeded to be punched and floored in Pigeon Forge, the home of Dollywood Theme Park. I documented an inconceivable line of vehicles making the left-hand turn into the facilities.

I spent the night in Lexington, Kentucky, while driving the next day nonstop except for filling the gas tank and the use of the restroom. I reached Oakfield in the evening hours. I was prepared to breathe in and out, care for Mom, teach my students, and serve the Lord.

Chapter 24
THE BUTTON

Since third grade I have had an inferiority complex in regard to misusing and mispronouncing verbs such as arise, bring, choose, sing, and swim. I quarreled with the tense forms of linking verbs or helping verbs. I tend to blame my poor grammar and writing mistakes on my Michigan upbringing. Sorry fellow Michiganders.

At Mott Community College in Flint, Michigan, the English 101 course in which I enrolled had twenty-three students attending the first day's lecture. We were a diverse group due to our ages and backgrounds. Five weeks into the classes I was fearful that even with my noblest effort, I would still be the recipient of a D grade.

With reluctance I dropped the course and four students remained in the class as I walked out and deserted my student's fee. Repeating the course the next semester I did receive a modest B grade.

In my authoring, I would toil through one sentence while rectifying my grammar and spelling. The process was time consuming and required a ton of effort. By the time I would accomplish one presentable sentence I would have dissipated my idea for the next sentence.

Adding to the toil of my meager output was the manual typewriter of the past era. In my high school years, I lethargically used all ten of my digits for a rate of twenty words per minute on my best days. The elimination of blunders with a delete button or backspace button did not exist. "Wite-Out" was a serious friend of mine, and unfortunately I would retype whole pages due to my voluminous errors, avoidance of vital facts, or misarranged notes.

As far as tackling a project like composing an entire book, I threw in the towel early by vacating the overwhelming proposal. My big break came through technology. The options in word processing programs to cut, delete, paste, and spellcheck my contents are incredibly helpful. Agitation regarding my mediocre grammar use and incorrect spelling is lessened due to the computer's assistance with my inaccuracies. Moreover, I have the option of voice activation on electronic devices as an aid in my rate of composing written creations.

When I was a student in high school or college, I dutifully followed along with the teaching techniques of lectures, discussions, and reading. I gravitated towards hands on learning. I was exhilarated with science lessons due to the experiments, yet I scuffled at memorizing the scientific theories and terms. At times I could comprehend the data, and then nothing clicked in my intelligence. Like most students my audio skills were not up to standards; I often displayed the shrewd tactic of selected hearing.

Because of my struggles with the learning process, I am constantly searching for the button that makes learning advantageous for students whether in a classroom, sports, or an occupation. Finding the button is discovering the motivational entity that will stimulate the students.

Perhaps the button is a smile, a good morning greeting, or a word of encouragement. The button may involve any number of manipulations with a visual aid, video, story, technology, field trip, or explaining a concept differently.

In my fifth year of teaching I taught grades five through eight while having the responsibility of being principal of our K-8 school. We held school in a township hall eight miles south of Oakfield due to the F5 tornado which destroyed our church and school. The LeRoy Township governing body was gracious in renting allotments of their building for our daily use for an entire school year.

At the conclusion of the first day of the school year I recited, "Well, one day is done, 174 days until summer vacation begins."

At the building's front door our lower grade teacher, Mrs. Tetzlaff, advanced to me. She anxiously informed me that she was missing a student, Bobby. Third grader Bobby and his family had moved to the Oakfield area in the summer. At the time of his enrollment his mother supplied records on Bobby's past status as a student at his past school and classroom. Bobby did satisfactorily academically, his growing challenges and banging resistance was his misbehavior and discipline.

At our temporary facilities in LeRoy a shuttle bus transported our students back to Oakfield. In Oakfield at the undamaged high school the students would transfer to their regular buses. As the report of Bobby's disappearance was announced, we had five minutes until the shuttle bus was departing.

Mrs. Tetzlaff and I completed a thorough inch-by-inch examination of the building. We began at the Township Hall's front doors and proceeded to the back door. We made a valiant effort in the examining the closets, behind doors, and in the cabinets.

Mrs. T and I finished at the back door of the 1960's one-story block building and we stepped outside as I browsed for Booby within our adopted playground area. The location had none of the normal playground equipment of slides, swings, or monkey bars. Yet, we did have ten acres of mowed grass where students could chase each other in tag, kick a soccer ball, or engage in touch football.

When I redirected my sight farther I determined the boundless acres of corn. The September corn stalks were a shade of green while exhibiting the start of the fall tan color. There were rows of the mature unharvested corn which served as an unfenced hideaway.

I had a notion Bobby may have wandered into the field and he was still fumbling around in the corn maze. I was predicting the need of policemen, a search party, and a helicopter at the site.

This mishap was coming on the heels of the Oakfield tornado only weeks ago in July. As principal I had depleted the last weeks of summer obtaining office and educational supplies. School events had to be reorganized and our church services were held at Winnebago Lutheran Academy in Fond du Lac. Prior to the tornado our church and school were housed in one facility with a few steps between the two associations. The new distance between the church and school was seventeen miles.

While standing a few steps away from the gray metal door of the hall, I was dreading the emergency phone call made on the school's phone.

Facing away from the back door, I heard the odd sound of a thud. I looked to my right and noticed on the ground a deserted backpack. Bobby wasn't in the backpack, as Bobby had flung the black bag to the ground. My senses traced the skyward path the cloth container had charted. Twelve feet in the air on top of the flat roof surface Bobby was sitting with his feet dangling over the outside wall.

Bobby gazed down on Mrs. Tetzlaff and me as if he had no worries. Bobby had scampered up the side of the building void of any apparent windowsill ledges, ladder, or built-in steps. From his perch Bobby was being entirely entertained by his teacher and principal.

I commanded Bobby to get his gluteus maximus down from the roof and I ended the formal demand with a concrete, "Right now!"

Bobby slithered down the wall as Spider-Boy and because of his raw talent I should have endorsed Bobby in an elite gymnastics program, or CIA training. At the very least I could have written a reference for him in connection with a job at the circus.

I entered the teaching profession too late to be a donor of spankings. I only had the thrill of receiving the method of discipline. I was persuaded to discipline Bobby in a variety of means when he reached ground level. I resisted all of the temptations including the wringing his of neck with my bare hands.

Instead I expressed to Bobby, "I will deal with you tomorrow. For now I want you to high-tail it to the bus. I will call your mom and update her of your stunt. There will be a meeting with the three of us."

Bobby picked up his backpack and scurried through the hallway to the bus with Mrs. Tetzlaff never leaving his side.

In the same school year, Mrs. Tetzlaff approached me in a desperate state reporting Freeman was missing. Freeman was not a student, but was one of the hamsters in Mrs. T's classroom. The furry creatures of Brooks, Driver, and Freeman were named after Green Bay Packers' pass receivers Robert Brooks, Donald Driver, and Antonio Freeman.

The LeRoy Township Hall besides our temporary place for school was the location for storing the township's snow removal and mowing equipment. The building was managed as a recycling center, township meetings, and hosting senior citizen functions.

With the news of the missing hamster I was haunted by delusions of Freeman scurrying through the building. My genuine woe was the elderly ladies playing cards and a beady-eyed rodent scampering along on the shining floor tiles disrupting their pastime.

Mrs. Tetzlaff and I were creating our plan of action which was comparable to our hunt for Bobby. We contrived to begin at one end of the block building and make a systematic search through the structure. We had no clue if Freeman was even in the building as he could have gained his freedom by joining the outside world.

Mrs. T and I began prodding in the bathrooms and we met in the hallway before entering the cafeteria. Mutually, we received the epiphany and hustled out to the bus. Summoning Bobby off the bus I noticed his fidgeting and I figured we were on the right track.

Explaining the situation to Bobby, I asked his knowledge of Freeman's whereabouts. Bobby offered me the deer-in-the-headlight glaze as part of me was fearful Freeman may have journeyed on a crazy ride in a swirling mass of water in a toilet bowl. Furthermore, I was bothered Freeman may have been a self-sacrificing grenade as Bobby launched the furry creature from Bobby's pad on the roof.

Once again I communicated to the tight-lipped Bobby, and I presented a short review of relaying truths, and the consequences of untruths. I asked Bobby if he had played with Freeman. Bobby shook his head side to side indicating a no answer.

Confident there was an association between Bobby and Freeman, I asked Bobby if he knew anything about Freeman's recent disappearance. For the third time Bobby denied any involvement and this time he spoke the word, "No."

My next exchange came from observing Bobby's hands maintaining a firm position in his coat. I inquired to see Bobby's hands deep in his winter coat's pockets and the third-grader produced one hand for my inspection. With a big sigh I expressed both hands had to be seen.

Bobby began staring at the parking lot asphalt as I again insisted for the other hand. When Bobby pulled out his other hand, cupped in his hand was a trembling Freeman. Evading the life of freely roaming in Bobby's bedroom, Freeman was returned to his cage in the classroom.

The next summer Bobby and his mom moved to a different location and Bobby did not attend our school. I'm unsure if we had switched on Bobby's button to motivate him as a student and person.

In my classroom there were rigid requirements for a learning setting. I think my classroom environment was organized, effective, and loving. With mixed results, I explored many motivational aids, reward systems, and discipline. One of the students' favorite diversions was dollar day. The activity was entertaining as it could be justified as a learning exercise due to the needed factors of concentration and quick reactions

At the conclusion of any recess the first person in line had a chance to win a dollar bill. Using their extended horizontal stationed index finger and long finger, a student won the bill if they pinched in their clasp the vertically dropped dollar before it passed through their fingers.

To make the game challenging I might ask as a distraction, "How's your boy/girl friend?" I might even stoop to saying, "I *might* drop the dollar on the count of three." Starting the countdown I would recite, "One, two," and before saying three drop the bill.

Guidelines for dollar day event included, no contest on windy days, no pattern of a challenge appearing, and no hanging around the entry door anticipating the recess whistle. I mixed variety by making it the third person in line or the tenth person in line.

I might modify the contest to be a $10 bill day, credit card day, or the celebrated wallet day. Yes, over the years dollar bills were forfeited as incentives, but no credit cards exchanged hands.

On Fridays, if we had a productive week in the classroom, we would have an alluring afternoon. I was able to pull off the lesson supplements since I was principal of our small school. Our activities might encompass a twenty-two mile bike ride on the bike trail, flying kites on our athletic fields, or fishing at the village pond. We took field trips hiking in the nearby woods or ice skating at an ice ring. While indoors we sang karaoke or watched a movie with popcorn.

In the classroom to emphasize a point or to connect a lesson, I might articulate a story from my past. The one past chronicle the students remember utmost is Brad, the pizza, and the maggots.

There is no doubt the narrative has become improved over time through the storytelling techniques of pausing and predictions being utilized. Incorporated descriptive language, colorful words, and a cliff hanger has helped. I am careful to hold back on specifics of the maggots to avoid a gagging episode by the students or me.

I usually presented the pizza story in September. During one school year pizza was scheduled on the menu for the fourth time of the school year in November. After the students received their food I grabbed a tray and placed my pizza, veggies, fruit, and dessert in the slots. I placed my food on our classroom's assigned table and returned to the counter to retrieve my silverware, napkin, and milk.

After receiving my utensils I turned around to witness Jake in the process of removing his hand from my food. A summary of my classroom rules always included, "A student will not touch another person's food and hands off Mr. Miller's grub."

I had instituted the rule when a fellow teacher caught a student secretively swapping his milk carton with one containing urine. The scenario made me be pro-active in avoiding a similar incident.

From my examination of the tray I uncovered white objects on the metal edge. Jake had placed uncooked white rice in between the layers of my pizza. I was impressed with his creativity, yet Jake and I had a serious discussion about deception and personal belongings.

I believe some students know the exact buttons to push to rile up or tease teachers and administrators.

The Lord grants us many resources to influence, motivate, and inspire each other. I thank the Lord for allowing me to be in the position to motivate children and adults in their lives.

Chapter 25
THE BUNNY RABBIT

Another story of a pronounced classroom performance was surrendered by twelve-year-old Judy. Judy thought outside of the box, and I seldom grasped the time zone she occupied in life. Judy was precious child of God and a special one of a kind person.

In our social studies class, the students and I were reading through a lesson, and the young scholars were taking turns reading a paragraph out loud. The pupils were progressing by continuing one at a time up and down the rows of desks. The oral reading procedure had been performed as a routine hundreds of times in the school year. When the person in front of Judy put the last touches on their reading it was now Judy's turn to read out loud.

Judy was a sixth-grader and this was the second year she had me as a teacher. Judy's characteristics implicated her as being introverted and shy. Not desiring to embarrass Judy, I waited five seconds and I expressed the familiar directions to Judy. In a helpful tone I reminded her, "Judy, it's your turn to read the next paragraph."

Judy monitored her textbook for an extended interval and afterwards Judy and I continued our staring contest. I guess it was of no meaning to her that the rest of the pupils had supplied their reading with a spoken voice. According to Judy's thinking, she had delivered the paragraph, as Judy had read the material silently to herself.

I expressed again to Judy it was her turn to read the paragraph for the class. Judy lurked at me with her eyes and surprised me by replying with a condescending attitude, "I did."

I didn't press the issue with her about the missing element. We skipped Judy's paragraph and we continued the lesson with the other students reading their paragraphs vocally.

Establishing a rapport with Judy was a complicated manner as I exhausted all the methods, tactics, and bribes I could tally as a professional educator. I could not sway her to have a dialogue with me at recess or at a sporting activity. The most I might receive in a conversation after school or at a church service was a standard yes or no. But that's more than she had ever relayed to her peers.

Judy was not a behavior concern, and she was an above-average student with her academics. Judy was dedicated and prompt with her homework, and she participated in our lessons. One day I believed I had made progress in our spoken relationship as Judy and I were starting her math lesson at my desk in the back of the room.

Normally, I had Judy hand in the day's assignment and I corrected her homework as she would begin work on her warm-up problems and activities. On this day Judy was motionless and she did not produce her homework.

I asked Judy, "Where is your homework? Do you have it completed?"

There was no reply from Judy and she did not make eye contact with me. Instead her head and eyes were fixed out the window. I was mortified at myself as I knew better than to ask Judy multiple questions in one individual time frame.

"Where is your homework?" I asked managing a modified outline.

For a second time I received no reply, and Judy had the identical stare out the window. This time I rotated my vision as I glanced out the window to make sure I wasn't missing out on an ecstatic element in the parking lot. Not seeing anything unusual, I moved to an amended tactic with Judy and the missing homework.

"Judy, did you do your math assignment?" I asked.

I received nothing from Judy except an accumulation of Judy's gazing out the south facing window. I was falling into her day-dreaming trance as I grabbed another glance out the window. I detected the bright sunshine, the asphalt parking lot, and the punctilious birds in the trees. Oh Judy, I wished I were outside also.

Worrying I would never coax her to reply about her homework, I was desperately searching for my next step. In general there was no harsh punishment for incomplete work in my classroom, so I knew Judy was not fearful of a possible grueling discipline. I wanted Judy to be comfortable with me in any communicative exchange.

Above all, my goal in dealing with Judy was I didn't want her to cry. In a moment of serenity, Judy shifted positions in her chair and fixed her eyes on me. She began her reply.

"Mr. Miller, in the middle of night my bunny rabbit opened his cage and escaped into my bedroom. Fluffy went over to my backpack and unzipped the main section. My pet bunny went through my math textbook and took out my homework. Fluffy then began chewing on the homework and she ate the whole thing, all of my math problems."

That was all she said as she sat staring at me with a blank expression. From the beginning to the end of the whole story Judy never blinked. She by no means altered her solemn representation, and she did not move any part of her body. I had no clue if she serious, sarcastic, joking, lying, fibbing, or crazy. I did know if I should bawl my eyes out or burst out laughing. I said to Judy I had to excuse myself as I receded through the classroom doorway into my connecting office.

As a teacher I had to do something. I stood at my desk and replayed the whole episode in my mind. I checked to make sure I was awake, while realizing I had to focus on the situation and develop a strategy concerning Judy and her missing homework.

Out of genuine curiosity I had all kinds of questions. I wanted to ask, "How did the rabbit open his cage door? How did the rabbit unzip the backpack? How did the rabbit turn the pages in the textbook? What did the rabbit do after he ate the homework? Did you witness this entire happening?"

One of my first reactions was to suggest to Judy to write the account in a diary or a daily journal. I would have the story in written form to prove that I was not making things up and hearing voices in my head.

I debated if I should discuss with her about fabricating stories. I'm sure she knew the difference between telling the truth and lying, even though we all need a refresher once in a while about fibs.

Maybe her resourcefulness was leading to future stories written by the talented and successful author Judy. She probably could come up with superb narratives uncertain whether classified as fiction or non-fiction.

Perhaps, it was best I left the episode intact as she was collaborating with me. Our interaction was an enormous achievement. I was proud in a way that Judy had the presence to articulate to me a vivid, detailed account of the incident.

My eventual reaction and my discussion with Judy was priceless. Perhaps our interchange and dialogue will be a fantastic future narrative either retold my Judy or me.

Judy and I did tread through the remaining school days in an accepted student and teacher relationship. Our alliance was a one-way street, with Mr. Miller fulfilling the vocal discourse. Judy soon reverted back to her plain head nods, or at best the familiar short replies of yes or no.

For years in the classroom, I facetiously held on to being twenty-nine years old. The students figured out there was no way I had become a dad at the age of twelve years old. For years I was stalled at being thirty-nine years old on all of my birthdays. Recently, I couldn't move off of being forty-nine years old.

I relay the birthday and age information wondering where Judy got her imagination and stretching of facts while telling a story. Shame on me for being a mentor of tall tale telling.

I believe the majority of educators are dedicated, loving, and hard working. I had noble teachers as a student and I have worked alongside remarkable teachers in my role as a principal. Thank you, teachers, for your work and dedication.

The extended daily hours, the endless administrative duties, and an aspiration for variation led me to step away from full-time teaching to a semi-retired position. I appreciate teaching and being around children while still exploring other untested hills.

I am blessed through my wife, Kris, who understands my desire to re-examine my goals. Currently, I am a substitute teacher and I have no correcting of homework, quizzes, research papers, or tests. I have no weekly staff meetings, no monthly board of education meetings, and no parent-teacher conferences.

The downside of the arrangement is my pay scale has a reduction and missing from my portfolio are the benefits of health care, personal days, and paid vacations. Even more significant I don't have the opportunity to daily connect with the students and establish constant interactions.

There is a diversity in changing schools, grade levels, and subject areas, yet I feel like a pinball bouncing around. On my sorrow's list is being void of a member functioning on a team.

In my recent semi-retired position, I have been assimilating the prospect of being a bum. I am a stay-at-home husband doing laundry, making meals, grocery shopping, mowing the grass, and snow shoveling the driveway. I donated a monetary contribution to our household by substitute teaching, basketball refereeing, and landscaping.

My midlife crisis isn't too far-flung. I have succeeded in climbing out on a limb working at home writing in my office in a gray hoodie, sweat pants, and an untrimmed gray beard. I have not procured a nose ring or body tattoos, not that I have anything against the propositions. Neither can I permit my graying hair to grow long enough for a ponytail.

On a cold February morning in 2013, I received a phone call from the principal at Winnebago Lutheran Academy (WLA). He was inquiring if I was interested in a long-term substitute teaching position at WLA.

I am connected with the high school through various paths. Jenny graduated from WLA, and Mrs. Miller has been an outstanding teacher at WLA for thirty-three years. St. Luke's Lutheran Church and School is a member of the WLA association, and for nine years I coached the WELS Jr. Viking football team that was a feeder program to WLA.

During the conversation with Principal Schroeder, he imparted I would have a week to decide if I wanted to take on the duties. The opening came about as the physical education teacher was due for the birth of her first child in eight weeks. My obligations would include two study halls, an English as a Second Language course, and two physical education (PE) courses.

The bulk of my energy would be in the two PE periods. The classes consisted of combined sections of freshmen and sophomore girls. The number of students in block six was thirty-nine, and forty-five students were in block seven.

My twenty-one year teaching profession and calls had been working in the grades of five through eight. My experience with high school students was the months accumulated while substitute teaching in local public high schools.

My assumption was I would not recognize the proper discipline procedures for high school students. As far as instruction and inspiration, I was totally uncertain as to the button involving motivating teenage schoolgirls in gym class.

On Sunday night, Principal Schroeder phoned me and asked if my status would allow me to begin the teaching duties the next day. The PE teacher had given birth to her first child that weekend. I replied I would be there ready to teach on Monday morning.

My first day at WLA was acceptable in the physical education classes. Unsure of an activity on the second Friday, I had the girls stationed in the middle of the gym floor after our lesson.

I proceeded to furnish them with a story about one of my past incidents as the girls were intrigued with my chance encounter with Muhammad Ali. They seemed interested in the description of my outfit, his autograph, and non-existing photo.

Developing a routine after our fitness exercise for our Friday's gym class, I told an additional fifteen stories over the succeeding weeks. I re-construed mini-stories about a child's quest of a hill, a man eating a piece of pizza blended with maggots, and a teacher's immersions on the Apache reservation. I depicted near-death incidents and a disappearing third grade student. I integrated in the Friday narratives the life lessons of curiosity, surprises, cultural differences, and our Christian faith.

At the conclusion of the narratives, the eighty-four girls' responses were recycled by me in defining the intriguing points and the boring parts. The storytelling was my rehearsal, my first rough draft.

That summer I began writing the first chapter using a pen and the retrieved blue spiral notebook once hidden in a dresser drawer. I had the familiar raw energy I had as a fifth-grader. I was enthusiastic and effortlessly compiled the first chapter. After two hours I yearned for a little break and not the old-fashioned twenty-two year recess.

The next day sitting on my backyard deck I pulled out the revised notebook. My poor grammar, weak sentences, and boring style was obvious. My repetition of details and over use of modifying words was awful. I was tempted to burn the pages in the fire pit. Better yet I could feed it to Fluffy.

In the fall while substitute teaching and after retelling "The Greatest" narrative, a high school senior announced he had never read an entire book. After our class the teenager approached me and he specified he wanted to buy a copy of the book. He offered a $20 bill as prepayment for a non-existing book.

At my house that afternoon I scooted up to my computer in our office. The crude words began to unfold into disorganized sentences, paragraphs, chapters, and a book.

Throughout the next year while substitute teaching I had considerable support from a prolific amount of students from various schools. Muddling through my stories in the book and in the classrooms, the students were encouraging with their questions, comments, and interest.

My motivational button for touching the students' minds, souls, and heart is through my narratives. I present a big thank you to all the students for being a great audience with reassuring words, carefree laughter, and heartwarming smiles.

Chapter 26
THE HEADACHES

On July 18, 1996, I traveled to work in the same matter as I had for several days that summer. I had been principal and teacher at St. Luke's for a year. Jill, Jenny, and I had moved to Wisconsin the previous summer after serving on the Rez in Arizona for three years.

There were a few headaches to our start in Oakfield, Wisconsin, due to facing the effects of reverse culture shock, trials with our living arrangements, and starting a new position as a teacher and principal.

The house we were scheduled to rent in the rural Oakfield area was not available, because the remodeling project was not completed. The revised timetable and living arrangement meant unloading our belongings from the U-Haul trailer for storage in a spare classroom at St. Luke's.

Our short-term residence was in a tow-behind trailer parked in the back of the facility. My family and I spent our first day in Wisconsin in the trailer cooking, watching television, taking care of household paper work, and sleeping. Besides being in the cramped quarters we ran out of hot water and the waste compartment was backed up by the next morning.

I performed modifications to our living arrangements through the manipulation of the church and school structure. The first task was to construct an operational shower in the school portion of the building. Part of a corner of the supply room across the office was transformed into a shower unit. At Fleet Farm I purchased the required showerhead, flexible hose, shower rod, clamps, and shower curtain.

Succeeding as a handy-man plumber, I moved on to the stumbling block of the camper's small area for meals. The solution required thirty footsteps to the church's kitchen located in the west back section of St. Luke's building. In the church's galley we had the amenities of a stove, table, chairs, and a stainless steel sink. The only drawback was we could only operate in the kitchen when other church or school groups were not using the space.

Our final dilemma was with the relaxing area in the miniature trailer. In the spare classroom with our unpacked belongings we carved out a space for our sofa, end tables, and entertainment center. We placed among the boxes our coffee maker, microwave, and television set. We mooched off the building's cable system as we roosted in our semi-private sanctuary in the evenings. We would slink into the building for watching television with popcorn in our pajamas.

At St. Luke's facilities, we were spread out with our activities as we slept in the sardine-can trailer behind the church, chilled out in our living room at the east end, showered in the supply room in the center of the complex, and dined in the kitchen on the west side.

The positive to the living arrangement was I could spend the hours during the day working in the building in my classroom or office preparing for the school year.

Seven weeks later, Jill, Jenny, and I made use of our Chevy S10 pick-up truck and moved our belongings into the two-bedroom pink house. The week before the first day of school, we emptied boxes while organizing our appliances and furniture in our new residence seven miles north of Oakfield.

Nearly one year after transferring to the rental house, I was driving my pick-up truck to St. Luke's to prepare for the upcoming school year. I briefly reminisced about the nuisances and headaches of the seven weeks in the trailer and the odd living arrangements the previous year.

My ideas reverted back to concentrating on preparing for the work ahead of me now after being at St. Luke's for a year. I was involved in making copies of worksheets, quizzes, and tests while utilizing the services of our two copiers.

The newer copier in the air-conditioned office and the older copier was in the faculty workroom. Persistently, both copiers were jamming and creating time-consuming annoyances. I was struggling to establish a routine of unjamming the copiers, reloading the machines, and filing away the reproduced articles.

The newer copier projected on the front screen the yellow digital letters HU. After a while I gathered together the clues to explain the letters as an abbreviation for high humidity level. The summer day in Wisconsin started out scorching hot and the humidity continued to rise throughout the day.

At noon I retreated from my work, and strode three blocks to the gas station and convenience store in town. In the summer breeze the mature trees lining the street provided a serene portrait. The trees were dazzling with their green foliage, towering height, and snarling limbs. Walking on the sidewalks, I grinned as the fat, healthy squirrels clawed the slabs of bark on the tree's main trunks while chasing each other.

The two-storied early twentieth-century homes had well maintained porches with frisky children, lazy mutts, and multiple hanging flower baskets. In the background were watchful babysitters, napping seniors, and a few stay at home parents. The Victorian-style homes from a past era formed etchings in my mind of meeting a horse and buggy trotting along the street.

My short break did provide me with a resurgence in energy to continue my task at school, even though later in the afternoon I decided to call it quits for the day. My schedule for the evening was set as Jill, Jenny, and I planned to attend in Fond du Lac the county fair and enjoy the night's country music act.

At school I was feeling ill. I had come to blows with these symptoms before. Typically, this well-rehearsed predicament begins with numbness in my left arm, or a tingling sensation on my lips similar to the freezing process at the dentist.

The next indicator is a thin round outlined blurred ring that appears in the center of my vision. The circle freakishly grows larger until it encompasses my whole vision making objects fuzzy and indistinctive.

Closely behind is the punctual reaction of stiffness and throbbing in the back of my neck, which is joined by the sharp stabbing in the front part of my forehead.

The exclamation mark to the terrifying torment is the fictitious clamp being tightened on the sides of my skull. Around this stage of the persecution I am positive my head will explode.

The first time I suffered a migraine headache I assumed I was having a stroke as I had all the symptoms of a blood circulation system gone whacko. The first time a migraine permeated me while driving, I nearly lost control of my truck on a curve in the road. My left arm went numb leaving me unable to grip the steering wheel with my left hand.

When a migraine headache punches me, I become disoriented and stating obvious answers to questions about my name and age are demanding. I can recognize faces, places, and objects, yet placing a name or label with the items can be unmanageable.

My first migraine headache arrived at the age of twenty-six and I began to investigate the symptoms, causes, and treatments. I started a journal recording my intake of food, coffee, and alcohol on the days around the headache.

One possible pattern explaining the rise of my migraines was a few of the migraines appeared after I had skipped a meal or two. Destructive to the food theory was the times I would eat regular meals and I would get pounded with a dreadful migraine headache.

As a Packer fan I tracked the commercials of the NFL Super Bowl XXXII while watching the Packers and the Broncos football game.

Through the first half Bronco's running back Terrell Davis had been playing well, but he was suffering through a migraine headache.

At halftime in the locker room, Terrell received medication for the migraine and in the second half he played well leading the Broncos to victory. During the ceremony after the game Terrell Davis he was awarded the MVP trophy even while enduring through a migraine headache.

A month later I received through my physician a trial sample of the matching medication Terrell Davis had been administered at halftime. During the warning signs of my next migraine headache I promptly treated myself with the nasal spray medication. Deplorably, the migraine turned out to be the worst pulsating headache I have ever suffered.

Another method I implemented at the first indication of a migraine is closing my eyes in a nap. A slumber party is not an option while teaching, driving, or at a meeting, but in other settings the possibility of sleep is my number one goal. Piling out at a dark, secluded location for a thirty-minute nap assists me in tolerating the headaches.

Likewise, I have had restricted success with drinking water for diverting the agonies in my head. The guzzling of gallons of water seems to ward off some migraines and the headaches I do have are not as intense.

Normally, it will take me seventy-two hours to fully recover from a migraine. On the first day I collapse in a sleep most of the day while experiencing dreams clogging my resting. When I am awake my head is pounding, I'm confused, and uncommunicative.

On the second day I have all the footprints of an alcoholic hangover. Things make more sense, but there is plenty of fuzziness and my head feels as if it is being squeezed yet.

By the third day I have a slight headache, and I have disbanded all the other ailments. My energy and appetite has returned, and I am ready to take on the world again.

Having migraines could have vigorously reincarnated my misfit perception, but my feedback from my research showed several historical figures and present celebrities have issues with migraines. Past figures include Vincent Van Gogh, Thomas Jefferson, Elvis Presley, Lewis Carroll, and John F Kennedy. Celebrities includes Kareem Abdul-Jabbar, Serena Williams, Ben Affleck, Janet Jackson, and Troy Aikman.

In my migraine journal I was diligent in retaining information about the weather, activities, and my stress level leading up to a migraine headache. Another possible connection is with drastic changing weather conditions. The weather theory came from the fact I experienced a migraine headache on the humid July day at St. Luke's.

On the muggy day in July of 1996, I felt the tingling sensation on my lips and perceived the aura in my eyesight. I halted my tasks at school and locked the front doors on my way out. In my truck I fastened my seat belt while losing the employment of my left arm.

I started for home with my disorientation crushing my perceptive, though I was able to drive the vehicle along the vacant village streets and rural roads. I drove the seven miles to the little pink house with my fuzzy awareness focused on maintaining the truck between the lines of the roads. I was heading north out of Oakfield and I was oblivious of the blustery skies to the west.

My plan of attending the musical performance at the fair was cancelled and I entered the rental house descending directly to the basement. Jill and Jenny had already left for the fairgrounds, so I had a quiet, empty house to pile out in for the evening.

In the dark environment I flopped on the twin bed stored in the concrete palace. My hammering head hit the pillow and my limp arm hung over the edge. Even with the pain in my head in the inside and with daylight hours outside, my eyes were quickly sealed shut. In my cave I became entrenched like a bear enduring a long winter hibernation.

Sleeping for nearly two hours the source causing me to be rudely awakened could have been a loud vehicle outside or the never ending brewing storm passing through our area. When I scampered up the stairs and walked outside to our driveway I was in awe of the uncanny sky.

Straining my eyes looking in the southwest sky, I inspected the fast moving gray clouds, the swirls of black strokes, and the blemishes of the yellowish background. I was hypnotized by the unnerving heavens as I considered the sky and its energetic movements.

Shaking my head and not retrieving the answer to my awakening alarm, I grasped my bearings and returned to the house's entry door.

I lumbered again down the stairs to my haven in the cool basement and I crawled under the blanket. For a few minutes lying while in bed I swept the cobwebs out of my mind while attempting to fall back to sleep.

My headache had appeared to have evaporated and I was hoping the wretched annoyance in my body was sucked up in the clouds. In my opinion the outside summer storm and my migraine headache were a perfect match for each other.

Because I had previously slept for about two hours, I was now restless and not able to fall back to sleep. I knew my headache was getting better as I was now hungry. I rolled off the bed and once again climbing the stairs to the ground level of the house.

In the kitchen, I leaned with my extended arms on the wooden sill of the double-hung window facing the adjacent farm field. I examined the southern sky that wasn't nearly as wacky as during the previous time frame. The subverting storm seemed to have passed through the region in a matter of minutes since I was last outside in the driveway.

When I made my way to the living room to turn the local news on the television set, I was startled and flinched as the phone rang that was hanging on the wall between the kitchen and the living room.

My head was still a little foggy, though I knew I was well enough to hold a conversation with a person on the phone. Besides, I was thinking it might be Jill or Jenny checking up on my health condition.

Picking up the receiver I heard a solemn Mrs. Ione Panzer say, "Mr. Miller, our church and school buildings are gone."

Chapter 27
THE TORNADO

The village of Oakfield is seven miles southwest of Fond du Lac, and is situated within a triangular location formed by three major cities in Wisconsin. Green Bay is situated northeast about ninety minutes away from Oakfield while Madison is located southwest about seventy-five minutes from our small town. Of the three cities, the Milwaukee metropolitan area is the closest to the village limits of Oakfield being a forty-five-minute drive to the southeast.

While listening to Ione Panzer, I was contemplating how an intact building could completely vanish. Ione continued, "The storm and a tornado came through and destroyed our church and school. There is nothing left. Everything is gone."

I got up to speed and I surmised from my day's memory of the humid weather and the dark skies that had existed, a tornado had plowed through the town of Oakfield.

Days later Ione relayed her personal account of the squabble with the tornado. On Thursday evening, St. Luke's was scheduled to have their weekly weekday church service at 7:30 PM. Vicar Finn was the guest preacher, and eight church members were in the church's narthex preparing for the evening's service.

Vicar Finn and the parishioners were in the identical predicament many of the Oakfield residents were facing. They were deciding whether to take shelter in a basement or to wait out the storm on ground level.

The small group within St. Luke's facility had the choice of two basements in the structure. The basement under the church was known to flood, and the basement under the school did not have electricity. The church members and Vicar Finn made the decision to seek protection in the 1970's school basement, which resembled a bomb shelter with its cement block enclosure.

The group was delaying near the school office contemplating the move to the black cavity. The village sirens began blaring and the assembly swiftly entered the basement through the stairs with the use of one flashlight. After a minute in the basement, the cluster of adults perceived the growl and roar of a rumbling train outside their sanctuary.

When both the roaring sound and the village's sirens stopped the nine allies clawed their way through the debris at the exit of the basement steps and arrived on the ground level.

At the time when Ione had phoned me it was only minutes after she had emerged from the basement. In the small community of Oakfield, churches, schools, and dwellings had been altered or erased in a manner of minutes. Life changes happening within a moment.

The next day and throughout the ensuing weeks there was state and national coverage of the Oakfield tornado. One of the reoccurring TV reports was the remaining wall among the St. Luke's rubble. The larger-than-real-life portrayal of Jesus knocking at the heart's door stood about twelve to fifteen feet above the ruins. Near the picture were the Bible's King James Version of Jesus' words, "Lo, I am with you alway."

When people, whether our members or strangers, would stare at the picture it was insightful as observers would gaze at the solitary interior church wall. Part of the brainteaser was brought on by the word "alway", which in modern English is translated as always.

A violent tornado struck the village of Oakfield at about 1815CST after it touched down 4 miles WNW of the village. During its approach on Oakfield it intensified to a F3 rating. When it tore through the village it intensified to an F4, but along its path 1 to 4 miles east of the village it intensified to F5 strength (estimated 265 mph winds).

In this span 4 homes were completely swept clean off their foundations and a couple automobiles became airborne missiles for a distance of about 400 feet. The core width of the most intense damage was about 150 to 200 yards, although at times, some secondary damage was observed in a 400 yard wide path. Oakfield residents heard local sirens about 8 minutes before the tornado entered the village.

Miraculously, no one was killed, but there were 12 injuries. Some of the injured were hospitalized. Along the tornado's path, 60 homes and 6 businesses were destroyed. An additional 130 homes and businesses were damaged. In Oakfield, a commercial canning company was devastated. Two churches in the village were also destroyed, as well as numerous vehicles. In the rural areas along the tornado's path, 18 barns and many sheds were destroyed or damaged, and about 500 acres of crops were wiped out. Total damage amounts were $39.5 million in public/private property, and

$900,000 in crop losses. Residents reported that they had difficulty "popping" their ears as the tornado roared through their neighborhood.

*Prior to entering Oakfield, the tornado hopped and skipped a few times, and multiple vortices were observed at times during its life cycle. Witnesses reported that the tornado "paused" for a minute or so on the southeast edge of Oakfield. As the tornado tore through Oakfield it changed its heading to east. Corn fields just east of Oakfield were reduced to short 1 to 4 inch high stubble, and burn marks were clearly visible in the fields. In the third segment of the tornado's life, when it turned northeast at a point 5.5 miles east of Oakfield, its strength diminished rapidly. Debris was found east to the Lake Michigan shoreline, and cancelled checks were later found 125 miles E/SE near Muskegon, MI! *4*

God did not allow anyone to die in the tornado.

I agree with the description stating it was a miracle no one was killed. The phone line to the Lord was never out of order, the battery did not go dead, and there was always a signal connecting us to God.

Immediately after the tornado authorities set up check stations on the roads entering Oakfield for the sake of safety, preventing looting, and preserving the pathways for emergency vehicles.

The next day I made my way into the village of Oakfield, and I detected the route of the direct hit. Many of the maple trees and oak trees I had admired the day before had been uprooted. They had been swept away to mysterious locations, or tossed around like toothpicks.

A number of trees were uprooted divulging empty craters and the fallen trees exposed their eerie root systems. The depraved standing trees broadcasted twisting limbs stripped of their leaves and their trunk's thick bark shredded away in large clumps.

The core path of the tornado suggested the grand opening of a five city block landfill. On the edges of the core's pathway the section resembled a war-torn bombed city. Houses were standing with exterior walls intact only to have missing windows and a vast opened sunroof.

Miscellaneous homes were missing half of their structure. To conjure up an appropriate vision, think of an oversized doll house opened sideways uncovering its inner contents. However, on these mutilated structures there were no hinges affixed to return the segments back together to create a functioning residence.

The homes on the outskirts appeared structurally fit. Further examination revealed shattered windows, shingles peeled off the roofs, trees stabbed into the walls, and power lines in tangled knots on the ground. Sprinkle in the shiny aluminum cans strewn everywhere and that is the sketch drawn up of Oakfield one day after the F5 tornado.

Over the years I have heard personal stories from residents and our church members. The stories are from primary and secondary sources, and they have left an impression on all who hear them.

One story shared is of an elderly man who resided diagonally across the street from St. Luke's. Mr. Redman was home in his living room's recliner shortly before 7:15 PM. As the community's sirens sounded, the man's wife, Elsie, implored her husband to descend to their basement. Rudy heard his wife's request and ignored her. Rudy was engrossed in viewing the fallouts from the raging storm.

As the winds spun around in circles within the community, Elsie stumbled her way down the flight of stairs. Rudy was left alone in his living room's chair viewing the projectiles swirling in his backyard.

After the siren subsided Elsie plodded up the stairs leading to the first floor. When she reached the top of the stairs the traditional two-story house built in the early twentieth century was gone and Rudy had come up missing as he was not in the vicinity.

An Oakfield resident was voluntarily patrolling the damaged buildings to verify the natural gas lines were not emitting dangerous fumes. Dashing from structure to structure, the volunteer came across Rudy sitting in his favorite recliner. Rudy outwardly appeared frazzled, yet he had no visible signs of injuries.

Bill, the active volunteer, figured Rudy had wandered out from his basement after the siren stopped and the elderly man had tracked down his favorite piece of furniture. Bill figured Rudy had probably decided to take a break from his examination of the tornado's destruction and he was resting.

Bill asked, "Rudy, are you alright?"

Rudy grumpily enunciated a few odd sounds as a reply, even though there were no particular words spoken. Bill made note of Rudy's apparently satisfactory condition, and the volunteer continued on his way as the emergency natural-gas monitor.

Later, the news of Rudy became a well retold account of the tornado. Rudy had not roamed out of the basement to the spot in the cluttered roadway. Rudy never made it to the basement as the reclining chair and Rudy had been lifted up by the tremendous force of the twister. The one track man had received a free swirling ride from his residence to the middle of the road within the interweaving debris.

The chair and Rudy were deposited upright on the street between his destroyed house and the demolished St. Luke's Church and School. Rudy was enclosed in debris, fallen trees, and tangled electrical wires.

The Redman's' car, similar to other vehicles in Oakfield, accepted a non-human escort out of their driveway. The vehicle traveled a tad farther than its owner Rudy. The car tumbled over and over concluding the ride by resting upside down on top of the ruins that was previously St. Luke's kindergarten classroom.

When I prodded through the rubble of the St. Luke's remains, I studied the area that was once my principal's office and classroom. The buildings' structural contents were mingled and disarranged with sections of the concrete walls positioned on the ground as if someone had pushed the walls over on its side. I did unearth my Lutheran hymnal and a few minor items, but nothing else significant in my schoolroom or office could be salvaged.

One year later in our new building, I displayed two objects rescued from other boundaries within the wreckage zone. The two reclaimed treasures were the United States flag from our church and an unframed painting depicting Jesus praying while kneeling on a stone. The impaired print of Jesus is a reminder of the tornado with its torn edges, needle-sized holes, and a stonewashed color.

Another snippet heard among residents was connected with the weather conditions after the tornado. Residents will relate that within minutes, the sky became clear with an obvious weather change consisting of a mild temperature and a low comfortable humidity level.

As the sun radiated in the calm evening hours the day closed with a thought-provoking yet normal sunset. One odd twist in those hours was the swarms of homeless mosquitos perturbing the people at dusk and well into the night hours.

In relationship to the National Weather Service report, the discovered chunks of debris mentioned were St. Luke's softball bleachers which were uncovered in a farmer's woodlot forty-five miles from Oakfield. A week later after the tornado, cancelled church checks were in our post office box retained from a person's lawn over a hundred miles across Lake Michigan.

For months after the tornado, if a person stood in any location in Oakfield, they would hear the constant beep from equipment removing the mountains of rubble. Add to that the chainsaws, which seemed to constantly hum as they carved up the trees, branches, and other wood fragments left behind after the storm.

During the next year there was constant village-wide construction as saws, drills, hammers, and generators were hard at work. Additionally, the replacement of the shingle roofs made the town an oasis for professional and amateur roofers.

After the tornado's devastation, the members of St. Luke's unanimously approved to rebuild both the church and school. St. Luke's building committee held weekly Tuesday meetings for twelve months at the Oakfield Bank's basement.

The committee members reviewed classrooms, offices, kitchen, commons, basement, and church nave. The seemingly never-ending decisions had to be made concerning the roof, air conditioning, windows, doors, floor coverings, and parking lot.

St. Luke's was blessed to rebuild a fantastic structure and the facility's costs were covered almost entirely by insurance. Additionally, St. Luke's received generous donations to aid in the rebuilding process.

St. Luke's pre-tornado building did not have a gym. After receiving generous monetary gifts from churches, schools, individuals, and various groups throughout the United States, a gym was added to the blueprints. The gym has been outstanding for our church and school functions, and the facility at St. Luke's is a blessing from a loving God working through compassionate and caring people.

Many residents, businesses, and churches of Oakfield received assistance from volunteers. General emergency medical care and other immediate provisions were provided by the first responders, the police and fire departments, concerned people, and the Red Cross. Everyone involved in the multiple tasks were fantastic.

Clean-up assistance was provided by numerous organizations and individuals. The time frame after the tornado was exasperating for the Oakfield residents due to the seemingly never ending process of cleaning-up and rebuilding.

Oakfield is known in many Wisconsin cities and towns exclusively from for the past tornado. In my talks with people in Wisconsin or throughout the country, their familiarity with the community of Oakfield will vary depending on a person's background and interests.

Besides oak trees, Oakfield is often identified with the ledge which is a limestone outcropping branded the Niagara Escarpment. The ledge covers area above and below the ground surface from the state of New York and well into the state of Wisconsin.

A section of the ledge contains wooden areas with hiking trials and startling views of the rocks, cliffs, and cavities. Scattered in the region around Oakfield are quarries making use of the rock for landscaping and building material in the retail and wholesale market.

Another popular landform attracting people to the region is the Wild Goose State Trail. The trail's passage spans thirty-four miles with the northeast trail head located in Fond du Lac. The southwest trail head is located on Highway 60 near Clyman Junction.

The rail to trail is used for walking, biking, running, and snowmobiling as it travels through the village of Oakfield. The Wild Goose Trail continues southwest as it skirts the boundaries of the familiar Horicon Marsh which contains the popular and well-visited National Wildlife Refuge and State Wildlife Area.

One outstanding commodity of the community is the girls' high school softball teams. The Oaks' varsity softball teams have won four Wisconsin State Championships in the last six years.

The current students in any grade level at Oakfield schools were not born at the time of the tornado. Yet, the Oakfield children are very observant to darkening skies and severe weather reports. The students are attentive to weather conditions due to being immersed with tornado anecdotes from parents, relatives, and friends.

A past student of mine, Ryan, was in my classroom many years after the tornado. Ryan had Mr. Miller as a teacher for four years and I was his basketball coach for seven years. Ryan lightheartedly indicated he survived the tornado. In 1996, Ryan was born in August surviving the tornado as a living individual in his mother's womb.

Several factors attributed to the fact that no deaths occurred as a result of the ferocious tornado. Many residents were not at their homes in the rural community due to them attending the county fair.

The people in the village were given an early warning because of the identification detection by weather spotters. The early recognition led to the advanced sounding of the sirens and people taking cover in their basements or in other selected areas.

Throughout my many retelling narratives of my personal account of the Oakfield tornado, I jokingly state that I slept through the whirlwind of events. There is a certain amount of truth in the statement. When I woke up at the pink house and pondered the threatening sky it was approximately the time interval the tornado had finished touching down and terrorizing Oakfield.

On one occasion about a year after the awful incident in Oakfield, I was overheard stating my displeasure with the loss of the mature trees that once were present on Second Street in Oakfield.

A close friend of mine retorted back with a shrug of his shoulder and replying, "It's no big deal. Trees grow back." The response seemed insensitive and made the trees seem trivial, though I recognize that change happens and life does continue.

As a person enters Oakfield from the east there are a series of connecting roads locals refer to as the *flat iron*. Scanning the west horizon while on County Road B viewers can detect a visual dip in the tree line. The wide alteration is the nearly twenty year-old alleyway of the Oakfield tornado which is becoming less and less noticeable.

As I approach Oakfield from the flat iron region I reminisce in regards to the devastating tornado and my years of teaching at St. Luke's. I sincerely thank God for His mercy and grace granted to the residents of Oakfield and myself on July 18, 1996.

Chapter 28
THE FIREFLIES

An untold number of WLA graduates refer to their past biology or anatomy teacher as Miss Clausnitzer. She has been teaching thirty-three years and is now known as Mrs. Miller. When Kris and I began dating we shared our childhood stories and pasts. Similarly, we shared related interpretations of our accumulated years of teaching.

Through our conversations we remarked that our fathers were large influences in our lives and our dads were alike in many assorted ways. The earliest obvious observation was them having the same first names, but our dads had parallel mannerisms, interests, and skills. Most significantly, our fathers are without any pain, worries, or sin as they are living eternally with their Savior, Jesus.

One occurrence that Kris, whose birth name is Kristi, broadcasted on our first date was her involvement on her family's farm of collecting fireflies. The account was relayed to me with sentimental emphasis and descriptions. At the end of the recollection Kris inquisitively asked if I had ever collected fireflies as a child.

"Yes, I caught fireflies as a child in Michigan," I replied.

Kris and I being raised 400 miles apart but with the comparable memories was a neat connection. Countless youngsters in the Midwest spend the summer evenings chasing the blinking illuminations of lightning bugs or insects referred to as fireflies. The fireflies are seized in residential lawns, city parks, and farm fields. The ritual entails the live capture of the bugs and retaining the insects in a clear Mason jar with air holes poked in the tin lid.

A running tally was not taken as Kris retold and asked the identical niceties concerning fireflies on our first four dates. On date number five we had strayed beyond the introductory dating level and I thought it was time to lay to rest the fireflies' narrative. I cautiously treaded in my reference to the fireflies hoping to handle the subject in a non-threatening manner.

Kris and I did reach a mutual pact about the future fireflies' inquiries, but shortly thereafter I was found repeating my stories. Possibly our mutual repeating of narratives was caused by the ruckus of our first dates, aging minds, or making sure the other person was listening to us.

Now as a married couple breaching each day further away from the honeymoon stage, the word fireflies remains in our vocabulary. Out of politeness or to clear ourselves of any premature forgetfulness, we often introduce a conversation with, "I know this might be fireflies, but…"

If one of us is telling a resurfacing account, the listener will politely interrupt and graciously issue the word fireflies to the storyteller. Our classifying decree is a thin line between slandering the story to a halt or a teasingly and affectionate reminder.

Kris and I had already been acquaintances for thirteen years before we first started dating. Kris has taught at WLA for thirty-three years and she has coached JV girls' volleyball all of those years. She coached girls' varsity basketball for twenty-five years and has over 300 victories in the sport as a past coach. Miss Clausnitzer had taught Jenny in biology and anatomy, and Kris guided Jenny in volleyball and basketball.

In March of 2008, Kris and I were talking in the WLA's hallway. I was there supporting our St. Luke's students taking part in a spelling bee. Miss Clausnitzer was at WLA working in her classroom on her daily school work. We talked for about ten minutes and the main topic of our dialogue was her recent stepping down as the girls' basketball varsity coach. The discussion ended with a supportive hug between two called workers and friends.

Our next conversation was two months later at the grade school track and field meet. I was there as a coach, and Kris was outside monitoring the WLA's gym period. We talked in the parking lot and Kris invited me to join her in the month of June as a volunteer at the Lombardi Celebrity Golf Tournament.

Six weeks later Kris and I traveled together in her PT Cruiser to the golf tournament in Menomonee Falls, Wisconsin. The dating obligations for the golf activity included carpooling and visiting with each other at our designated location on the course. Our responsibilities as volunteers included leading the celebrities to and from their tee box or putting greens. Another duty was working crowd control of the fans seeking autographs and photos at our particular spot.

The day of the golf outing ended with our arrival back in Oakfield at eight in the evening. The date concluded on my patio deck rehashing the day's experience. After ten minutes of chatting, we said our good-nights as we both had other plans for the evening.

Good-humoredly Kris and I have disputed the declaration of our first official date as we became a couple. One possibility was our attendance at a Thursday night church service at Faith Lutheran Church in Fond du Lac. After the church service we went for dinner at a local restaurant.

Even with our mild discrepancy of our first date we both agree July 12 was an official date. On the summer day we traveled to a Brewers baseball game. I merged my truck in the steady traffic in Milwaukee as Kris revealed the day was her birthday. I had already agreed to prepare and serve our evening dining orders, so I proclaimed the full-service tailgating catering act as my birthday present to her.

The weather was great, the Brewers were victorious, and the tailgating activities were fascinating. Kris often jestingly reminds me that Jenny texted me numerous times during the date. Checking up on her dad, Jenny inherited her grandma's calling as Nosey Rosy.

Fifteen months later, Kris and I were winterizing the Taj. Before we drove back to Wisconsin, we read a devotion on marriage. My best friend sat at the fireplace and I knelt down proposing to her. A weeping Kris nodded her head vertically up and down in reply to my question.

In the classroom I will not accept an answer to a question through a head nod whether it is from a fifth-grader or a high schooler. Through the sobbing I did rustle up a suffocated, but audible yes answer.

Being teachers with hectic schedules, I figured it could be beneficial to have our wedding ceremony held in the summer months. Kris' rationale was we would be married in March and then we could spend our honeymoon in April on the east coast of the United States.

One of Kris' duties at WLA is to organize and lead the junior and senior classes' bus trip to Washington, D.C. The trip endures ten days and includes engagements at Jefferson's Monticello, Jamestown, Colonial Williamsburg, Richmond, Washington's Mt. Vernon, the memorials on the National Mall, the Capitol Building, the Naval Academy in Annapolis, and the Gettysburg National Battlefield.

After occupying nine school months with children, I was hesitant to be surrounded by high school students for the entire duration of our spring break. I was merely the groom so I agreed to a honeymoon traveling nearly 2,000 miles on buses transporting one hundred teenagers and twenty adult chaperones.

Kristi and I were married in March at St. Luke's in Oakfield, Wisconsin. Kris and I were blessed as Kris' brother, Tom, walked Kris down the aisle presenting his older sister to me in marriage.

Less than one year later, Tom was taken to heaven at the age of forty-four years old. The evening before Tom's death Kris had a wonderful phone conversation with him in regards to ice fishing reports and God's unconditional love for his children. Missed by his family and friends, Tom's passion for NASCAR, friends, cooking, hunting, fishing, and his love remains in our precious memories.

The well-organized field trip to DC was informative as we visited historical and important locations of our country. The large group traveled on coach buses with talented drivers while enjoying meals and agreeable hotel lodgings. The impressive adventure was a blessing among the Christian teenagers and adults.

The same year over Christmas vacation, Kris and I journeyed to Costa Rica and we labeled the excursion our real honeymoon. The opportunity came about as we lodged with our friend Rhoda as she house-sat in the Central America country. The house was in the village of Fortuna, about four miles from the active volcano Arenal. For three days we were unable to perceive the volcano due to the persistent cloud cover and light rain in the tropical rainforest.

In Costa Rica, we trekked through the curving mountain roads with our guide Carlos while we viewed and closed in on iguanas, sloths, monkeys, caymans, toucans, and Jesus lizards. The lizards were almost miraculous as they scooted across the water in a running motion.

On day trips we viewed the sugar cane, pineapple fields, a national preserve, and a white-sand beach. My old imitating antics aroused during a one on one howling contest with a male howler monkey. The monkey standing high on a tree branch was confident I was a threat to his large harem. The intense monkey won out as I drifted away from the scene after a few minutes of arguing conversation.

On the Pacific Ocean beach, Kris and I hiked along the seesaw tide and studied a tiny island in the isolated bay. Sparkling blue water encircled the landmass and the island's terrain was rich with swaying palm trees and a rocky shoreline. The island could have been an unspoiled setting for the novel *Robinson Crusoe*.

Broadening our walk, we came upon a functioning cantina. There was no blatant commercialization strategies within this shack's décor and its matchless personality. The exterior siding was fashioned from faded boards resembling drift wood obtained from the shoreline.

The main entry door was wide open, authorizing any stray person to enter the structure on a whim. For a free glance around there was a good sized framed opening on each side of the door. Comparable to the front door the two windows were wide open.

The hut sat within the margins of a group of beautiful shade trees, as the thatched roof of palm branches complemented the entire setting. Our ears heard the upbeat music from the establishment, which supplied a brisk background for the patrons on the outdoor dirt patio.

The estimated time of day had no purpose as we were completely ignorant to which day of the week we were inhabiting. Kris and I ordered two bottles of *cerveza* and sat on tall stools facing the ocean. We toasted our day as we watched an eight-inch lizard scurry in front of our table. Our buddy knew exactly where he was going taking up residence under an upside down fading wooden rowboat.

While viewing the scenery I announced, "Time can stop right now. I'm not leaving here."

Kris in her life has traveled to England, Scotland, Ireland, France, Italy, Switzerland, Germany, Austria, Denmark, Sweden, Finland, Norway, Poland, Russia, Japan, Mexico, Canada, and Alaska. I have not traveled as globally as Kris, but as a fortune hunter at heart I do enjoy traveling within the United States and to foreign countries.

Our mutual love for traveling has lead us to surprise each other with birthday gifts involving journeys. For my birthday Kris arranged an outstanding weekend at an Illinois State Park Hotel and acquired tickets to the theatrical act of *Wicked* in downtown Chicago.

My ordinary trips for Kris include:

2008—Milwaukee Brewers game, tailgating feast.

2009—Panfish fishing, Lake Emily, cookout at my house.

2010—Walleye fishing, Lake Winnebago, local pizza buffet.

I wasn't very creative with my birthday practices in the past, so Kris and I join forces as we invited coworkers, spouses, friends, and family members to her fiftieth birthday party. The get-together of forty people was held at our house in Oakfield and the hours of the festivities would be from two in the afternoon to seven in the evening. The early conclusion of the party concerned Kris as the evening hours are when parties are establishing their recreational worth.

Midway in the party, Mrs. Miller sat front and center opening her birthday gifts. There were gag gifts and heartfelt presents. When it came to my present to Kris, I confessed to the assembly my past dull gifts.

I then explained the festivities' odd hours were because the birthday gal and I had to be at Chicago's O'Hare Airport for an early bird flight to San Francisco on a five day vacation in California.

2011—Surprise excursion to San Francisco.

In a historic, vibrant district of San Francisco, Kris and I stayed at the refurbished San Remo Hotel. We tested menus in Chinatown, and sampled sourdough bread and clam chowder along the wharf. As out of towners we visited a Subway restaurant, but we also shopped at a nearby grocery store conjuring up our own homemade meals.

Kris and I briefly indulged the tourist traps, yet we scoped out and blended into locations off the beaten path. We verified the anonymous saying, "If you really want to explore our country in its truth and purity, get off the interstate and hit the back roads of America."

I had been fascinated for years with California and in particular San Francisco. My tactical exploitation of Kris' birthday to fulfill one of my dreams is typical of both Kris and I multi-purposing our trips.

Kris and I have reveled in year round outdoor activities of hiking, campfires, and cribbage. In the appropriate seasons we gear up for deer hunting, cross-country skiing, and ice fishing. In the summer months we find time to enjoy bike riding, kayaking, and gardening.

Our common interests in athletics and the outdoors is unmistakable. As a high school student in Medford, Wisconsin, Kris was distinctly successful in varsity volleyball, basketball, and track. In her years at DMLC, Kris received acclaim in volleyball, basketball, and track. As a Christian mentor Kris has had notable successes as a coach and as a teacher. I'm quite certain Kris ranks being a loving grandma to Peanut and Spike as unbeatable.

Kris and I are competitive in our pursuits and at times we do modify some competitions to avoid hostilities, acknowledging Kris is a loyal Badger fan and I am a devoted Wolverine fan.

However, we compete in the fishing trifecta first introduced by Davey Lee. Our outcomes determines who cleans the fish, prepares the meal, and has the bragging rights as the champion fisherman for the day.

Recently, we have conceived a trifecta in regards to the luminary bodies of the night sky. The contest involves locating the first star, the moon, and the first constellation. The dry land trifecta game is a fabulous pastime while sitting around a campfire. The winner of the challenge secures relaxation as the loser has to restock the beverages, maintain the camp fire, and prepare the popcorn.

The pathway leading to Kris and me arriving together could have derived through various avenues. God's timing is always right. We were brought together to support each other, worship together, and love each other. Thank you, Lord, for fireflies and guiding Kris into my life.

Chapter 29
THE PLANE RIDE

Our westward flight left Chicago's O' Hare Airport without any delays and without turbulence while cruising at 35,000 feet. Kris fell asleep as soon as we were in the aircraft. Initially, I struggled with sleep as I played over in my mind our upcoming itinerary in California. The first day in San Francisco we were exhausted from the party at our house and the early bird flight. We picked up our rental car and checked into our hotel. We sought to explore the late-morning sites on foot as we walked from our hotel five miles encircling our way through San Francisco.

On the jaunt we toured the now-departed Candlestick Park, the modern AT&T Park, Fisherman's Wharf, Lombard Street, Pier 39, Chinatown, and the city's famous cable cars. Meandering through the downtown area we decided to take a short break around noon on a black metal grated park bench.

Being out of towners we were certifying the tour buses dropping off the throngs of tourists. Additional entertainment was provided through our game of speculating where the people had come from as they entered the frenzied city. We had conjectures of visitors coming from Oregon, farms in Iowa, the Texas hill country, and the suburbs of Boston.

Swapping games, we then engaged in the common performance of head-bobbing for sleep as our eyelids rested, our equilibrium shifted, and our noses drifted toward the sidewalk. When our necks would no longer support the tension, our nervous systems jerked our thick domes back to the upright position. Yet, our eyes remained closed.

Finally, we caved in and zonked out as sleeping aliens on the park bench in the hectic city. When we awoke thirty minutes later, the sun's rays had repositioned with the sunlight was now blocked by the buildings. I did an assessment of our surroundings and behind us was a sprawled-out person pilfering an afternoon catnap.

Dusting off my eyelids I clutched our new ecosystem containing pigeons, seagulls, and sea lions. I shuddered at the obscured shadows and the vast movements of human and vehicle traffic. The high-rise buildings appeared as towering beacons in the bewitched forest. Kris and I certainly weren't on a farm in central Wisconsin or at the Taj Mahal on the St. Mary's River in Michigan.

We loitered on the bench, and I'm sure most tourists assessed the three bench personnel as homeless allies warming themselves in the summer's sun. I was downcast we were not offered any spare change or bites of food.

On the second day of our excursion in San Francisco, I learned we would be unable to tour the intriguing site of Alcatraz Island. Because I had not attained advanced tickets, we now had time to maneuver a side passage to Yosemite National Park.

Before leaving the Bay Area, Kris and I visited the Muir Woods National Monument with its coastal redwood forest. In our rental car we arrived at the park entrance around 8 AM as the trails and gift shop were beginning to stir. Our Chevy Cruz was the third car in the large parking lot as we spent the morning hours spiraling through the majestic redwoods on the foot trails in the park.

Two hours later the Millers were leaving the park and we detected vehicles parked at least two miles away from the entrance. Sometimes the early bird does receive the good parking spot.

We continued our adventure as we drove our rental car four hours east to Yosemite National Park. The last ten miles prior to entering the park boundaries were overwhelming due to the approaching mountains, valleys, and waterfalls.

In the park the breathtaking vistas were up close and personal. The isolation, rough terrain, and sheer grandeur were marvelous features. At our first stop in the valley the panoramic view caused a wave of elated tears on my cheeks. God is great!

Kris and I squeezed in limited characteristics of the valley and this was one of my scheduling gaps. As darkness fell on the valley, we had serious considerations of snoozing in our undersized rental car. This wasn't anything new for me-I years ago depended on a truck bench seat and a blanket as a bed to dispatch with my sleeping hours.

I had read the highlighted paragraphs of the park's brochure mentioning sleeping overnight in vehicles was not permitted. The written paragraphs mentioned the restriction was stringently enforced by the park rangers. Being interrupted by a ranger in the night didn't bother me, it was a hefty fine that I wasn't looking forward to having in my possession. The perturbing fine appeared more costly than a hotel room booked for the night.

Driving into the night, we were seeking any motel room we could deploy for our few hours of sleep. As an unprepared guide I was compelled to carry our luggage to our room after finding lodging miles away from the entrance of Yosemite Park in the town of Sonora.

Sonora, California was established in 1848 as a mining town during the California Gold Rush in the Sierra Nevada Foothills. Sonora's population is approximately 5,000 residents and the town turned out to be an agreeable unscheduled side visit. The next day Kris and I roamed on a leisurely walk while exploring a museum, downtown shops, and the hillside residential areas.

Through our years together, Kris had heard me divulge versions of my eccentric uncle and the influence he had rendered in my life. Hence being in California we were duty-bound to manufacture a social call to my Aunt Barbara and my eccentric Uncle Dick near Wilseyville, California. Wilseyville is sixty miles north of Sonora and is similarly located in the Sierra Nevada Foothills.

My Uncle Dick was born and raised on the Dowell farm in Montrose, Michigan, and he graduated from Montrose High School in 1940. He had served in the United States Navy in World War II, and after the war he resided in the bay area of Oakland. A number of years ago, my Aunt Barbara and Uncle Dick transferred to the hill country near Wilseyville.

After my high school graduation in the spring of 1978, I was presented by my parents the equivalent opportunity my siblings had been offered as a high school graduation gift. All three of us were accorded the option of a monetary gift or an all-expense paid week in California. Our room and board would be provided by our Uncle Dick. Yvonne chose the California trip while Mike and I selected the monetary gift.

I applied the money toward my first automobile purchase, my black '68 Chevy Camaro. According to my adolescent cognizance, I could journey to the Golden State any time in the near future for a visit with my relatives. So now thirty-one years after my graduation from Michigan Lutheran Seminary, I was summoning my uncle and aunt in the hill country of California.

My mother's older brother in his lifetime had collected and displayed toothbrushes in his personal abode. Perhaps the jamboree adorning his wall becomes more provocative when the feature of the past toothbrushes being exhausted by other individuals is cited.

My Uncle Dick's living arrangement at the time was an old train depot converted to his bachelor pad. To complete the configuration he had converted a wooden hot tub on the premises outdoors. Pictures of my uncle's wooden lounging apparatus reminds me of the opening scene in *Petticoat Junction* where the striking daughters are captivatingly leaning on the inside edge of the railroad's water tank with their towels swung over the side.

In my childhood years, my Uncle Dick was a machinist which permitted him to travel around the United States. The specialized worker maintained the equipment that contrived the jam and creamer packets utilized by restaurants. Uncle Dick would combine his business trips with stopovers in Michigan to visit his relatives.

My uncle would hop around the country using commercial airlines, but one summer I truly revered the avenue he used to pop in to mingle with his relatives in Michigan. My Uncle Dick piloted his own single engine Cessna airplane across the United States and he landed it in the hayfield next to my grandma's farm.

As a thirteen-year-old rogue, I was entranced in listening to my uncle's adventure of directing his prop plane across the Rockies, the Mississippi River, and the Great Plains. When my Uncle Dick and his plane were in Michigan, he extended to his nephews and nieces free rides in the aircraft. In my cerebrum I was ecstatic with the thought of the airplane's journey in the air, but in my multilayered subconscious I had confusing issues concerning the escapade.

The order of the rides was completed and I was the finale of the revolving airplane rides. Minutes before the flight, I was antsy about fainting, peeing my pants, or running away scared. I was a pimply teenage boy pacing the hayfield, checking the skies, and watching my uncle's every move.

Crawling into the tight quarters of the airplane my uncle informed me of the usual preflight checklists of securing the seatbelts, starting the engine, checking the gauges, and taxiing to position.

Uncle Dick mentioned he had been detecting odd noises and erratic behaviors with his plane's engine. As a precaution and to receive a check-up on the plane's engine and instruments, we would be concluding the expedition at a nearby airport in the township of Clio. I was familiar with the highway signs about four miles away pointing out the direction to Cagney Airport, another two miles down the township road.

My once pony-tailed uncle conveyed his apprehension about the shaky functioning of the engine. Uncle Dick critically spoke of his trepidations concerning the drainage ditch and power lines at the end of the field. My uncle's fear was pitching the plane too steeply, and thus enduring a catastrophic conclusion to our takeoff.

Only within the year had my uncle attained his pilot's license and he was now whispering to me the backup plan if the engine's performance was not effective. To avoid the ditch and power lines, he would back off the throttle and steer clear of the hazards while remaining on the ground. My silent reflection and reaction to the announcements was, "I would hope that would be the plan Uncle Dick."

My uncle relayed there could be a strong possibility of not completing the voyage at that time. In my uncle's defense, his warning was meant to assist me in understanding a possible termination of our act of aviation. My uncle may have been attempting to throw comforting words in my direction, but I would be devastated if we didn't ascend into the sky with the clouds and birds.

I wasn't jumpy about the takeoff or suffering a harmful and life-threatening crash. I was too young for that type of rational thinking as I was only anxious about choosing the best viewing opportunity from within the plane.

My Uncle Dick started the engine while performing all of the pre-flight checks. The plane started south bound down the grass covered field as we bounced along the rutted ground.

I was struggling with the numerous options as the Nosey Rosy in me was worried about missing out on a once in a lifetime special view. I had to decide if I wanted stare out the front window at the upcoming trench running perpendicular to the field. With that angle I could also keep an eye on the slingshot style of electrical power lines.

I had an abundance of possibilities as I could elect to spy-on the ground beneath the plane or even sample my uncle's piloting maneuvers. There were lots of gauges, needles, and gadgets on the instrument panel for be to monitor if I selected that observation. Another option had me glancing at the faraway detachments out my side window.

I was ready to make a final ruling and decision, and then it happened in a flash. I peeked out of my side window witnessing the harmless ditch and the non-threatening power lines below the plane. The two items were rapidly transferring out of our vision. Uncle Dick and I were suspended in the sky with me not wanting to utter a single word.

On the edge of my seat, I surveyed the landmarks below. Immediately after takeoff, I recognized Brent Creek where we went sucker spearing as young children. We then swerved around north as I detected the Flint River and my family's ranch-style house.

When we circled over my childhood brick house and veered south, I didn't smile or wink while marking the water treatment's bypass. At that time, I did not realize the future drag races and parking engagements I would witness and experience on the secluded road.

The next subsequent item came into view well in advance and it seemed we hovered in the area for an extended period. Over the top of the engine and through the rapid spinning propellers, I could observe ahead of us, my past antagonist-the opposing hill.

In the two seats of the airplane with my Uncle Dick, I was able to investigate and scrutinize the other side of the haunting hill. I assessed the creek and the hill as one commodity in one panoramic view. As a matter of fact I observed numerous peaks along the voyage. Many of those same inclines I would explore in the future wandering up and down the hill and countryside.

I was hundreds of feet above all the landforms in the region, and I was the king of all of the hills.

Relaxing and sitting back a bit I distinguished the highway leading into Montrose with the toy cars and trucks putzing along the asphalt path. The vehicles' occupants had no worries about me high above them in the tiny airplane while I gawked down at them.

From the air I spotted the static green woodlots with their mature trees. The trees appeared as if I could yank them up by their roots akin to a gardener with unwanted weeds. The organized farm fields embedded with crops resembled the lines sketched with a stick in a sandbox. Even the farm ponds were suggestive of water puddles I could run and stomp through creating a sloppy mess in the area.

With my eyes, I examined the portrayal of the farm buildings layouts. Their purposes were certainly disclosed from my vantage point. The houses in the subdivisions were organized in my young brain as an orderly distinction of planned development. While in town the vehicles in the parking lots appeared as if I could wipe all of them out with one swat of my authoritative hand.

The objects below me imparted a pretend intuition. I was merely examining a train set and the petite items connected with the toy model displayed on a sheet of plywood.

I knew my time was limited. I decided to focus into the far horizon observing the clouds, and holding my surveillance on alert for the other side of the world.

The voyage into the atmosphere was finished way too early for my overzealous cravings. The plane ride was amazing while soaring like on eagles' wings. The adventure was the highlight of my childhood.

The trip in the air with my uncle was forever sealed when we safely arrived at the asphalt runway at Cagney Airport. The landing on the well-marked air strip was professional versus the barbaric takeoff in the neighbor's hayfield. I praised all aspects of the adventure and I wouldn't trade the expedition for any other experience. In Heaven I will soar like an eagle again.

When Kris and I were visiting with my aunt and uncle in California, I recalled why I have been in awe of my uncle. In a number of ways I perceive his characteristics and mannerisms in me. I'm proud of the many attributes I have inherited from my free-thinking uncle. My misfit ideas are his normal thinking and daily acceptable conduct.

At his residence between Yosemite National Park and Lake Tahoe, my uncle constructed a bed and breakfast, created and installed a horizontal garage door, and converted a computer monitor to a bird feeder. He rehabilitated the inside metal tub of a washing machine with new life as an elevated rotisserie fire pit.

In the house Uncle Dick recycled his Craftsman metal tool chests as kitchen cabinets and mounted a frosted-glass railroad depot door as the sliding bathroom door.

Kris and I spent an evening with Aunt Barbara and Uncle Dick conversing in regards to our trip, their house, family members, and neighbors. I confirmed my uncle's passion for swimming, his past work in a bakery, and his years of being a talented handyman for hire.

The whole encounter was encapsulated during their Thursday morning social campfire. In the hill country my aunt and uncle have an open-invitation to the mountain's residents to gather at the Dowell's wash-tub. The neighbors fondly embrace the fire, conversations, coffee, and treats. This was my aunt and uncle at their best as they were entertaining, outgoing, and interesting.

I had conceived a short list of questions for my uncle and one of the inquiries concerned his beginning involvement in aviation. My uncle cheerfully conversed about himself in the 1930s on the family farm in Montrose, Michigan. Routinely, the neighbor flew his small airplane towards town as the young boy would stand in their farmhouse's plot in the morning probing the sky. The dreamy boy was roused to develop his own flying abilities.

As a fifty-year-old divorcé, Richard Dowell was introduced to a female flight instructor at a social party of their mutual friends. My uncle asserted he was not attracted to the woman nor could he visualize a long-term relationship with her.

After their introductions at the party and through the dating process in the near future, Uncle Dick secured reasonably priced flying lessons with the young lady. My uncle perkily confessed that once he received his pilot license, the dates diminished between the beginning aviator and now ditched instructor.

The inquiries I had for my Uncle Dick in connection with his hobbies, occupations, and family were all courteously answered. But my Uncle Dick had a snicker during my version of a certain narrative.

My uncle was nearly laughing out loud when I relayed my version concerning a thirteen-year-old misfit and his uncle in a tiny airplane. I stomached a mental squashing as his rebuttal of the account generated my jaw to drop, my mind to blur, and my head to tilt cockeyed.

My uncle shared there was no engine conundrum, and there was no way he was apprehensive about the bumpers at the end of the field in the form of the ditch and the power lines. My irregular uncle had embellished the entire preflight communication to craft the voyage as more dramatic for his naïve nephew.

I had desired for years that my Uncle Dick could see his unique qualities in me, and I secretively petitioned to be his favorite relative or at least his favorite nephew. The final dagger to my absurd ego was when he replied he had specified those ingredients to everyone seated in his aircraft for the free airplane rides.

My fairytale flight would now be forever changed with these minor facts revised. However, nothing could crash my elevation in the atmosphere as the experience will always remain marvelous.

Spending two days with my vegetarian aunt and uncle was too brief. We said our emotional good-byes while trading gigantic hugs. Uncle Dick firmly hugged Kris and stated to her in a tone exclusive to only him, "We like you."

Kris and I drove back to San Francisco and concluded our trip to California by renting bicycles and riding across the Golden Gate Bridge.

In my lifetime, I will forever view a small plane in the sky and reminisce about my Uncle Dick. I will always cherish my plane ride with my special uncle. I love you, Uncle Dick.

Chapter 30
THE HALL OF FAMER

For 45 years, celebrities from the sports and entertainment fields hit the links for the fight against cancer at the annual Vince Lombardi Golf Classic. As one of the oldest two-day charity golf events in the United States, the Vince Lombardi Golf Classic doesn't just have history it has tradition. Bob Hope and President Gerald Ford helped establish the tradition and mystique of the Vince Lombardi Golf Classic in the 1970s and the Vince Lombardi Cancer Foundation is proud to carry on the legacy of Coach Vince Lombardi. *5

On the day when Kris and I were yakking at Winnebago Lutheran Academy near the tennis court, Kris had invited me to join her in volunteering at the charity golf event in Menomonee Falls, Wisconsin. At the golf outing, Kris and I would be the marshals at the tee box of the fourteenth hole. We were to guide the personalities to the tee box, making sure the spectators were respectful and quiet for the celebrities' tee shots.

The celebrities were on teams of four players with the other three non-celebrity players paying a hefty entry fee for the privilege of golfing with the famous personalities.

In the years Kris and I volunteered, I was fascinated with receiving autographs and pictures from various well-known athletes and celebrities. I basked being in the presence of Robin Yount, Pat Richter, James Lofton, Gorman Thomas, Bob Uecker, Bart Starr, Mason Crosby, John Elway, Jerry Kramer, and Ron Kramer.

Pat Richter the past athletic director at the University of Wisconsin was one of the first celebrities I was fortunate to interact with at the outing. Kris had spoken to Pat and had arranged for him to give me a "Go Red" as he pointed to my Michigan maize and blue chair.

After Pat had teed off, he delivered the provoking jest to me while he proceeded to climb into his golf cart. Before he pulled away, Pat commented I would appreciate the celebrity golfer appearing in a bit.

Ron Kramer approached our tee box and I will concede I was unable to distinguish him from anyone else. All I knew was Ron Kramer had played football for the Green Bay Packers in 1960s. From Pat Richter's comment, I figured Ron Kramer was connected in some way or manner to the University of Michigan.

As a Michigan fan, I have had my favorite coaches such as Bo Schembechler, Lloyd Carr, and Jim Harbaugh. I hold precious memories of players such as Rick Leach, Rob Lytle, Anthony Carter, Tyrone Wheatly, John Navarre, Braylon Edwards, Jake Long, Leon Hall, LaMarr Woodley, Brandon Graham, Desmond Howard, and the exceptional and distinct Charles Woodson.

Ron Kramer, I did not recognize as a Michigan man. Ron Kramer was an alternate golfer at the outing added to the field of play due to a last-minute dropout. Being a replacement, Mr. Kramer didn't have a biography in the program. Smart phones did not exist, so I was left in the dark concerning information on Ron Kramer.

After Ron Kramer teed off and as I stood by my chair, Ron approached his golf cart and put away his driver. At that moment I became aware of his maize and blue Michigan Wolverines golf-club head cover. I was dumbstruck and my heart became revved up noticing the block M on his straw hat. Before I had time to say anything Ron said, "Go Blue!"

I did not go into shock as I returned to the celebrity, "Go Blue!"

Ron Kramer moved his cart along the path and he paused his golf cart by my chair. I extended out my hand and we shook hands as I introduced myself.

I asked him casual questions about the status of Michigan's football program, and I could tell he was passionate about the University of Michigan. Ron replied with his opinions on a wide range of subjects as I was captivated with his willingness to chat with me.

After the first meeting with Ron Kramer, I made it my mission to acquire as many facts as I could about this former U of M football team member.

In the long tradition of outstanding Michigan athletes, Ron Kramer deserves to be ranked among the best. A nine-time letterman (three each in football, basketball, and track), Kramer's credits include two consensus football All-American selections, the retirement of his jersey number by the Wolverines following his senior season, and the selection as basketball Most Valuable Player for three years standing.

A native of Girard, KS, Kramer's family moved to East Detroit when he was five. Prior to attending the University of Michigan, he won Michigan all-state honors in football, basketball, and track.

As a Wolverine, Kramer was an excellent two way player on the gridiron, occupying at some point the positions of offensive and defensive end, running back, quarterback, kicker, and receiver, often all in the same game...

As captain of the basketball team during his senior year, Kramer set Michigan's all-time scoring mark at 1,124 points, a standard that stood until 1961. As a member of the Wolverine track squad, Kramer was a talented high jumper, despite his 230-pound frame...

Kramer went on to play for the Green Bay Packers under Vince Lombardi in the early 1960's. As the prototype of NFL tight ends, he was named to the all-Pro team following the 1961 and 1962 seasons, as the Packers went on to win consecutive World Championships...

After retiring from football in 1968, Kramer was elected into the Michigan Sports Hall of Fame in 1971. Later, in 1981, he was named as a recipient of the NCAA's Silver Anniversary Award in recognition of significant professional and civic contributions spanning 25 years after completion of his college eligibility. *6

I came across photos of Ron Kramer wearing the number eighty-seven at Michigan and the number eighty-eight for Green Bay. Ron was on the cover photo of "Sports Illustrated", and I found a photo of him as an elderly man wearing a casual sweater while signing a Michigan winged helmet.

The next year, Kris and I once again volunteered at the celebrity golf outing. Pat Richter approached our area and remembered Kris, me, and my Michigan lawn chair. Pat and I exchanged memories of past football games between the Badgers and the Wolverines while Kris and I thanked Pat Richter for his participation in the golf event. I also thanked Pat for alerting me of Ron Kramer's presence.

Pat responded, "Ron Kramer is a good man. Enjoy your conversation and moments with him."

This time in the tournament Ron Kramer was a scheduled golfer listed in the official program. Approaching the tee box area, Ron and I shook hands and we re-introduced ourselves. I asked Ron if he would sign the eight by eleven colored photo of him I had brought to the tournament. As we discussed the photo, I caught sight of Ron smiling and approvingly nodding.

The subsequent year the foundation established a new policy in connection with celebrities signing only certain items, so my autograph from Ron on the photo became even more exceptional to me.

The thoughtful discussions I had with Ron Kramer were over head coaches, athletic directors, and presidents. In all of our talks, Ron never spoke negatively of any situation or anyone.

Ron Kramer was a mind-boggling athlete in his glory days with spectacular accomplishments and recognitions, but he was a modest person throughout his life.

For several years the retired athlete had maintained a tradition of taking apples to the Michigan football players during the weeks within the football season. Many Wolverine fans and Packer fans have a sincere admiration and respect for Ron Kramer.

In our spontaneous discussions, Ron Kramer and I unveiled the polished facts and personal sentiments of countless past Michigan football games. In our exchange, Ron recited his tailgating spot in Ann Arbor and he invited us to visit him before a game. I was familiar with the location as we had often tailgated near there. I was bubbly and thrilled with the invitation.

Ron Kramer was in his 70's, with a personality and mannerisms similar to my dad. I understand that is part of the reason I was enthused by being in his presence. However, the idea of absorbing minutes with one of the ultimate Michigan football players of all time was unquestionably an honorable occurrence.

That fall I was unable to meet up with Ron prior to a Michigan home football game in the Big House. The only Michigan football game I attended that year was in Evansville, Illinois.

The following year Kris and I we were assigned as marshals at the Lombardi Classic on the fourth putting green. The tee box for the fifth fairway was a few steps away from our green, so as a veteran volunteer I predicted conversing with Ron Kramer at both locations.

Ron's group aced a long putt on the fourth green and Ron didn't have to clamber out of his cart at the location. As the group's carts entered the next tee box area Ron stayed in his cart as the other three men teed up their golf balls. The men detonated the small white objects far into the lush downhill fairway.

Approaching Ron in his cart I was excited as I once again shook hands with my mentor. I reintroduced myself while we recalled together our past interactions.

Presenting my black sharpie and the official program I asked Ron if he would sign his name on the cover. I presented to him I would be pleased if he would sign the front cover as I didn't intend to hide his autograph on the inside pages.

In Ron's proximity, I unearthed satisfaction in spending the moments with an honest, genuine, and caring man. In our dialogue, Ron and I shared obsessions devoted Michigan fans ridiculously ruminate on during their discussions and time together.

As a die-hard Michigan fan I had sung, hummed, and blared out the Michigan fight song countless times over the years. I sang the tune as I watched on television a ball-boy, Jim Harbaugh, pat the Michigan's quarterback in the end zone. The boy was electrified that Rick Leach, wearing number seven had scored the winning touchdown.

On a rainy Saturday afternoon when the Wolverines hosted the University of Iowa Hawkeyes the dedicated Michigan fans and I sang "Hail to the Victors" although Michigan lost on a last-second field goal. The contest was my first live game in the Big House.

I chuckle in regards to the time I arrived at a game early enough in my seat in the Big House to observe the U of M band entering the playing field through the tunnel. As they high stepped onto the field I became frozen with joyful stage fright. I did not sing one single word as I hummed along with over 100,000 singing fans.

While chanting the greatest college fight song, I surveyed my beloved Wolverines on TV in the Rose Bowl on New Year's Day in 1997. The University of Michigan football team won a national championship and were indeed the champions of the west!

The first time I played the melody on a piano, I used the sheet music I received from my relative Danielle. She presented the notes to me when she was nine years old, and the measures of pencil drawn notes are composed on notebook paper. Someday soon the treasured item will be used by my grandchildren on a piano.

Jenny and I once yelped through the song as we jumped up and down on the couch on a wild warpath. We were, after all, on the Rez in Arizona. Miles away in South Bend, Indiana, a last-second field goal by Remy Hamilton gave Michigan a 26-24 victory over Norte Dame.

Now in Menomonee Falls, Wisconsin, I was carousing with an All-American, Ron Kramer. I have no clue how it happened as Ron and I began booming out our rendering of "Hail to the Victors."

Among the spectators of our public presentation were the other golfers, Kris, and about three dozen spectators. After we finished our carousing, Ron and I provided each other with a high five as the people around us awarded our musical rendition with their healthy ovation and their smiling faces.

Mesmerized by the moment, I barely noticed Ron descending out of the golf cart. While grabbing his driver from his golf bag, I recognized myself coming a long way with Ron Kramer since first spotting his maize and blue golf club cover. I was all grins thinking of my first stunned reaction to his straw hat with the block M.

Ron made his way to the tee box and proceeded to hit a decent drive. I'm positive I wore the happiest smile of any volunteer on the golf course. For one abnormal moment I wanted to be the guy at golf tournaments who yells out after a tee shot, "You're the man!"

Respectfully, the gallery and I presented Ron Kramer an appreciative round of applause. Ron situated himself back in the cart and he courteously posed for a photo while I stood alongside him.

I expressed to Ron I would for sure meet up with him at a Michigan game. We shook hands and I thanked him again. His cart pulled away as I barked out, "Have a great round of golf, Ron. Go Blue!"

Ron returned to me a fist pump and a solid, "Go Blue!"

I never did acquire a connection with Ron Kramer tailgating at a game. In September, three months after our singing rendezvous, Ron Kramer died. Two years later, I was able to attend the football game at the University of Michigan dedicated to Ron Kramer. Standing in the Big House remembering Ron Kramer, I had pleasing tears on my cheeks and an overwhelming happiness in my heart.

At the golf tournament again the ensuing year, I was able to share with Pat my chats with the Michigan alumnus. The next spring at the Crazylegs Classic Run in Madison, Pat Richter was the official grandmaster and we had a brief chat near the vicinity of the registration.

I had two outstanding men I had the privilege to meet through the Vince Lombardi golf outing, Pat Richter and Ron Kramer.

When Ron Kramer hit the tee shot from the fifth hole at the Lombardi Golf Tournament, I watched as he returned to his cart and motored down the asphalt path. I was standing motionless and thinking of the blessings I encountered through such a fantastic person.

The remaining group's carts stopped next to me and one of the men motioned for my attention. After I wiped my watery eyes, the man announced to me, "Hey, you made a huge impression on Ron. All day he has not moved from his golf cart due to health reasons. He did not even attempt a golf swing until now. Ron went to the tee box and hit that ball for you."

I had a few more tears to shed.

The program with "Ron Kramer #87 H of F" now resides in my office. Thank you, Ron Kramer, for your friendship and furnishing me with tremendous memories.

Ron Kramer, hall of famer, my favorite Michigan man. Go Blue!

Chapter 31
THE LEFT TURNS

One excursion Davey Lee, Nanny, Yvonne, Mike, and I embarked on when I was a young child was shuffling off on weekends to the stock car races. At the nearby race tracks, my family would follow the banged-up cars with their roaring engines and crazy dashes out of the corners. In the grandstand, we shadowed the hectic sprints down the straightaways and were deranged by the electrifying crashes. We were not regulars in the crowd, but we attended a few races in a summer.

On Saturday evenings my parents, siblings, and I might position ourselves in the wooden grandstands at Auto City Speedway near Flint, Michigan. Cheering on our favorite drivers we would pick a certain car to win a race or at least finish ahead of everyone else's pick. On the oval speedway at Auto City there were two high-bank clay surface tracks, an inner quarter-mile track and the outer half-mile track.

From time to time we would travel on Sunday afternoons to Dixie Motor Speedway near Saginaw, Michigan. Dixie Motor Speedway also had a quarter-mile inner track and an outer half-mile track. At Dixie the asphalt oval tracks were primarily flat with the turns having a miniscule degree of banking.

The hours as a spectator at the racetracks had a strong influence on my brother, Mike. At the age of nineteen Mike and two young friends bought a used racecar. The car was prepared for racing by being stripped down to the bare frame with the engine and transmission left in factory condition.

Added to the inside compartment for safety purposes was a metal roll cage, a racing seat, and a window netting. Under the hood the setups swapped in and out included a larger radiator, a racing carburetor, and a fuel cell gas tank. On the vehicle's outer shell, racing tires and a supplemented paint job were the last NASCAR type of touches added to the racecar.

The racing automobile resembled the General Lee automobile from the TV show *The Dukes of Hazzard*. The main variances in the two autos were numbers and models of the vehicles. Mike's racecar was labeled number eighty-five, and Mike's car was a Plymouth Roadrunner.

None of the three young entrepreneurs drove the street stock division racecar as an unconnected fourth person was behind the wheel. The agreement was forever tainted after the driver halted the car by crashing into an idle water tank truck on the back side of the track.

Mike's partners dropped out of the enterprise because of the supposedly comprehensive damage to the car after the violent crash. Mike became the sole owner and driver of the racing machine.

After Mike made the necessary repairs during the week, he settled into the racing auto the succeeding Saturday. When the night's racing was complete Mike went up to the pay window to collect his winnings. That night at Auto City Speedway, Mike was forever hooked on stock car racing.

Over the next twenty years Mike would win a few races, rarely crash, and finished most of the contests. Seldom did Mike have a contributing sponsor even though from time to time he received discounts on car components, and the racecar did receive a professional paint job in exchange for advertisement on the car.

The racing measures as a hobby was a lavish pursuit for Mike's finances, and my friend Tim and I helped Mike as his amateur pit crew. Mike and Tim were the authentic mechanics as I was inept as a mechanic. In spite of my lack of skills I was eager to perform other supportive tasks in the garage at Mike's house or in the pit area at the race track.

My learning curve with working on automobiles did enable me to change the engine oil, tires, and spark plugs. In the garage I glided through charging the battery, cleaning the carburetor, and checking all the fluid levels. Though, as a glorified gopher I was liquidated from the hands on superior developments of changing an engine, swapping out a transmission, or replacing a rear axle.

Being a tag along brother, I found pleasure in driving the car on and off the trailer, and hot lapping the automobile at Auto City Speedway. The clay oval track was watered down and the slippery surface had to be driven over to create a suitable hard racing surface. The process in the mud began with slow speeds. As the dirt became packed the velocities of the cars amplified to near racing speeds.

The hot lapping was tedious for the real drivers, so Mike would frequently permit me to perform the duty. I was enraptured buckled in the car's seat and besieging the high bank turns even if the process was with slow speeds and lots of sliding around. In the straightaways I was ecstatic with the engine's growl and its unleashed power.

My favorite car of Mike's collection was a '69 Camaro painted as a replica of a gold Miller High Life beer can. Two large white parallelogram Miller High Life symbols were decals on the hood and the large white words Driver Mike Miller were painted on the roof. Near the rear corner panel in black lettering was the name of the shop that had painted the car and in red lettering on the rear window panel were the names of Tim and Brian, the two pit crew members.

Mike had prepared in an unusual manner for the race venture with the Camaro. The engine of the car had overheated and the big block engine was damaged, so Mike invested in a custom built engine. The modified engine was a gigantic investment, but it would deliver more horsepower. Throughout the racing season the fresh engine was never a hindrance as it had pleasing breakaway speed and plenty of torque.

The handling of the car was the confusing nemesis. In racing terms the car was either tight or loose in the curves. As a 3,000-pound car the vehicle would push through the corner's midway segments aiming to sashay in a straight path toward the outer concrete wall. When the car was loose the car's rear end would fishtail around causing the automobile to spin out on the inside of the track. Throughout the season we tried correcting the car's path by adjusting the air pressure of the tires, tie rods, leaf springs, and the sizes of the racing tires.

The racing season had begun with high expectations, but Mike won just one race in the season with the lavish car. I believe Mike was less aggressive with his style of racing due to the price tag piggy-backing the Miller High Life car.

Numerous times in a variety of types and times of races, Tim and I would cheer as Mike advanced through a race by passing lesser cars. Just as quickly we would find ourselves groaning when Mike would be thwarted by the drivers re-passing Mike's sassy, independent car.

Most racetracks have season-ending races not on the regular schedule and one of those crowd-pleasing races are the mechanics race. At Auto City Speedway the season-ending races were a fan's delight as the owners of the racecars were placing their valued vehicles in the direct path of danger and costly damages.

For years Mike's racecars were not available for the end-of-the-season races due to mechanical complications, a wreck in a previous race during the evening, or cancelled races due to inappropriate weather.

The final night of racing had clear skies and cool temperatures. I prayed Mike would have safe races and I snuck in a prayer to safely preserve the gold colored car from any technical hitches. I didn't have to express my selfish intentions to God that evening, yet I appeased my worries by reciting the same prayer over and over.

Mike and the '69 Camaro made it through the races. The mechanics race wasn't cancelled and I climbed through the window of my highly prized thoroughbred. The peppery Camaro had one more race.

Our childhood friend, Tim, could have been selected to drive the racecar as he was more qualified when comparing his driving practices and mine. Tim was well-known in our neighborhood for operating all vehicles with a heavy foot while driving on the edge of reckless.

Tim drove fast and furious whether on the Belill, Marshall Road, or on the Interstate systems. Nothing was out of bounds for Tim as long as it had a workable engine. At that time in our lives Tim had already compiled a nice quantity of driving awards from law officers in Michigan and neighboring states in the Midwest.

Tim though knew how much I craved to dive through the window into the car race. The mechanics race would be authentic racing, not some wimpy hot lapping of the car. Cladded in Mike's fire suit and helmet I harnessed myself in the high-back leather seat. The one-piece fire suit was exceedingly oversized on me because Mike is every bit four inches taller than me.

I snapped the window netting closed and moved the toggle switch to the on position. My heart was pounding louder than the engine as I was ready to get it on with the other drivers on the oval race track.

Due to our last-minute adjustments I was struggling to make it on the track for the start of the finale. Flying out of the pit area I progressed through the gears and was unyielding on the gas pedal.

On the racetrack the mechanics race was beginning with the officials' indifferently waving the green flag. Standing proud on the podium the official was oblivious to my race entry. At the start of the race while coming out of turn four I smooched up to last place in the field of eighteen racecars.

On the first two laps of the ten-lap race I concentrated on becoming comfortable with my steering through the corners. In those two laps I unintentionally passed three slower cars. The three snails were sluggish because of orders to circle the track conservatively by the owner or they drove slowly due to their grim fear in the racecar.

In the next racing laps, I started to surge up to cars through the straightaways. I even became audacious enough to pass cars by sneaking underneath them on the inside side of the curves. Gaining confidence and beginning to comprehend the heavy car's handling, I even bettered some challengers on the difficult high side of the turns.

The left turns had become a hoot, and operating a vehicle displaying such raw breakaway power and an overabundance of acceleration was exhilarating. I would lunge forward as I dove into the corner and I was propelled backward as I was exiting the turns.

By letting off the gas pedal as I entered the turn the engine was effectively decelerating. The racing device glided through the high banks and I absolutely had no need for the brakes. There was no pushing or pulling with the fabulous Camaro.

I couldn't conjure enough accolades in my mind. The Camaro was my BBF, my Best Buddy Forever.

After several revolutions on the track, I was compensating for the noticeable car's fishtailing exiting the corners. The right hand turning of the steering wheel was my strategy to avoid spinning out, and within a lap it became a rhythmic motion enacted out of instinct.

In the front straightaway I kept an eye on the flags being exhibited, as I didn't want to be seen as a novice and miss a yellow flag. In the same way I was quizzical if the official had crisscrossed the white flag and the checkered flag, signifying the halfway part of the race. No matter how many laps were left, I was on my way to being pompous about excelling beyond the weaker cars and minor drivers.

I went into the dimly lit turns with both hands working the steering wheel. My peripheral vision was emerging and the complete view out my front and side windows were theatrical.

As I was zipping through corners three and four, I spotted another Camaro ahead of me. I was familiar with the white Camaro containing the red sixty-five painted on the door panel. Denny had been winning races with the car in his division, but his brother, Ron, was now driving the auto in the mechanics race.

Ron in previous years had been a proficient driver, and he had regularly guided his car to the winner's circle. This was dreamlike as I was making a pass on a veteran driver and a great car. This was a fantasy transformed into reality for this daydreamer.

Propelling out of turn four with our Camaros side by side, Ron provided a nod with a spark in his eye. I zoomed by Ron and he supplied the businesslike wave to me implying, "Go have fun, Brian."

Nailing the gas pedal to the floor coming out of turn four, the track in front of the grandstand was a clear corridor in my view. I had no clue my position in the race or the number of laps left in the race. Expectedly, the car was sliding higher in the groove, yet the wide tires were holding their grip as they were kicking up fresh clumps of dirt.

In the banked bends of one, two, and three, the danger of running the high groove was veering off the track and plummeting down the steep embankment. The result of the rude tactic was putting your human anatomy and the car's future at severe risk.

I exited turn four and I could distinguish the ticket-purchasing crowd of people in the grandstand. There were the rowdies encouraging their favorite driver or car with their swinging arms and fist pumps. Both children and adults were turning their heads back and forth on a swivel as if following a professional tennis match.

In my opinion the race could last for an infinity. I knew the memories from this one magnificent racing night would assist me through the upcoming gray and depressing winter months.

Glancing ahead on the oval raceway, I was gloating about roping in victims and dispatching them with a smooth pass. I had become cocky, while seriously overlooking the fact that pride does come before the fall.

On the next lap, as I rocketed through turn four, I sensed a slight thump in the car's rear end. My reaction was another driver had hustled his way through the field of cars and was dispensing a love tap to let me know of his presence.

Unfortunately, the nudge was my car's right rear bumper making contact with the uncompromising wall. This was the three-foot-high concrete wall with its chain link fence separating the gooey racetrack and the fans. One slight elbow on the wall turned my world around even though I had now removed my foot from the gas pedal.

The car spun hard to the left and I received a bird's eye interpretation of the deserted clay infield. As the car continued in its mad whirlwind the car was now heading towards the concrete divider. I was expecting to be vaulted in the side by another car coming out of turn four. My main objective to steer away from the wall.

Trouncing on the brake pedal, the Camaro was retaining its roaring path toward the unbending barrier. The inevitable was accepted by me and with both hands I death gripped the steering wheel.

With a solid wallop, the car and I smashed head-on into the obstruction. My world went cold, dark, and silent with my brain switching to the off position. The car also went silent. As my wits returned, I was viewing the lonely dirt infield as the silent Camaro was sulking toward the loose dirt.

The car oozed down the incline and came to a halt facing the secondary flag man in the infield. I was predicting the fire-suited official would stroll to my car window with the encouraging words, "Hey kid, nice run, tough break though. Better luck next year."

But the dispirited man said nothing. The grim delegate stood ten feet from the car and was shaking his head sideways. For all pragmatic purposes he was probably saying, "You idiot! Get that piece of junk out of here and learn how to drive before you come out here."

I didn't know if I should restart the car or wait for a wrecker. My infield adversary was growing incredibly impatient with me as he rolled his index finger in small circles and developed his final firm instructions by snappily pointing to the pit area.

Starting the smoldering racing machine, I muttered to myself, "Wow dude, you could at least examine the car and make sure I'm not causing more damage by driving the car."

I would imagine that after my hitting an unyielding hurdle at a high rate of speed, my crawling to the pit area wasn't his top priority on that last night of the racing season.

Hobbling the wounded car onto the trailer and weaseling out the window, I sustained a respectful distance between Mike and me. In other words, I stayed on the opposite side of the car from Mike.

Our initial examination disclosed the radiator and engine fan were crushed. The engine was pushed back twelve inches and certainly the interior of the costly engine was damaged. The transmission gears were shattered, the drive shaft was bent, and the rear end was dangling in place and riding crooked between the rear wheels.

The matter was further humiliating as every individual in the pit area had to produce their two cents' worth of stares and comments as they approached the mutated Camaro sitting immobile on the car trailer.

People on Mike's no-fly-zone never had to guess about his status or viewpoint on events. Mike was known to express his inner ideas through strong language, radical facial demeanors, and course loud speaking. In due course I stepped within Mike's reach, but only because I had to ride home with him in his pick-up truck.

I was prepared to dispense with the tongue-lashing, the shunning, and the long-term loss of my brother. I had no excuse for my actions and I could only reply, "I'm sorry."

Mike's reaction to everyone around the car was that the Camaro was a complete loss. Mike tacked on the fact he would be unable to remain in racing due to the significant damage to the car and the future costs involved with replacing the car. Not only had I annihilated the car, my actions were leading Mike to terminate his hobby.

During the ride home and throughout the following years, Mike never called me an idiot and did not shun me or slap me around. In time, Mike once again tolerated me as we continued as brothers.

Weeks later an educational comment on that night of racing was shared with me as I was recalling the event with a spectator of the mechanics race.

I was informed the winner of the mechanics race had won a large, fashionable trophy. Foreign to my knowledge there was one lap left in the race and I was holding onto first place when I tapped the wall. No other car was threatening my checkered win. But I was careless in letting the victory and trophy slip out of my lackadaisical grip.

Mike did race the ensuing years, but he never had another car with the speed, showmanship, and appeal similar to the '69 Chevy Camaro.

Mike performed well in a new trend of races called Endurance Races. The races had about 150 cars entered and the contest was usually 200 laps on a quarter mile track. There were no yellow or red flags and the oval track would be littered with exhausted cars.

Retiring from racing and becoming a fan himself in the grandstand, Mike created one last way to satisfy his competitive spirit. The one-lap spectator drag races during intermission allowed fans could to participate with the vehicle they drove to the track. Mike won several trophies in the drag racing style of competition.

After the season with the Miller High Life car, I moved on with my life my working, starting a family, and heading off to college. I would never again have my name on a racecar as a pit crew member.

In fact, I have visited only two race events within the last twenty-five years. Last summer Kris and I went to a Saturday night short track race in the Wisconsin Dells. We cheered on WLA student, Nick, as he competed at the asphalt track.

My forty year love affair exists with the late 1960s muscle car the Chevy Camaro. My first automobile was a black '68 Camaro which eventually was stored in our family's barn for thirty years. I was captivated to be acquainted with a certain gold '69 Camaro that delivered an astonishing ride. As a young adult, the left turns I encountered at Auto City Speedway were incredible.

Chapter 32
THE MARATHONS

Not all races in my life have been in an automobile or on a race track. Much later in life I was exposed to running races with my legs. For years I have noisily confessed I despise any type of running. The side-aches, heavy breathing, and cramps were not my idea of recreational fun. As children, my cousin Paul ran long distances for training for various activities. He solicited me to join him for runs in our neighborhood, but I wasn't persuaded to join in the misery.

Until three years ago, I had only run a mile twice in my life and I had never run more than one mile. For the first practice of our college football season we ran one mile at the beginning of the practice. The mile was timed primarily as a gauge to track our physical condition and our readiness for the football season.

I have made statements before using the adverb "never" and I had voiced I would never run over a mile in my lifetime. When Jenny ran a 5K race in Oshkosh, Wisconsin I was awestruck. Jenny's theory on long-distance running resembled her dad's pessimistic philosophies. After Jenny's exploit I placed running a 5K race on my bucket list.

After a two-inch snowfall on a February day, I was walking on the Wild Goose Trail in a scene worthy to be on a postcard. Nearing mile four of my five mile walk I decided I would run the last mile. I was wearing sweatpants, a cotton hoodie jacket, and ordinary walking tennis shoes. I started trotting, and one mile later I exhausted my lope at my house's garage door. On the scamper I stayed away from any excessive sprinting with my pace being one level above the tempo of a feisty walk.

On my walk the next day I decided to expand the challenge and run the last two miles back to our subdivision. The two miles were harder to complete due to my abrasive breathing and heavy legs

However, I was on cloud nine back at my homestead. Dressed again in my gray hoodie I raised my arms above my head as I bounded up the two steps leading up to my front porch. Once I reached the pinnacle, I spun around and executed the victory dance from the movie *Rocky*.

The following week I ran a two mile duration on four different occasions. Two weeks after my first one mile jog I finished a morning run and shower, and I bellied up to the kitchen island for a cup of coffee. Before I rummaged my way through the newspaper, I noticed on the top of the heap of papers, a pink flyer advertising a 5K race.

The Bunny Hop Race sponsored by the Solutions Center was scheduled for the next Saturday the day before Easter. The race was being conducted eleven miles away at Lakeside Park in the city of Fond du Lac. According to the flyer's information, the race would fit into my schedule if I ventured to register.

I conveyed to Kris the amazement of God tailoring the flyer to be at the top of the papers. The full page circular was in clear view as an intervention stating it was the proper time for my wish list race.

Throwing me a curve ball, Kris admitted positioning the pink advertisement on top. At first I was disenchanted my miracle hadn't happened, but God does use diverse means to accomplish his plans. Besides, I was flattered Kris took the initiative to share the information.

Signing up for the race I had a mild phobia of becoming lost during the run, finishing last, or collapsing from exhaustion. An incentive to perform well in the race was that Paul and his two grandsons would be visiting from Michigan that weekend. I was hopeful Paul would run in the race, but due to his constant knee dilemmas, Paul was unable to participate. Instead Paul, Bryce, and Lane fished on the park's canal banks and cheered for me.

The Saturday morning of the Bunny Hop 5K was sunny and the day's temperature was in the mid-forty's. Runners beforehand were in the warming house. I noticed the veteran runners and the beginners like me. Entering the start of the race I examined the racing bibs, music devices, and volunteers on the course. I was amazed at the supporters, finish line, and post-race amenities.

Everything went well in the race as I correctly navigated the route, I wasn't the last finisher, and I didn't gag to death. Likewise, I wasn't upset about being passed by children and elderly women.

After the race I received an e-mail promoting a road race at the University of Michigan in Ann Arbor, Michigan. The Big House, Big Heart 5K/10K Runs were scheduled for the following weekend.

After viewing Wolverine football games as a youngster on TV, I longed to run out of the mysterious tunnel onto the field. In my childhood fantasies, I would enter the stadium prior to the Ohio State game as a starting defensive backs for the Wolverines.

At fifty years old, I certainly wasn't playing tackle football. Instead, here was an opportunity to run my second 5K race and run onto the fifty-yard line of the football field in Michigan Stadium.

In April of 2012, the day after the annual Wolverine intersquad spring football scrimmage, I lined up with 1,300 other runners outside the stadium. On East Keech Avenue in Ann Arbor, I experienced for the first time a corral start of a race. The race route went through the campus and the regal buildings while we were encouraged by cheerleaders and several clusters of Michigan band members.

My highpoint of the race was running through the tunnel under the bowl-style stadium. In the tunnel on the overhead beams are painted three times the repeated phrase The Team. As "Hail to the Victors" was pumping through the tunnel's speakers, I ascended out onto the field.

Being two feet off the ground and running with ease, I ran the finishing route to the south end zone. The course turned near the goal post and tracked along the middle of the field to the finish line.

Stretched across the fifty yard line was a replica maize and blue banner used on game day. I jumped and touched the banner as I perceived 109,901 Michigan fans cheering.

I did not have a long range running plan, yet my first three organized runs were distinctive. My next run after the Big Heart, Big House Run was the Mackinac Bridge Memorial Day Run.

The Mackinac Bridge or Big Mac was completed in 1961 and spans the waters of the Straits of Mackinac. The Mighty Mac connects Mackinaw City in the Lower Peninsula and the city of St. Ignace in the Upper Peninsula. The Mackinac Bridge is nearly five miles long and rises to a height of 250 feet, with the water being 290 feet deep below the mid-span of the bridge.

The Saturday morning road race begins on the north end of Mackinac Bridge and the run starts at 6 am. School buses transport the runners from Mackinaw City across the bridge to the start line until 8 am. The early morning start sometimes provide a sunrise over the water, or a view of a freighter traveling along the shipping routes.

The view of the Great Lakes while running back to Mackinaw City is unparalleled knowing Chicago is on the right side about 400 miles south on the shores of Lake Michigan. On the left side of the bridge is Lake Huron with the city of Detroit roughly 300 miles to the south.

The spring run over the bridge has about 800 runners whereas the Labor Day walk across the bridge in September enrolls 30,000 people. On the Saturday morning of Memorial Day weekend, the outside lane of the southbound lanes is closed for vehicles. Runners on the first mile of the bridge are presented with a five percent-grade incline.

I have been in my life a passenger or a driver crossing the bridge hundreds of times, and many times I have inched across the bridge in diverse weather conditions. I have struggled with thick fog, down pouring rain, freezing rain, sideways sleet, and blinding snow.

The day before the Mackinac Bridge Memorial Day Run, Kris and I arrived at St. Ignace with gusty winds of 30 mph blowing across the bridge. Driving across the bridge, our truck was shoved sideways as we noticed four foot whitecap waves in the straits. I had serious doubts of stepping foot on the bridge's surface the next day.

The next morning the winds calmed down, and I was on a yellow school bus riding over the Big Mac while witnessing a beautiful sunrise. Pacing myself the first mile, I enjoyed the view of the upcoming pillars as I was starting to find a comfortable stride.

Running closer to the railing, I stole a look or two at the expanse of water. I arrived at the spot on the expansion bridge between the two enormous concrete columns holding the 42,000 miles of cable, and I said an impulsive hello to Davey Lee in Heaven.

In the past Dad would make one of two comments at the spot in the past. "We are at the highest point of the bridge and it is all downhill from here." Or because we would be heading to the Taj Mahal, "Well gang we are almost back home to paradise."

Runners in the race descend the south side of the bridge as the wooden stockade enclosing Fort Michilimackinac is in view on the shoreline. The Mackinac Bridge Memorial Day Run finishes near the high school indoor hockey rink.

Kris and I delight in the breakfast after the run while having interesting conversations with many individuals from all over Michigan, the nearby Midwest states, and other regions of the United States.

After finishing the Mackinac Bridge Memorial Day Run, I had an ambition to climb the ladder of feats by taking on a 10K race. One month later I ran my first 10K race in Waupun, Wisconsin.

According to most running sources, the largest-growing road race in popularity with new participants per year is the half marathon. The name itself is enticing and adventurous.

To determine if I could run a half marathon, I went on a twelve-mile run prior to an early evening meeting. By walking a large chunk of distance, I was able to scarcely arrive at the meeting on time. The informal twelve-mile run taught me I could not venture out for a long-distance run without properly training.

As a newbie, 13.1 miles appeared an insurmountable amount to run and I wanted to run an inspiring half marathon. I happened upon the Detroit Half Marathon held in October which I could combine the run with a Wolverine football game. The Detroit Half Marathon fit the bill as inspiring because of the need for a passport on the run and the one mile portion of the running route under a water source.

I had spent the first twenty-eight years of my life as a resident of Michigan visiting as a child the Detroit Zoo, Henry Ford Museum, Greenfield Village, and Detroit Tiger's baseball games. As an adult I attended Lions and Pistons games, and I had traveled across the Detroit River to leave a donation at a Canadian casino.

The Detroit Half Marathon begins downtown and within minutes runners negotiate the lighted International Ambassador Bridge. Runners continue the morning strides into Windsor, Canada and follow the Detroit River for about four miles.

The final steps on the Canadian soil scampers through the mile long Detroit/Windsor Tunnel. After the competitors enter the USA the route consists of a dozen turns with one extended straightaway and concludes in downtown Detroit.

During the half marathon, the early morning sight from the Ambassador Bridge was inspiring and it was engaging to read the Canadian signs and hear their boosting shouts for the runners.

In the one mile Detroit-Windsor Tunnel connecting the two countries, the air was warmer and stale. At the passageway's mid-point and seventy-two-feet below the surface of the Detroit River, I pondered the colossal cubic centimeters of concrete and water weighing down on the structure. I concede I did dramatically pick up my pace in the tunnel, and I was very pleased when I reached the USA's border.

As the half marathoners and the marathon runners split at the thirteen-mile marker, I had perhaps 300 hundred yards to the finish line. The marathoners meanwhile had over thirteen miles to endure. I peeked at the marathoners while contemplating the energy and effort needed to complete a marathon. I would *never* run a marathon.

I was relieved when I made it to the finish line of my half-marathon. Driving back to Wisconsin, I was whining about my throbbing arches. I was trying to persuade myself the four months of training and the race were delightful triumphs, but the fork splitting the marathon and half marathon routes was racing in my lopsided head. I suddenly blurted out I was going to run a marathon.

Arriving back in Wisconsin, I received a good night of sleep and I was physically healing with my mind still being corrupt. I began browsing for a training plan for a first-time marathoner.

My winter months of training went off without a hitch while I combed through marathons to register for one in Arizona. The Arizona marathons were either filled or not feasible to my schedule.

My first marathon was the Southern Indiana Classic in Evansville, Indiana. The March marathon of 2013 was satisfying, but I struggled the last four miles because of hitting the wall. In addition, the last mile had a fierce headwind and a long gradual hill.

By the time I crossed the finish line, the celebrating bells and whistles were gone. To add burden to my wretched body, my vehicle was a half a mile away. Shuffling to my vehicle, I sat in the passenger seat fussing over the photo of a misfit in his Michigan maize shirt wearing a marathon medal. I had completed a marathon.

In late June, I ran Grandma's Marathon on a rainy morning in Duluth, Minnesota. Days prior to the race I was stung in my calf area by ground wasps. Usually in long runs my arches begin throbbing at the nineteenth or twentieth mile mark. During Grandma's Marathon the throbbing started at mile two because of my swollen calf muscle.

In October, I reunited with Detroit and I ran the Detroit Marathon. Kris and I witnessed the Wolverines beat the Indiana Hoosiers the day before and the weather for the marathon was sunny with mild temperatures. The race route again traversed the Ambassador Bridge and the Detroit-Windsor Tunnel while this time I snapped pictures along the route with my phone. I read most of the spectators' signs, thanked the volunteers, and recognized the people's support.

In June of 2014, I ran the Maritime Marathon in Manitowoc, Wisconsin. The weather was rainy, though the scenery along Lake Michigan was grand. Through the twenty-six and two-tenths miles I had no physical ailments and while running I began irrationally organizing the strategy of running a marathon in each state. The goal is not unique among marathoners, yet for me it seems an incredible goal.

In November of 2014, I ran my fifth marathon the Naperville Marathon in Naperville, Illinois. My last marathon to date is the IMT Des Moines Marathon, which is six marathons in six states.

Running has been wonderful for my peace of mind, creating goals, and exploring new locations. Thank you, Lord, for all my blessings and opportunities in my life.

With the Lord's strength I will keep running marathons and living my life to His glory. *"Let us run with perseverance the race marked out for us. Let us fix our eyes on Jesus."* *7

Chapter 33
THE HABITS

I have extremely ugly and painful thorns as a sinner, but I have a merciful Savior who loves me unconditionally and completely forgives my repentant heart.

For the last decade I have been on the thirty year and out plan with an addiction to nicotine. I began puffing away on my first bummed cigarettes when I was a teenager. My progression of panting away on the cancer sticks depended on my workplace, friends, or availability of cigarettes to be purchased.

Finding some obscure means to obtain a cigarette, I would join another eighth grade juvenile delinquent at the city park for a nicotine fix after school. The tactlessly devious cigarette drags were conspired before our lung-bashing basketball practices.

In adulthood I never categorized myself as a heavy smoker. I lacked the talent to create perfectly formed smoke rings from my exhaled smoke to classify me as an elite smoker. Since I did own a Zippo lighter and I would regularly buy cigarettes by the carton I was definitely an established seasoned smoker.

In my teaching years, I did not smoke at school or in the presence of students and this was an age when it was allowable to smoke on school grounds. I refrained from smoking while playing college football, but I was ineffective with attempts to totally ditch the disgusting habit through hypnosis, patches, or medication.

I quit cold turkey in January 2004, as I woke up in the morning and exposed through my inventory I would be required to buy another pack or carton of cigarettes that weekend. The expectation of spending the money and being controlled by the nicotine irritated me. I flung my remaining cigarettes in the kitchen's garbage can.

One side effect of successfully quitting smoking was the increase in my body weight. My weight would fluctuate as much as thirty pounds between the inactive large-eating winter months and the active less-eating summer months. Nine years ago I tried to disassemble the weight roller coaster and fight the battle of the bulge in my life.

The statistics of people losing weight through any diet plan is ten percent. The percent keeping the weight off for five years is six percent of the first successful dieters. Using the village of Oakfield as an example this means only six people out of 1,000 dieting residents would maintained weight loss over the span of five years.

I am a foodaholic and I am a sincere eating activist as I hold food in high regard 24/7. I relish all types of cuisine and I am passionate about my cooking adventures in my kitchen. During the course of years there has been a cyclone of emotions, effort, and results within my eating lifestyle. I can have only healthy foods in my house because if corrupt fare is present I don't perform well rejecting the temptations.

In my childhood, peanut butter was an ingredient enjoyed on my toast in the morning and in my sandwiches at lunch. PB mixed with maple syrup also found its way into my bowl of vanilla ice cream. As an adult, I appallingly can consume a jar of peanut butter like it is a bowl of cereal.

Jars of crunchy or smooth peanut butter were in the past hidden in my house by Jenny. Currently, Kris has volunteered for the sneaky duty. Concealed throughout our home are full, partial, and empty jars of peanut butter. An adjustment has been amended in the house as I'm permitted one spoon of the nutritious snack per day. The biggest spoon in our house is my measuring device and personal delivery tool.

When I became critical about controlling my body weight and changing my lifestyle of eating, sleeping, and exercising, it was due to the fact that my suit coat was not fitting me anymore. In my frugal mind, I had squandered enough of my finances by buying larger clothes.

I couldn't pull myself away from the dinner table, evening's snacking ritual, and midnight raids to the refrigerator. Even during the daylight hours I had terrible eating practices. The transformation became fruitful when I denied myself unhealthy foods, ate smaller portions, accomplished regular exercise, drank gallons of water daily, and establish a proper sleeping routine.

Every portion of the dietary rule for weight loss and maintenance is based on fewer calories in and more calories burned off. When I lost nearly a third of my weight, seventy-five pounds, I alleged the rabbits in my subdivision were eating better than me. I was eating low-nutrient iceberg lettuce whereas the rabbits were feasting on my vibrant red roses, thriving spirea shrubs, and tantalizing red, yellow, and orange tiger lilies.

In my dietary equation, my sleeping behavior is an ever evolving conquest. For years I survived with only five hours of sleep a night. I would have a crash day about once a month sleeping however long I desired. With proper sleep I do much better maintaining a suitable weight. As with the case of all obsessions and bad habits, it's a lifetime of brawls. There are steps taken forward and hijacked steps backwards.

A friend of mine would ask every now and then how the race was going. I would decipher he was referring to a car race or a running race and I would reply, "Hey silly, I'm not in a race."

My friend would ask me the question again with a different phrasing since he now had my full attention, "How's the human race going?"

Our lives are like a race and we are part of the human race. My life has been touched by admirable people I dearly love. Many of those people remain in my life and others have exited this race on earth.

When my dad was undergoing his last days of cancer treatment I was privileged to visit with family and friends. Many individuals expressed sadness over Dad not being at his Taj one more time. They were compassionate and sympathetic as I would thank them for their reflections.

My joy was sharing with them that Davey Lee had progressed to the point of focusing on heaven. Dad had said goodbye to the human race on earth. His declaration of living with Jesus had strengthened my assurance and hope of eternal life in heaven with Jesus.

Thank you, Lord, for all of my quests, and I eagerly anticipate more escapades here on earth and in the future in Heaven. I have many designs for exploits in my aging mind and it is staggering to dream about all of the possibilities. Here's a quote from a re-invented misfit and a big dreamer at heart.

Growing up as a youngster and as a young adult, I imagined being a cowboy, a professional singer, a songwriter, a pianist, a magician, a pastor, a soldier, or a truck driver.

I had visions of playing or coaching football, basketball, or baseball at the high school, college, or professional level.

There were the daydreams of racing stock cars, or being employed as a hunting or fishing guide in a remote area like Montana or Alaska.

Crossing my mind was the prospect of being a world-renowned chef, a teacher in a foreign country, a caring nurse, a valiant pilot, a patient social worker, a world traveler, and even an author.

The possibilities were magnificent to dream about in my youthful mind, but I perceived myself as abnormal and uncertain about life. "

As a twelve year old boy, I craved to explore the other side of a hill. Over a decade after high school I traveled to the other side of the world, and I enjoyed relations within different cultures and societies. In my life as a husband, father, and teacher, I desired to unleash the motivational button in people.

God has answered all my dreams and prayers. I am in awe of the blessings God has granted me through His love and mercy. My prayers were not fulfilled in the manner I always desired, but my prayers were satisfied in God's way and time.

Past thrills and contentment came for me while in a flight in a small plane, working years at a lumberyard, laboring at a printing press facility, and working at a cheese factory.

The almighty God watched over me crashing a racecar, suffering head concussions, experiencing near-death incidents, surviving life altering accidents, sleeping through a tornado, enduring a ruptured appendix, and having thoughts of ending my life.

I was blessed with memorable hunting and fishing excursions, and being allowed to wear a cowboy hat among the Apaches. I was given the opportunity to safely participate in athletic competitions and coach various sports at different levels and competitions.

While I have been showered with the joy of cooking, traveling, and singing, I now have a fantastic partner, Kris, with me in all my adventures. Along the way I have re-discovered contentment in fireflies, family, friends, running, traveling, and writing.

I didn't set forth to compose a book forever hidden in a dresser drawer. I desired a story to entertain and encourage readers, a simple book about the adventures of a presumable misfit.

The Lord answered my heart's desire, prayers, and dreams. I pray that He will answer your dreams and prayers.

To God be the glory!

Sources Cited

1. *Taj Mahal, History Channel Website, January 2016*

2. *The Halloween Storm, History Channel Website, January 2016*

3. *Jeremiah 29:11, New International Version Bible, 1984*

4. *Oakfield Tornado, National Weather Service, January 2016*

5. *Vince Lombardi Classic Golf Tournament Website, January 2016*

6. *Ron Kramer, Wikipedia, January 2016*

7. *Hebrews 12:1-2, New International Version Bible, 1984*

Made in the USA
Charleston, SC
08 April 2016